AF594896

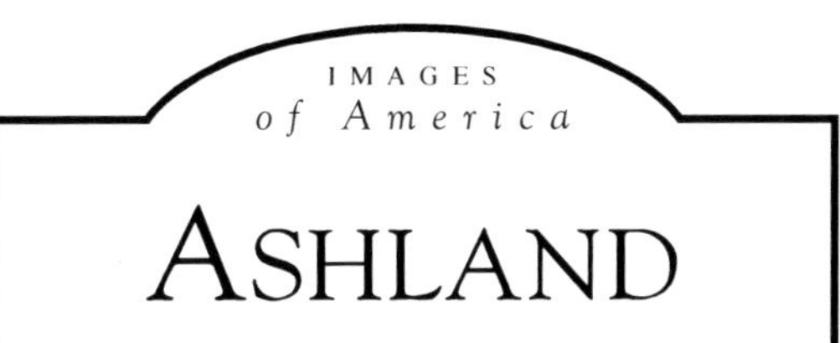
IMAGES
of America
ASHLAND

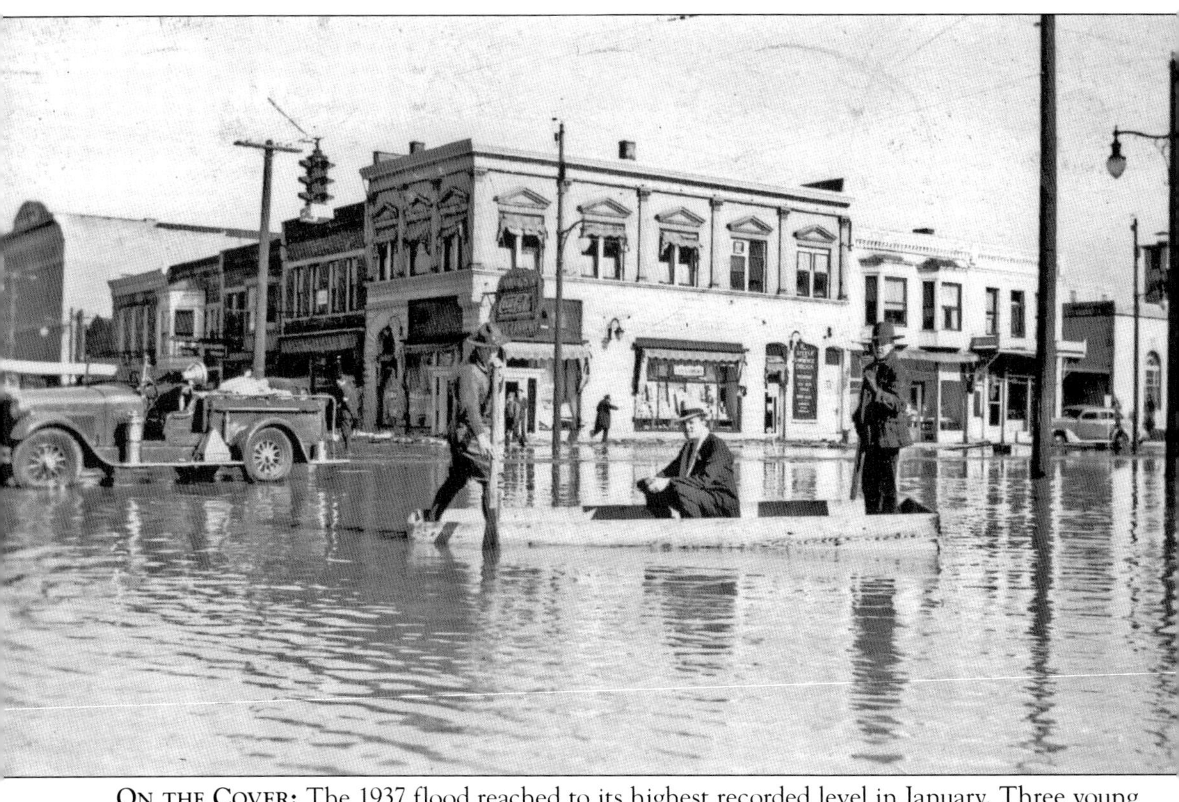

On the Cover: The 1937 flood reached to its highest recorded level in January. Three young men forge ahead in their boat across the intersection of Sixteenth Street and Winchester Avenue. The familiar Steele and Lawrence Drug Store on the northeast corner is in the background. (Courtesy of the Arnold Hanners Photographic Collection, Minnie Winder Room, Boyd County Public Library.)

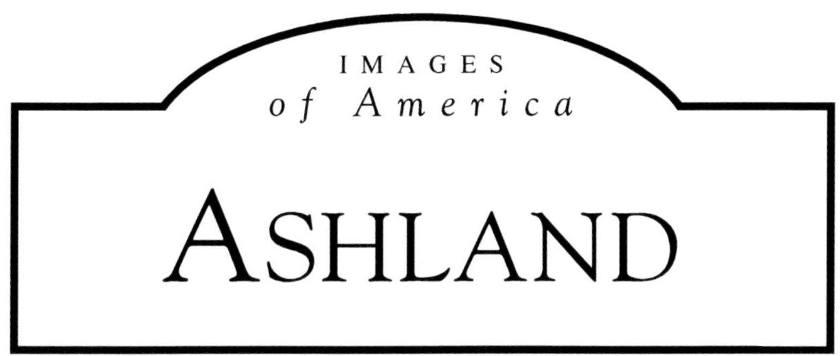

James Powers and Terry Baldridge

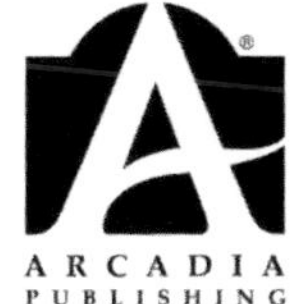

ISBN 978-0-7385-6744-0

Published by Arcadia Publishing
Charleston, South Carolina

Printed in the United States of America

Library of Congress Catalog Card Number: 2008929802

For all general information contact Arcadia Publishing at:
Telephone 843-853-2070
Fax 843-853-0044
E-mail sales@arcadiapublishing.com
For customer service and orders:
Toll-Free 1-888-313-2665

Visit us on the Internet at www.arcadiapublishing.com

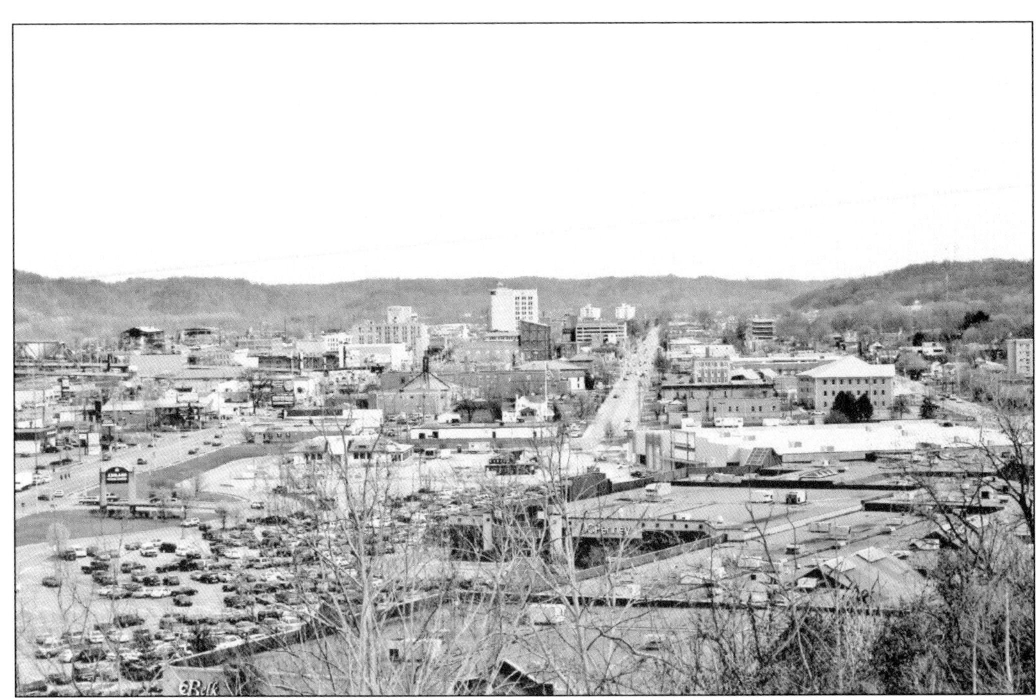

LOOKING EAST AT ASHLAND TODAY. Like all towns and cities around the world, Ashland has had its share of memorable and forgetful historical periods. Very few structures with a century or more in their foundations decorate the skyline, as shown in this photograph from the hill on which Wal-Mart is located. (Photograph by Keenan MacLean Baldridge.)

Contents

ACKNOWLEDGMENTS

We would like to thank the following for their varied forms of assistance on this project: Arnold Hanners Photographic Collection, Minnie Winder Room, Boyd County Public Library; Virginia Hanners; Arthur Greene Sr.'s Greene's Memorette, 1938; Collection of Boyd County Historical Society, Inc.; Historical files of Boyd County Public Library; Eastern Kentucky Genealogical Society, Inc.; Greenup County Public Library; the Jesse Stuart Foundation; the Eastern Kentucky Railway Historical Society; Miner's Coins and Antiques; Kings Daughters Medical Center; the Paramount Arts Center; Highland Museum and Discovery Center; *Ashland Daily Independent*; WLGC Ashland; the *Herald Dispatch*; WGOH/WUGO Radio Grayson Olive Hill; the *Greenup News Times*; Department of Veterans Affairs Hospital in Huntington, West Virginia; Brown's Grocery; Tackett's Grocery and Pizza; Stultz Pharmacy, Inc.; Greenbo Lake State Resort Park; Carter Caves State Resort Park; Camden Park; Wal-Mart of Ashland; Hitchins Historical Society; Chesapeake and Ohio Railroad Historical Society; Greenup Old Fashion Days Celebration; Ashland Poage Landing Days; www.ekrailroad.com; Greenbo Railroad Days; Grayson Memory Days; Allen and Brown; Keenan Baldridge; Heather Baldridge; and family and friends.

INTRODUCTION

Ashland, the largest city in eastern Kentucky, is located on the banks of the Ohio River in Boyd County. This second-class city, when first incorporated by act of the legislature in 1856, was located in Greenup County. Boyd County was created four years later.

Ashland, first known as Poage Settlement, was settled by the Poage family of Virginia. Robert Poage and sons, with Maj. George Poage and his son, held title to thousands of acres obtained by assignments from the William Bell patent and treasury land warrants. The first recorded land grant in the area was made to Gen. James Wilkinson in 1783, from which Robert Poage purchased a 5,000-acre grant. It was from these early families that land was acquired by industrialists later on. The area was rich in the timber, coal, and limestone needed for production of pig iron, making the area attractive to early iron producers, who used the Ohio River for transport. The first iron furnace was established in 1818 by Richard Deering in Greenup County. The Ashland furnace opened in 1869, the largest of its kind in the country, and was one of 60 at that time located in the area known as the Hanging Rock iron region. The furnaces later converted from charcoal fuel to coal.

Early industrialists formed the Kentucky Iron, Coal, and Manufacturing Company, incorporated in 1854. The town laid out on land they had purchased was named Ashland after Henry Clay's home in Lexington. Martin Toby Hilton, an engineer, was hired to lay out the town with streets running parallel to the river 100 feet wide and those perpendicular to the river 80 feet wide. Among the early families attracted to the area by iron and coal were the Means, Coles, Peebles, and Seatons. During the Civil War, the Aldine Hotel was used as a government hospital. The building, several stories tall with 50 rooms, had been built by a promoter who hoped to give Ashland an air of permanence.

The region's furnace towns were linked through Ashland, and transportation of coal and raw materials was centered there. The first railroad, the Lexington and Big Sandy, reached Princess, 10 miles away, by 1857. Other rail lines, such as the Ashland Coal and Iron Railroad, the Chattaroi, and the Eastern Kentucky Railway, developed to meet the demands of industry. In 1924, the Chesapeake & Ohio Railway (C&O) acquired the rights to most of the lines and became the major railway through Ashland. The steamer lines on the Ohio River transported iron to ports as far away as Cincinnati and Pittsburgh and returned with goods for the city. Among these lines were the Cincinnati, Portsmouth, Big Sandy, and Pomeroy Packet Company and the Pittsburgh and Cincinnati Steamboat line.

The government of Ashland started as a council of five trustees. Ashland incorporated as a city in 1876 with H. B. Brodess as its first mayor. The first postmaster was H. B. Pollard (1847), the first police chief was John Casebolt (1868), and the first fire chief was Jack Spicer (1885). Today the city has a city manager with a mayor and four city commissioners.

Ashland's lumber industry flourished from the 1880s until the beginning of the 20th century. The period of greatest growth was the 1920s, when the population increased from 14,729 to 29,074. The American Rolling Mill Company (Armco), headquartered in Middleton, Ohio, bought the Ashland Iron and Mining Company in 1921 and Norton Iron Works in 1928. The company continued to grow; it started up the first continuous sheet rolling mill in 1934 and a hot strip mill in 1953. In May 1989, Armco Steel entered into a partnership with Kawasaki Steel that brought $350 million into the company. Ashland Oil, the 13th largest petroleum refining company in the United States, was founded in 1924, when it was headed by Paul G. Blazer.

In 1981 it became legal to sell liquor in downtown Ashland. The Simeon Willis Memorial Bridge opened in May 1985, followed by the Ashland Plaza Hotel in September 1985. The business district extended west to the $42-million Ashland Town Center shopping mall in 1989.

One

Our Ashland

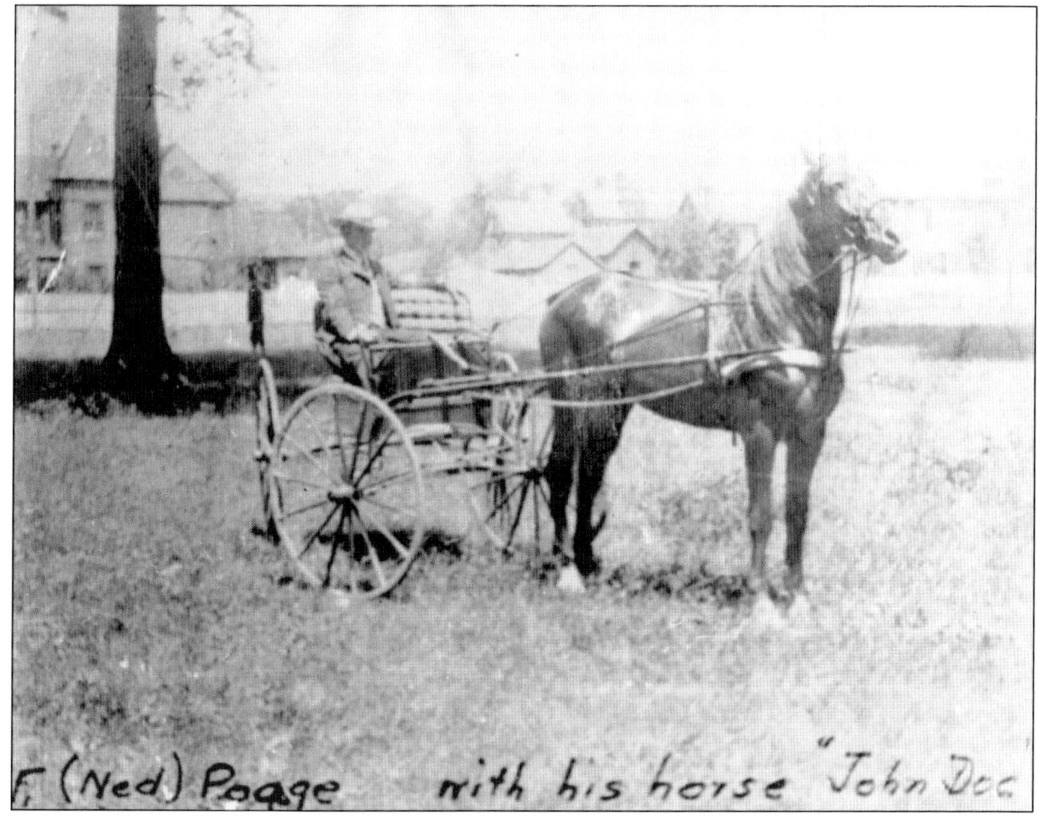

A Rare Poage Family Photograph. Shown in this photograph from the mid-1800s is F. "Ned" Poage and his horse, John Doc. This is one of very few surviving images of a direct Poage descendant. The Poage family started what came to be known as Poages' Settlement in the 1780s. The Poage family and Ashland are celebrated every summer with Poage Landing Days. (Courtesy of the Arnold Hanners Photographic Collection, Minnie Winder Room, Boyd County Public Library.)

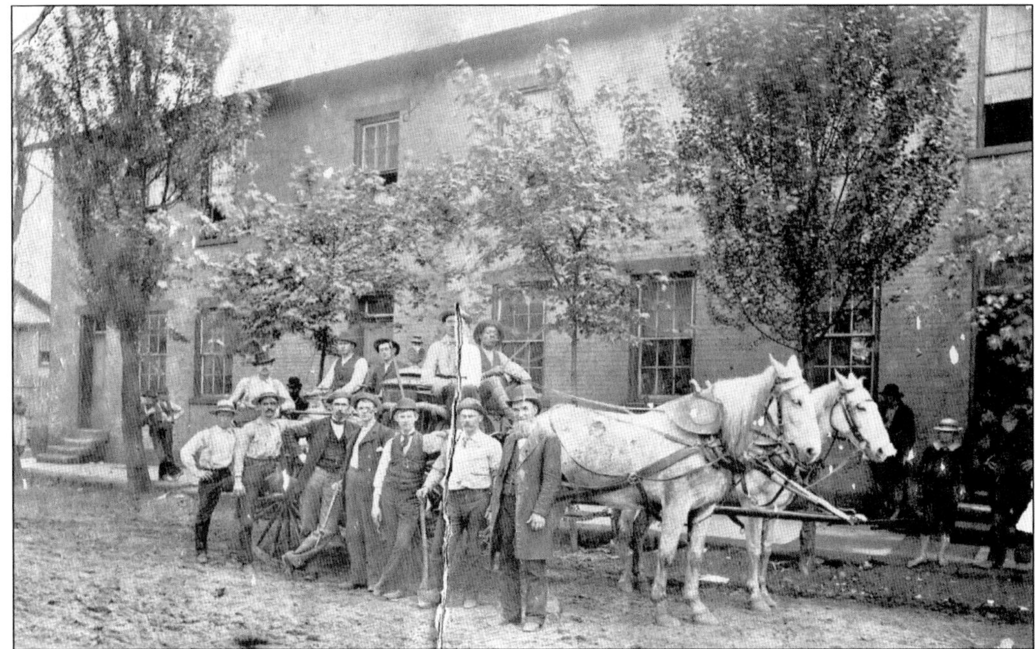

ANOTHER VERY EARLY ASHLAND PHOTOGRAPH. This picture, taken around 1885 along Carter Avenue, shows a beautiful team of white horses with a group of Ashland men. The pump on the back of the wagon may give a clue to the activity of the men. This could be the very first photograph of Ashland firefighters. (Courtesy of the Arnold Hanners Photographic Collection, Minnie Winder Room, Boyd County Public Library.)

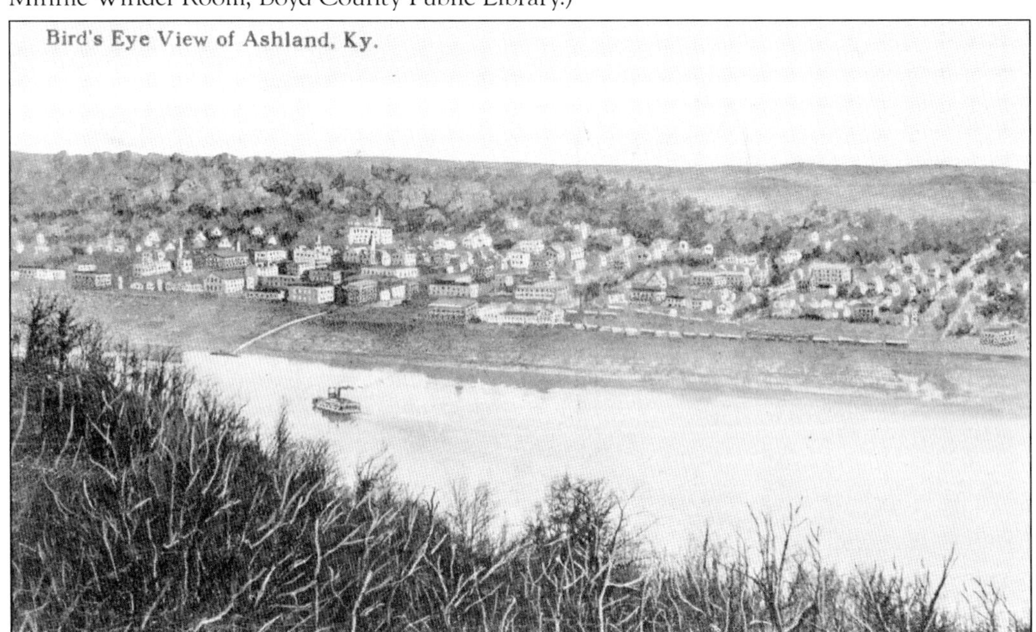

AN UNFAMILIAR CITYSCAPE. This postcard from around 1900 depicts an Ashland with very few recognizable landmarks and several decades before bridging the Ohio River was even thought of. The view comes from a hill that appears to stretch uninterrupted down to the bank of the mighty river in Coal Grove, Ohio. (Courtesy of the James C. Powers Collection.)

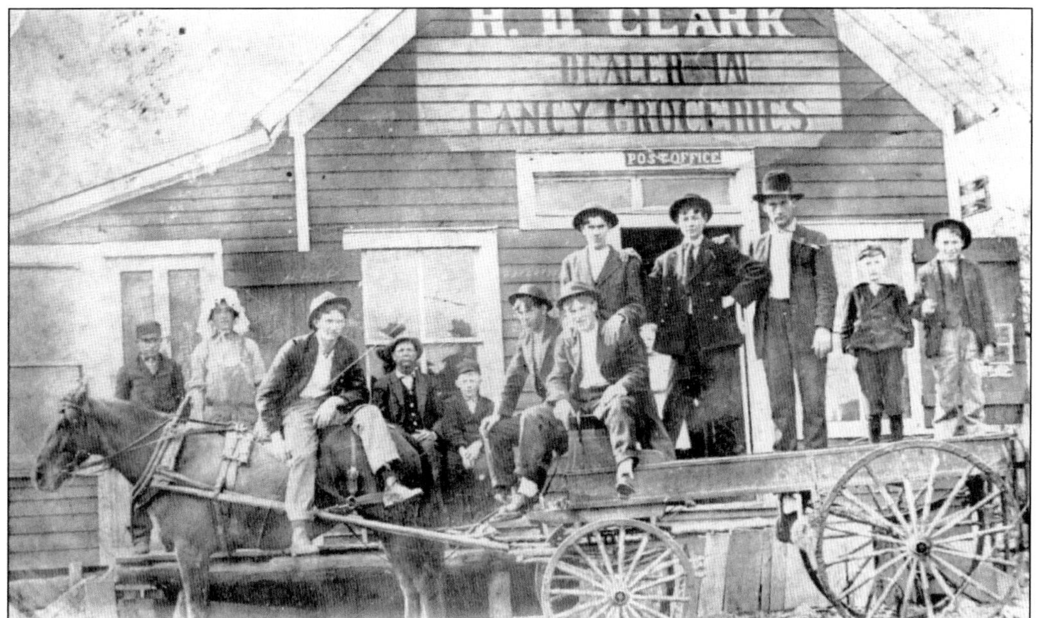

HANGING OUT AT H. D. CLARK'S. Young men gather for this 1880s photograph in front of a grocery store and post office on Twenty-ninth Street near Blackburn Avenue. Notice that the sign in the background says "dealer in fancy groceries." Every crowd of young men seems to have a clown, and this group is no exception. Notice the young man second from left wearing a woman's bonnet. (Courtesy of the Arnold Hanners Photographic Collection, Minnie Winder Room, Boyd County Public Library.)

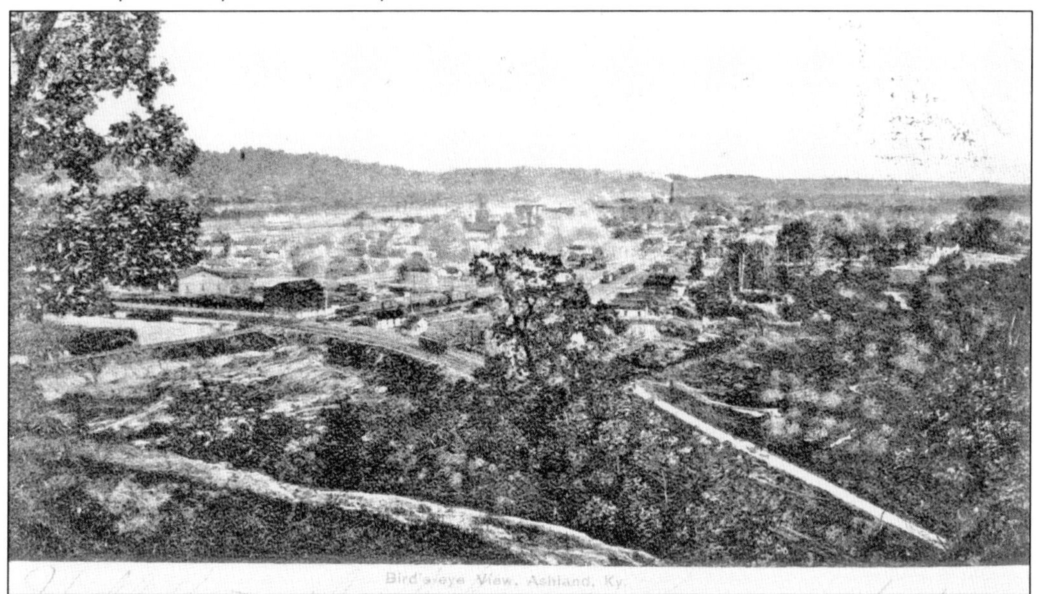

SENDING GREETINGS FROM ASHLAND. This postcard with a bird's-eye view of Ashland dates from the early 1900s. On the front is written, "Hello Virgil, where is Leo now days?" This type of greeting was the cheapest and most convenient way to relay quick messages. Postcard mania was most popular during the late 1800s and early 1900s. (Courtesy of the James C. Powers Collection.)

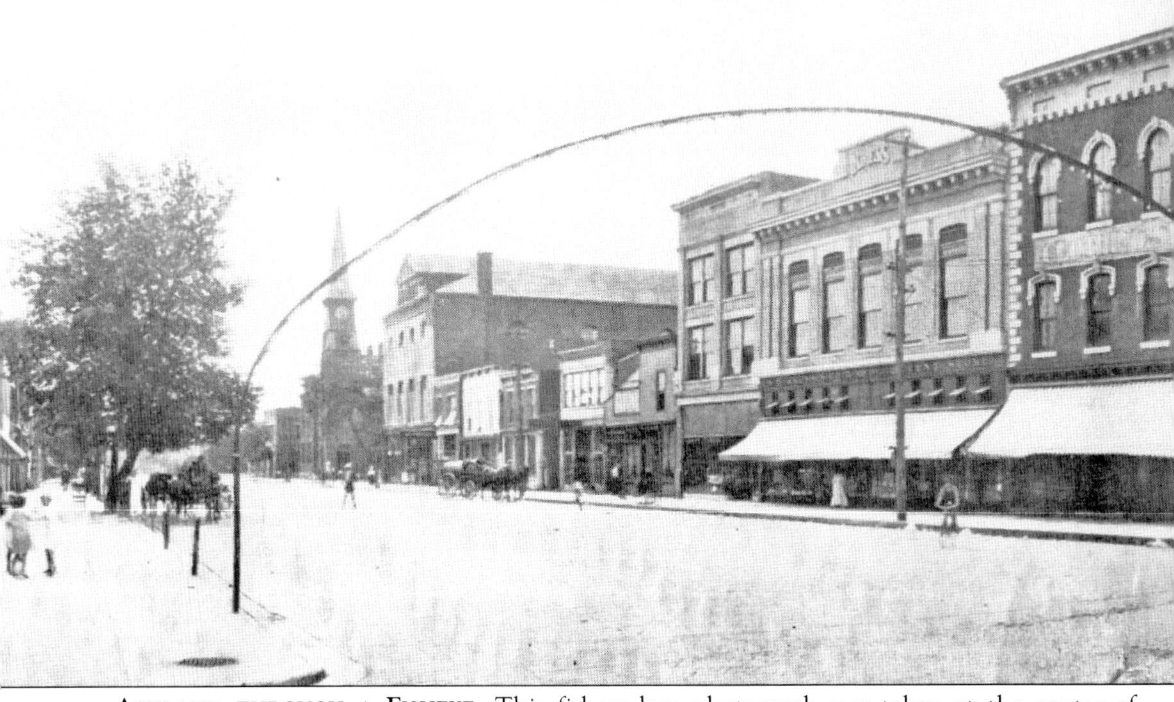

ASHLAND THROUGH A FISHEYE. This fisheye-lens photograph was taken at the center of Sixteenth Street looking north in the second decade of the 20th century. Greenup Avenue stretches eastward to the left. There are very few wagons and buggies, and children play outside an apartment building on the south side of Greenup and Sixteenth, indicating that this

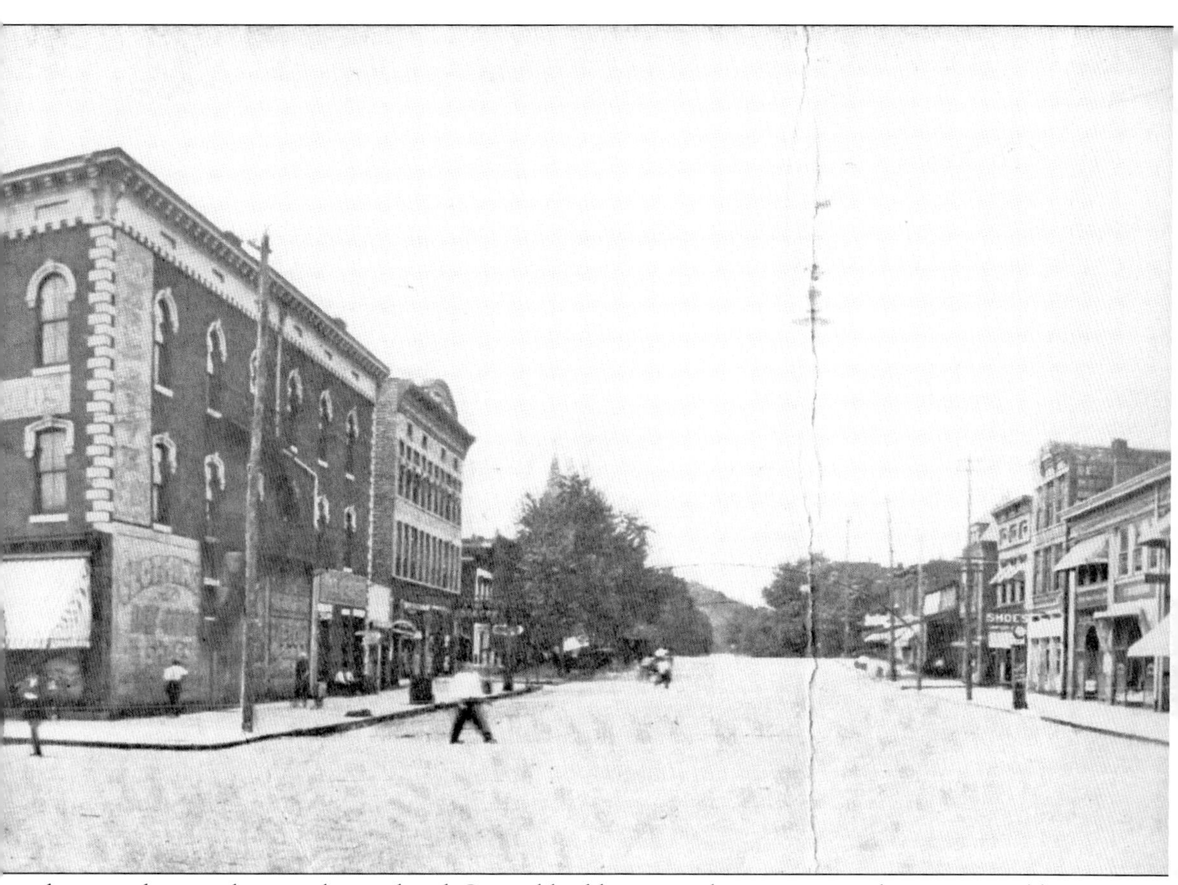

photograph was taken on the weekend. Several buildings seen here survive today, most notably the building that houses the Boston Beanery restaurant. When this photograph was taken, Sixteenth Street was known as Broadway and was 100 feet wide, unlike streets both east and west, which were 80 feet wide. (Courtesy of the James C. Powers Collection.)

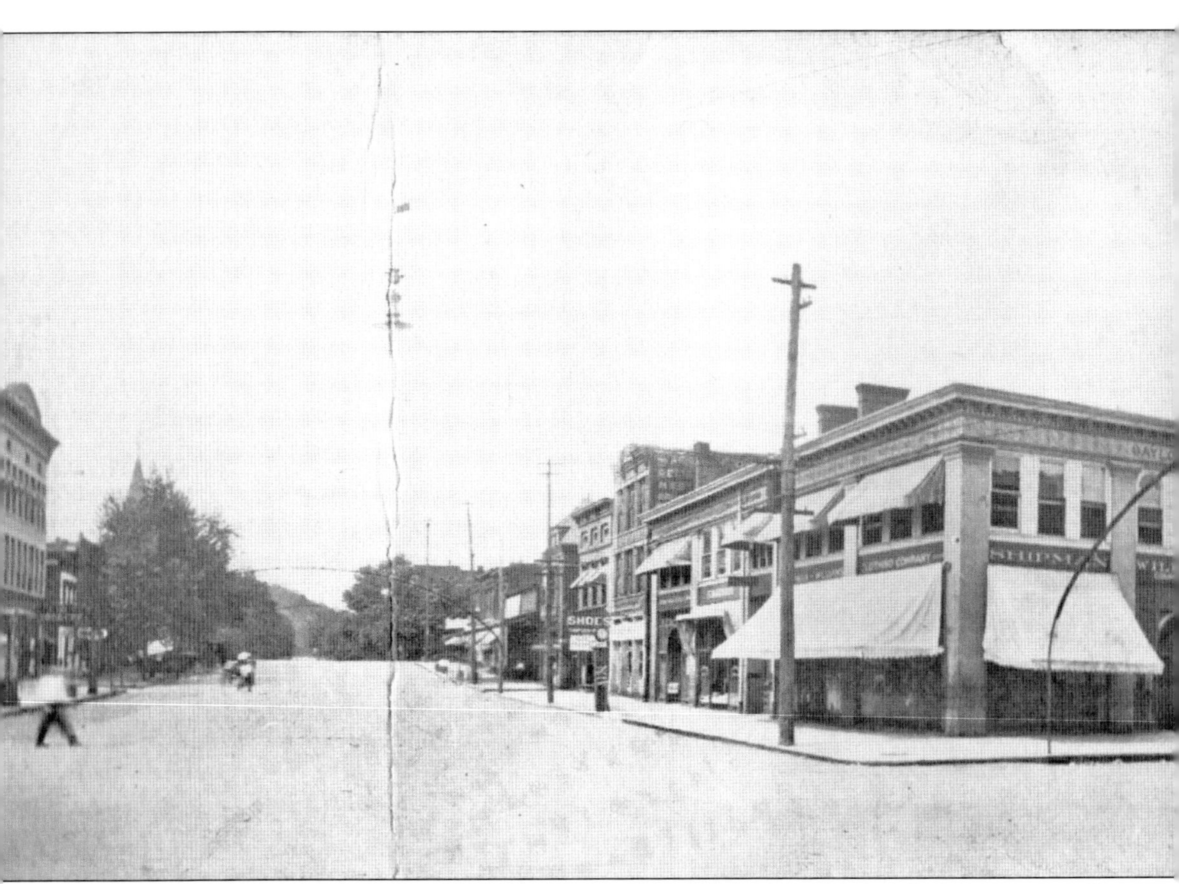

A Rare Street Panoramic. The right side of this panorama is Sixteenth Street or Broadway and Greenup Avenue west toward Fifteenth and Sixteenth streets. Just a couple of structures in this 1910s view are standing today. Seventeenth Street was called Central Street, because it led to Central Park. The streets east of Central—Eighteenth to Twenty-eighth Streets today—were

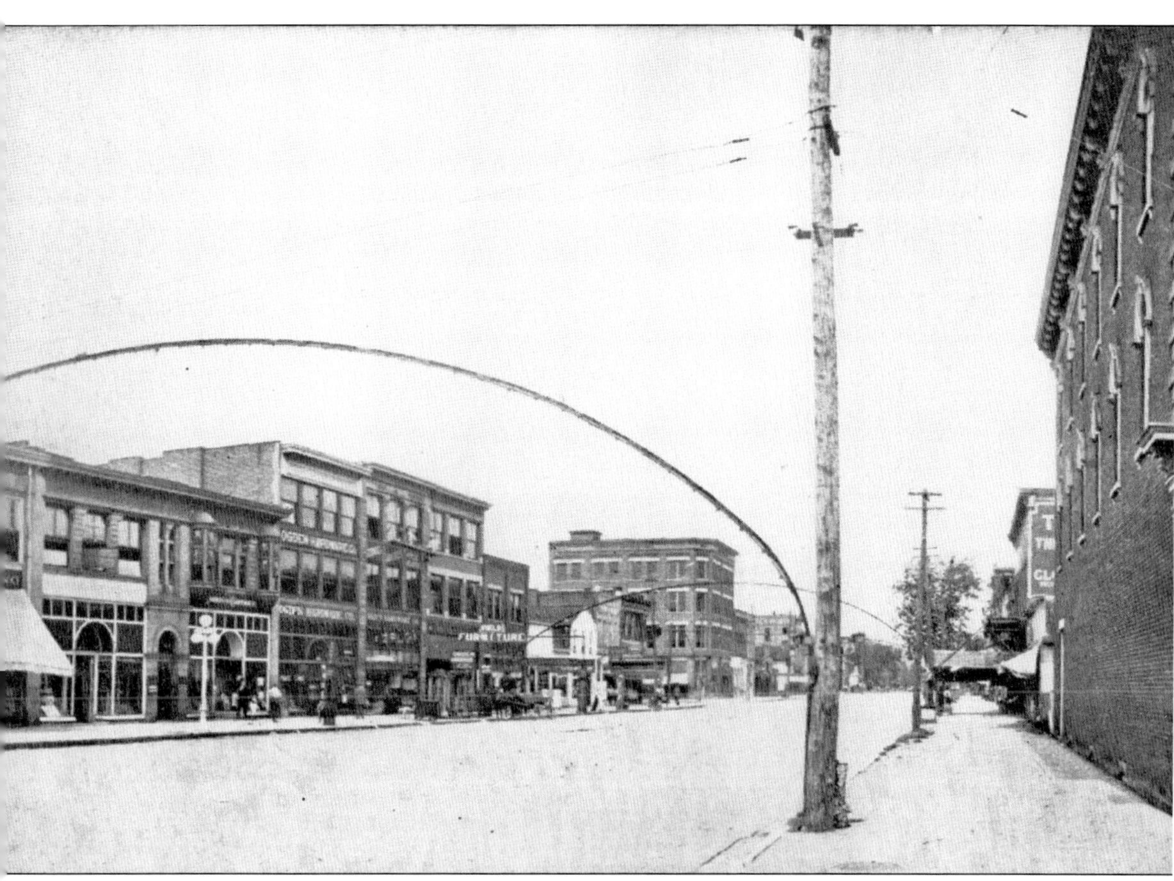

named C through M Streets. The population of Boyd County at the time of this photograph was around 25,000. In the late 1850s, a hotel was built on Broadway called the Broadway Hotel. (Courtesy of the James C. Powers Collection.)

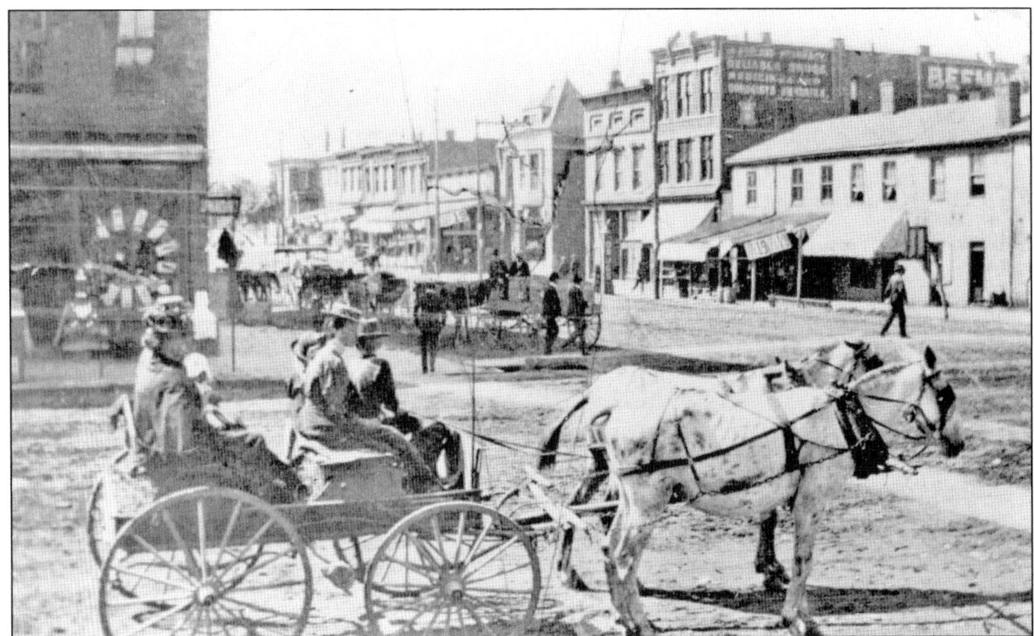

ANY ONCOMING WAGONS? This photograph was taken as the young man and women came upon the intersection of Broadway and Greenup Avenue. Several structures from this 1890s image can easily be picked out of the previous panorama photograph. The wording on the two-story structure across the street advertises "Reliable Drugs" for a druggist. (Courtesy of the Arnold Hanners Photographic Collection, Minnie Winder Room, Boyd County Public Library.)

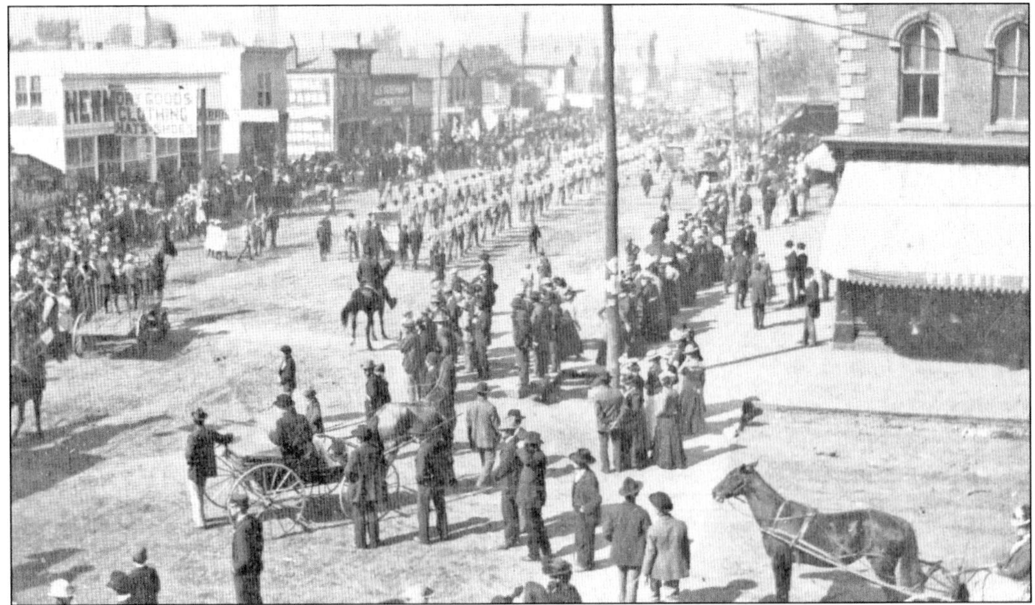

A PARADE THROUGH TOWN. Several groups of men in matching dress march down Winchester Avenue in the 1890s. Perhaps they belonged to an early Ashland club or group. They are parading past one of several "Dry Goods, Clothing, Hats & Shoes" stores in the city. Almost everyone during this time wore a hat. (Courtesy of the Arnold Hanners Photographic Collection, Minnie Winder Room, Boyd County Public Library.)

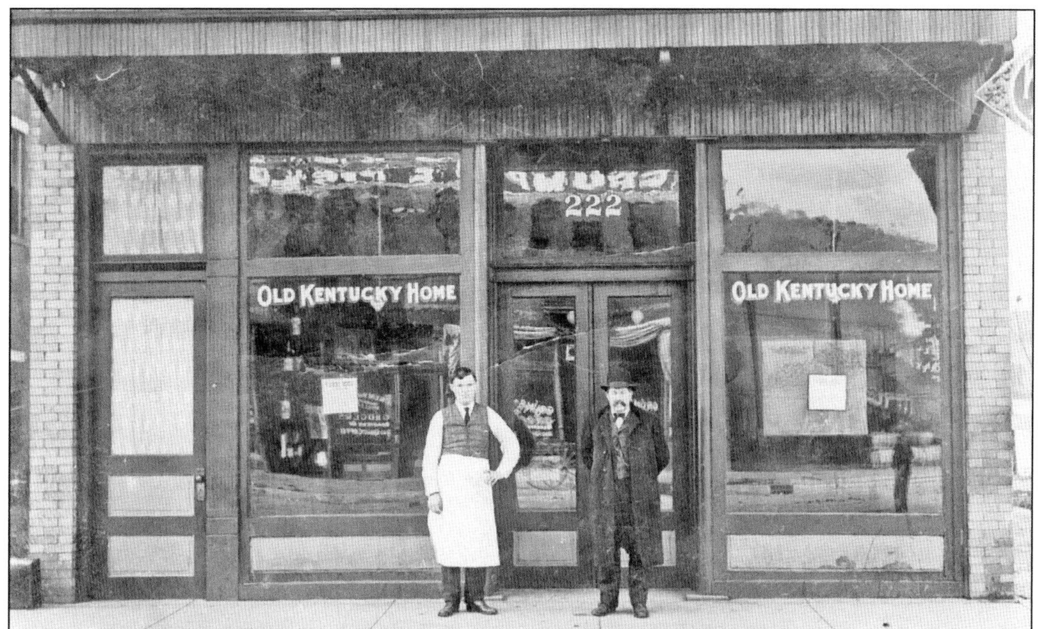

TAKE THE PICTURE. Two gentlemen pose for this 1900s photograph taken outside of Old Kentucky Home on 222 Greenup Avenue. The hill across the river in Ohio is easily seen in the reflection in the glass behind the men. So is the "Crump Grocery Roasters of Coffee" on the structure located on the north side of Greenup Avenue. (Courtesy of the James C. Powers Collection.)

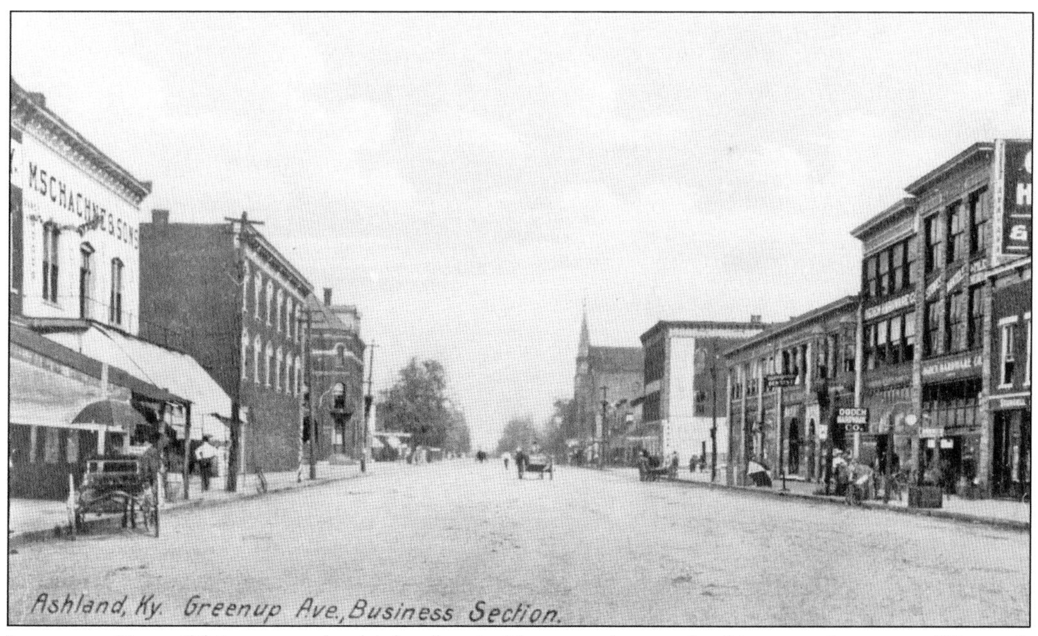

LOOKING EAST. This postcard, which takes in Greenup Avenue looking east from near Fifteenth Street, dates from around 1900. Notice there are no half-circle streetlights running along the avenue—they will not appear for nearly a decade. The Second National Bank's familiar corner entrance is several buildings up on the left. (Courtesy of the James C. Powers Collection.)

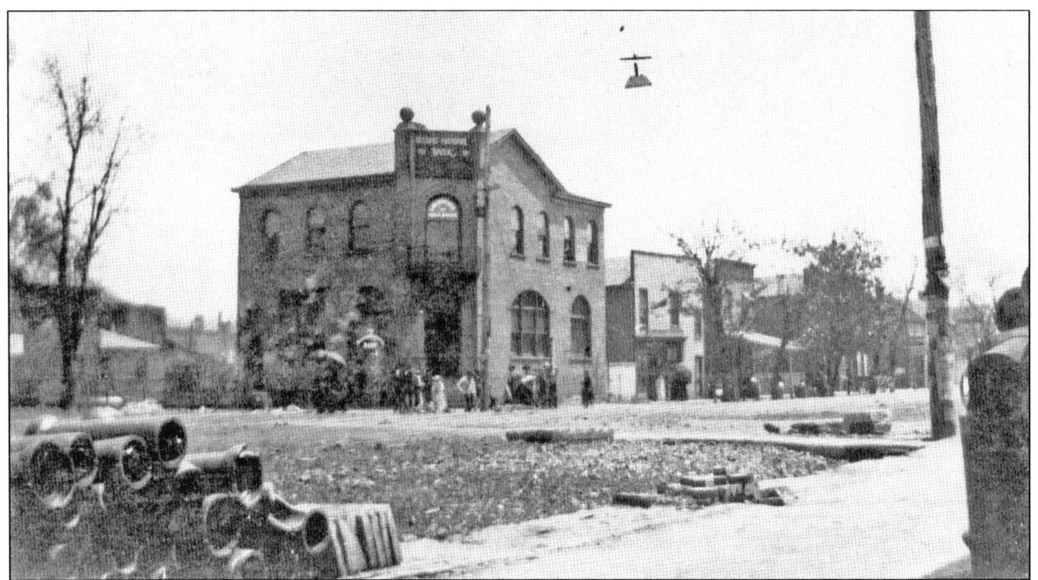

BUILDING OF BRICK. The Second National Bank on the northeast corner of Greenup Avenue and Sixteenth Street is shown in the late 1800s. Notice that the streets are not in a manicured condition as in the photograph below, as drainage pipes await better use. The bank is the only brick structure in the photograph. (Courtesy of the Arnold Hanners Photographic Collection, Minnie Winder Room, Boyd County Public Library.)

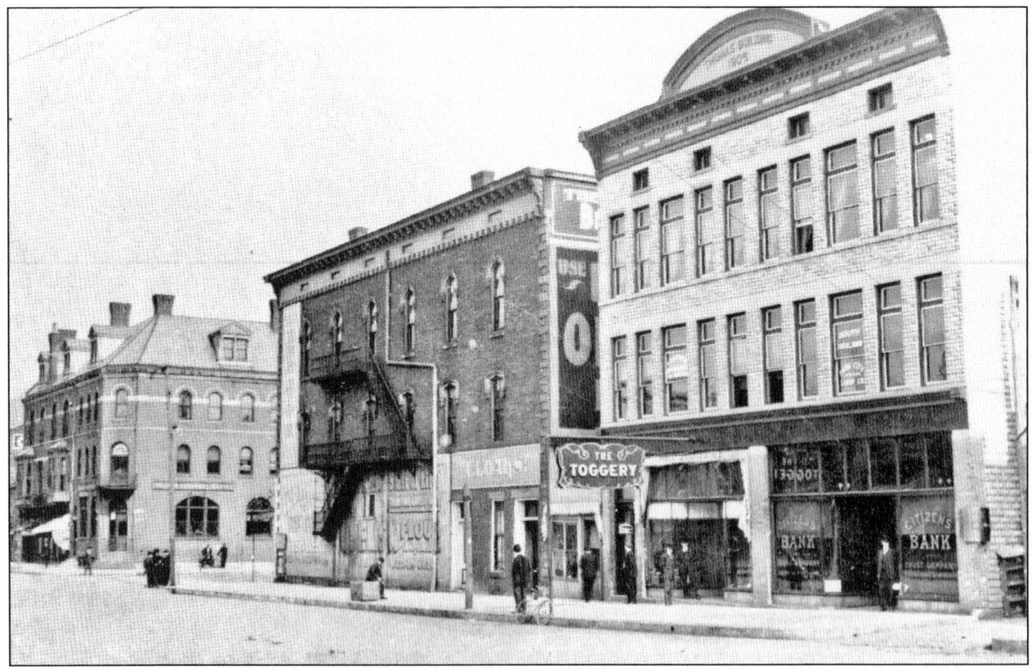

THE TOGGERY. From almost the same position as the photograph above, the Second National Bank appears renovated and larger here around 1918. Also shown is the Thomas Building on Broadway, which was built in 1906. The Toggery and the Citizens Bank occupy the Thomas Building's first floor. (Courtesy of the Arnold Hanners Photographic Collection, Minnie Winder Room, Boyd County Public Library.)

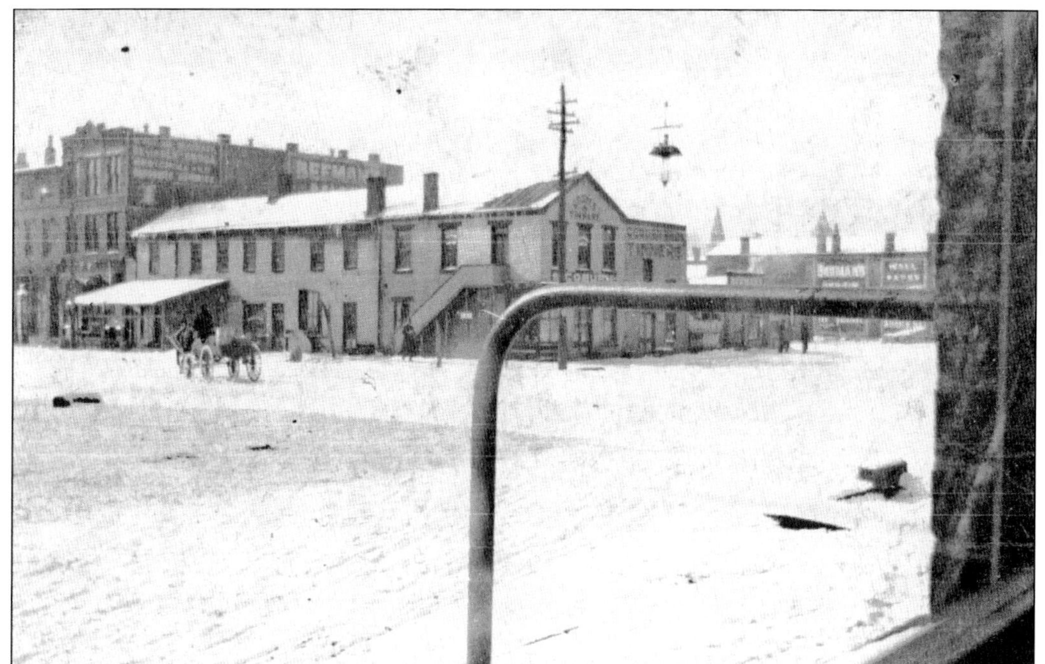

COLD INTERSECTION. In a rare photograph of winter in Ashland from around the early 1900s, a wagon carries supplies to an unknown destination. Note the business across the intersection, S. Coburn. The business sold tinware and stoves made in nearby southern Ohio. (Courtesy of the Arnold Hanners Photographic Collection, Minnie Winder Room, Boyd County Public Library.)

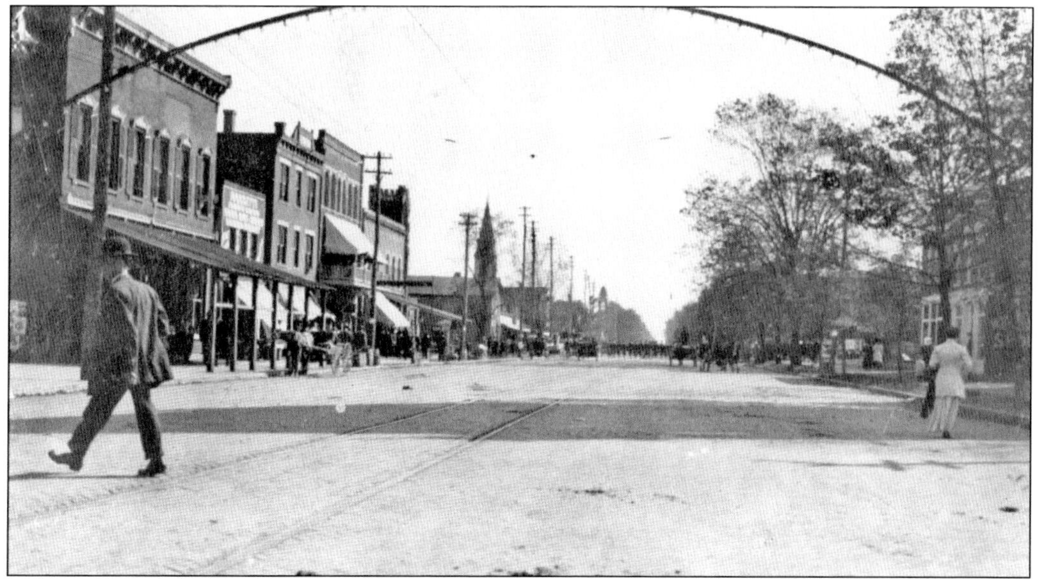

A STROLL. A gentleman walks in one direction and a lady walks in the other across the street. The streetcar rail runs down the center of the street. Ashland streetcars, which used electricity as indicated by the cable running above the street, ran through the business district on a regular schedule. (Courtesy of the Arnold Hanners Photographic Collection, Minnie Winder Room, Boyd County Public Library.)

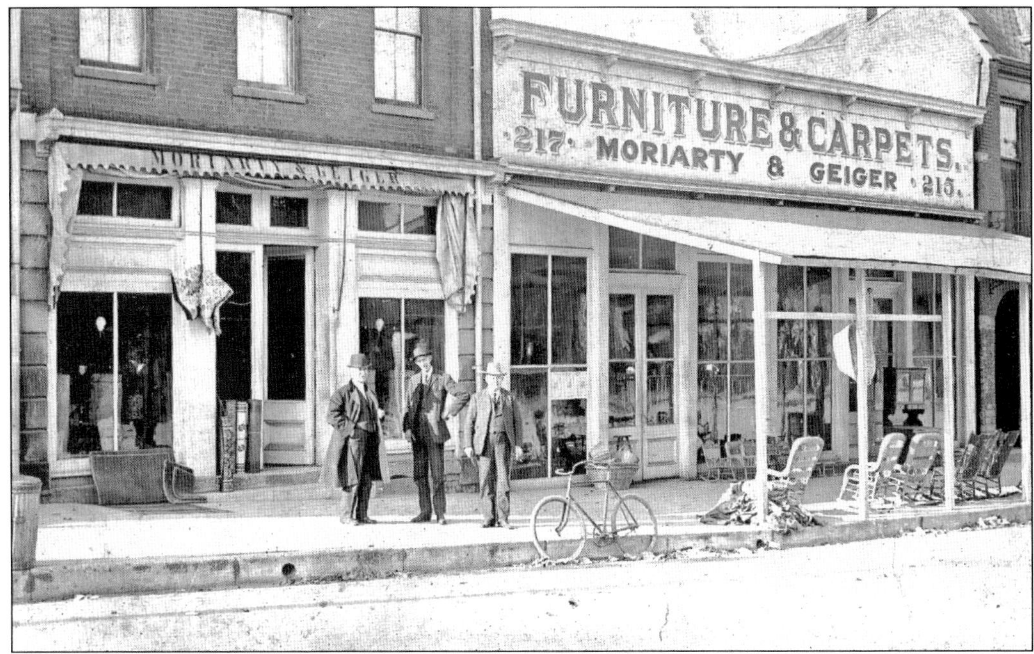

A LONE BICYCLE. Three men stand for this photograph taken in the early 1920s outside the Moriarty and Geiger Furniture and Carpets store. Customers would travel to Ashland from Webbville, Grayson, and Greenup to purchase household luxuries. (Courtesy of the Arnold Hanners Photographic Collection, Minnie Winder Room, Boyd County Public Library.)

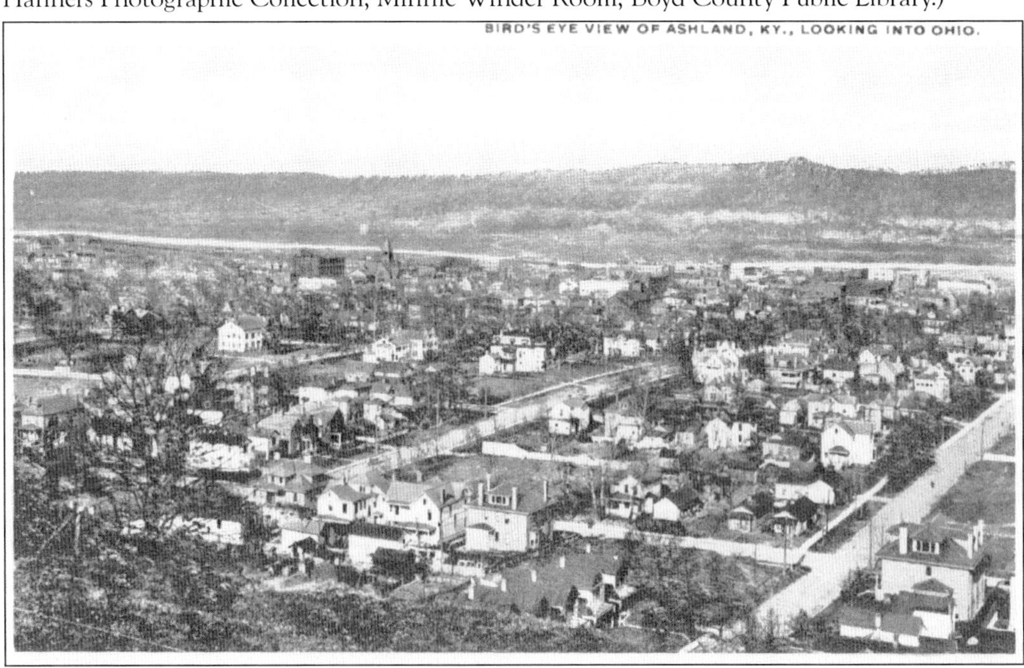

A BIRD'S-EYE VIEW. The Ashland that we know today is hardly noticeable in this early-20th-century postcard. Many of the structures from that time no longer stand due to progress, age, and accidents. Postcards with bird's-eye views of several local cities were produced during this time and are highly sought after by collectors. (Courtesy of the James C. Powers Collection.)

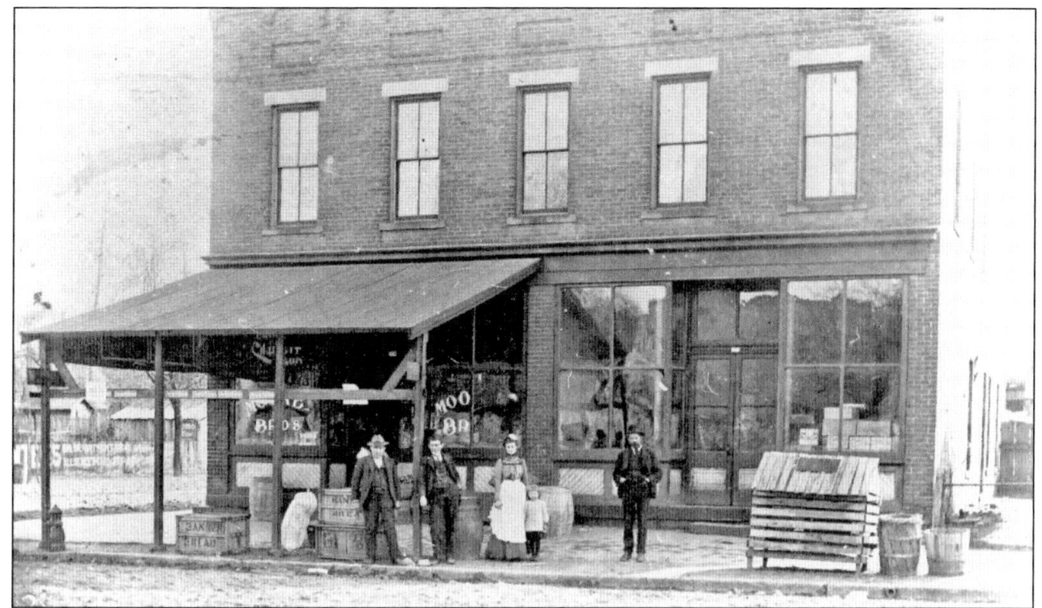

A FAMILY GROCERY. Owners and family proudly pose for this *c.* 1900 picture of Moore Brothers' Grocery. Ashland has seen its share of family-owned businesses come and go throughout its history. Several national and regional grocery stores are available today. (Courtesy of the Arnold Hanners Photographic Collection, Minnie Winder Room, Boyd County Public Library.)

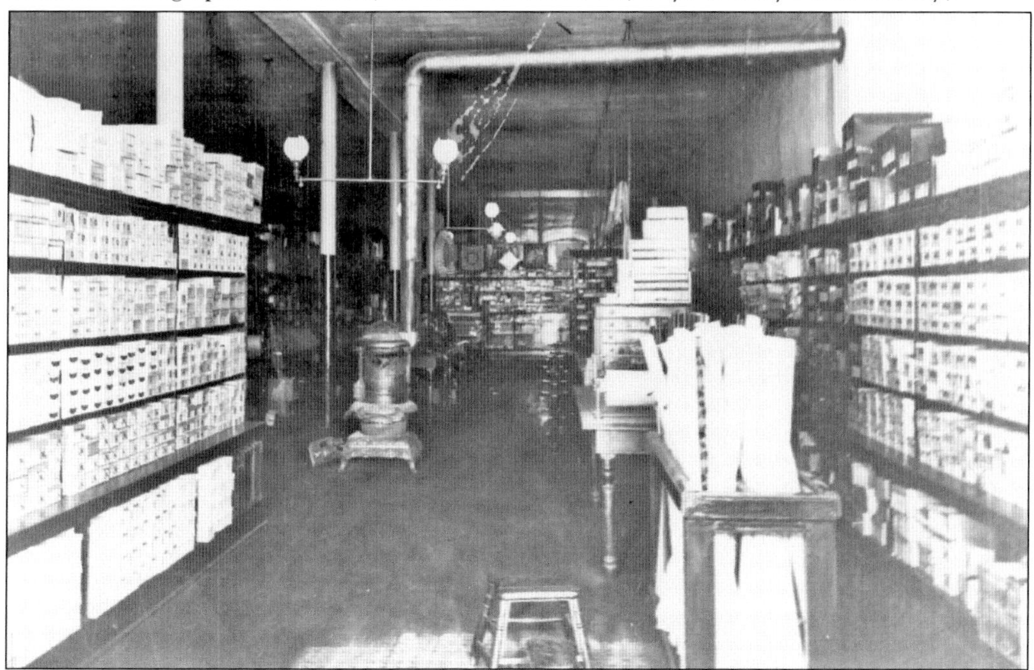

A PEEK INSIDE. This interior photograph of Moore Brothers' Grocery from around 1900 shows a coal or wood stove used to warm the business during cold hours. The store clerk was responsible for inventory, sales, bringing in coal or wood, and emptying the ashes into the street. (Courtesy of the Arnold Hanners Photographic Collection, Minnie Winder Room, Boyd County Public Library.)

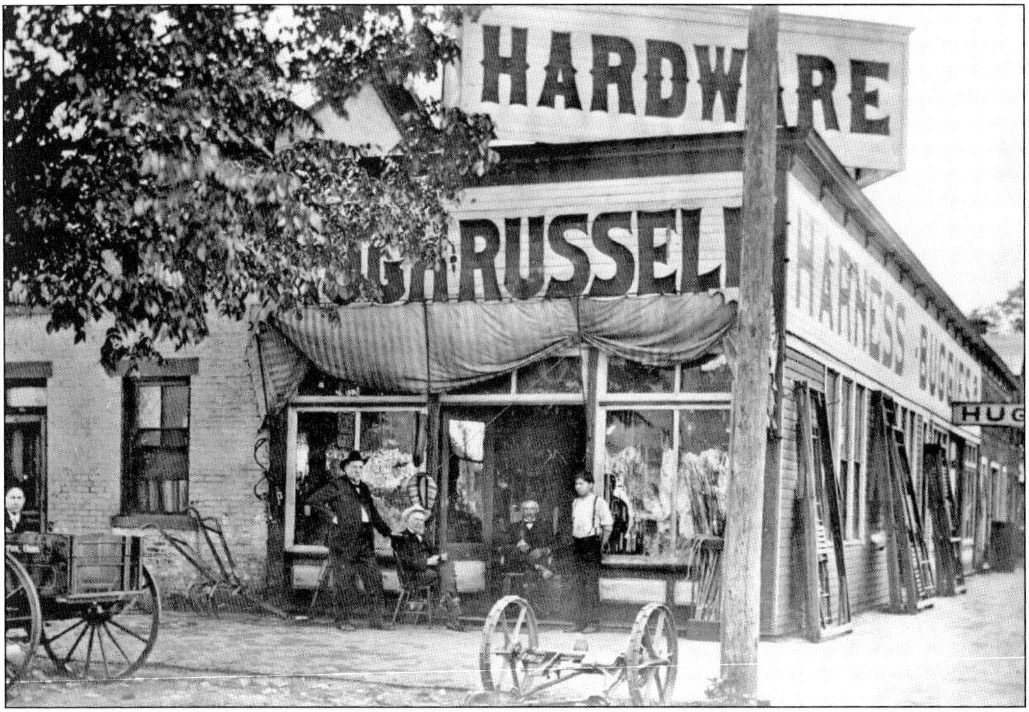

Need a Plow? This photograph from around 1900 shows a horse-drawn sickle bar mower in the foreground and Hugh Russell's Harness Shop on the southwest corner of Greenup Avenue and Fourteenth Street. Farmers from rural Boyd, Carter, Greenup, and Lawrence Counties came to this one-stop farming shop. (Courtesy of the Arnold Hanners Photographic Collection, Minnie Winder Room, Boyd County Public Library.)

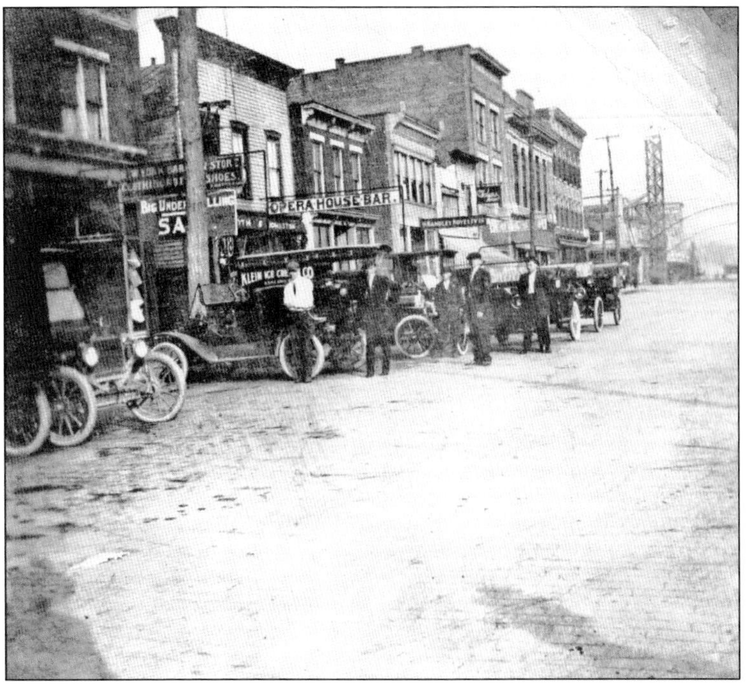

Posing on Greenup Avenue. Several young men are watching as the picture is snapped of them and Greenup Avenue running to the west in the background. Perhaps the men are taking a break at the Opera House Bar after working for the Klein Ice Cream Company, as displayed on the back of one of the vehicles from 1915. (Courtesy of the Arnold Hanners Photographic Collection, Minnie Winder Room, Boyd County Public Library.)

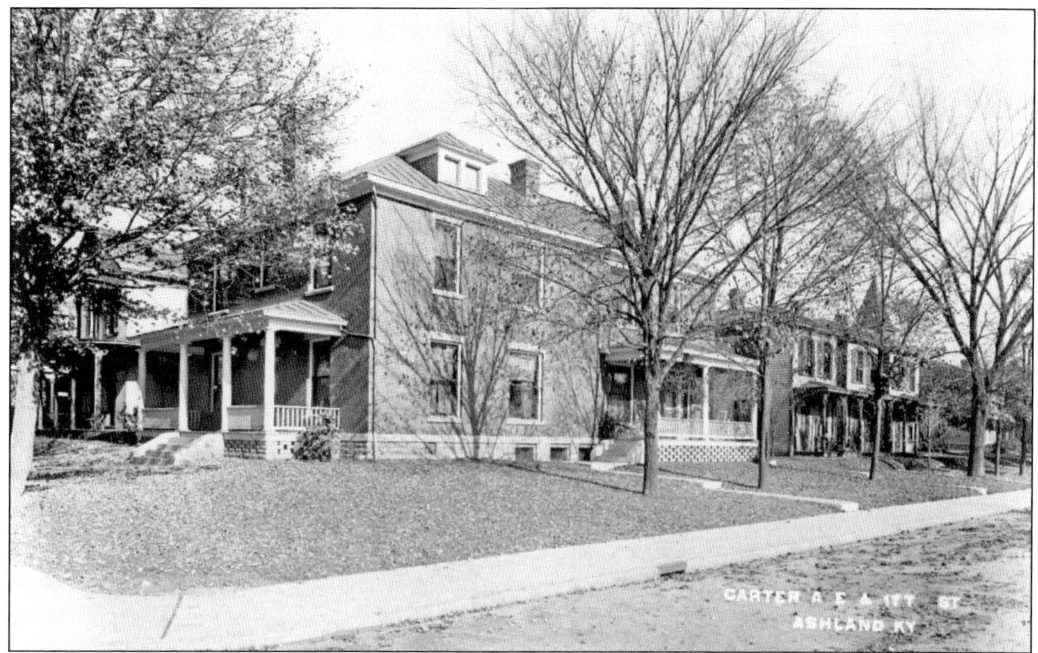

THE DR. SPARKS HOME. Photographed at Seventeenth Street and Carter Avenue around 1930 is the home of Dr. Proctor and J. C. Sparks. Dr. Sparks retired from delivering generations of Ashland citizens only to come out of retirement for the delivery of James C. Powers, one of the authors, in 1938. (Courtesy of the Arnold Hanners Photographic Collection, Minnie Winder Room, Boyd County Public Library.)

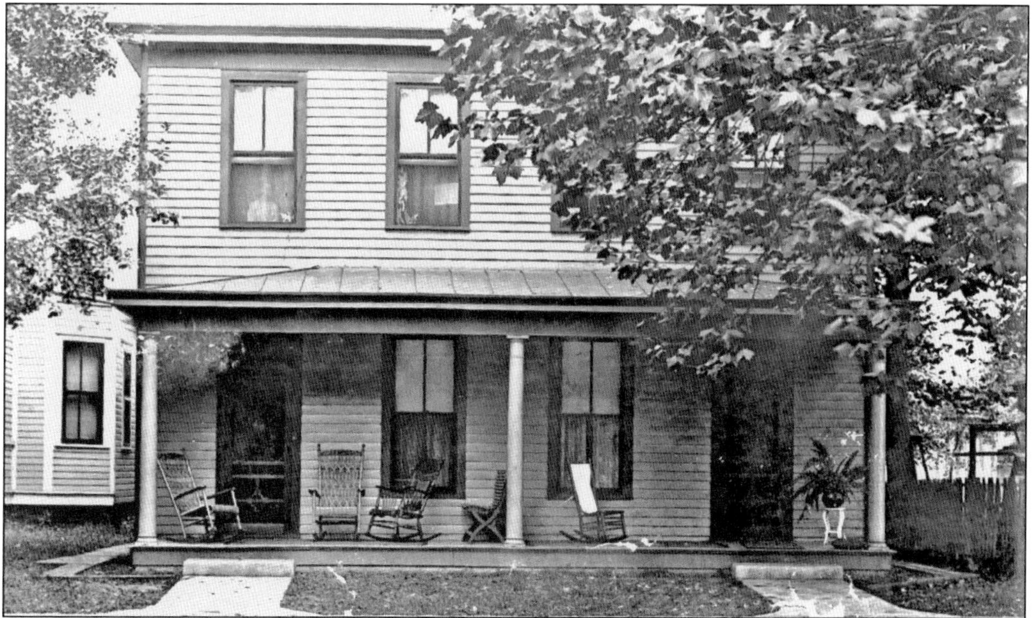

A QUIET, COOL PORCH. The home at 622 East Winchester Avenue, photographed here in the early 1900s, belonged to James K. Ellis. Many families during this time sat on their porches and conversed about the day's activities. The Ellis sisters, pictured on page 28, grew up in this house. (Courtesy of the James C. Powers Collection.)

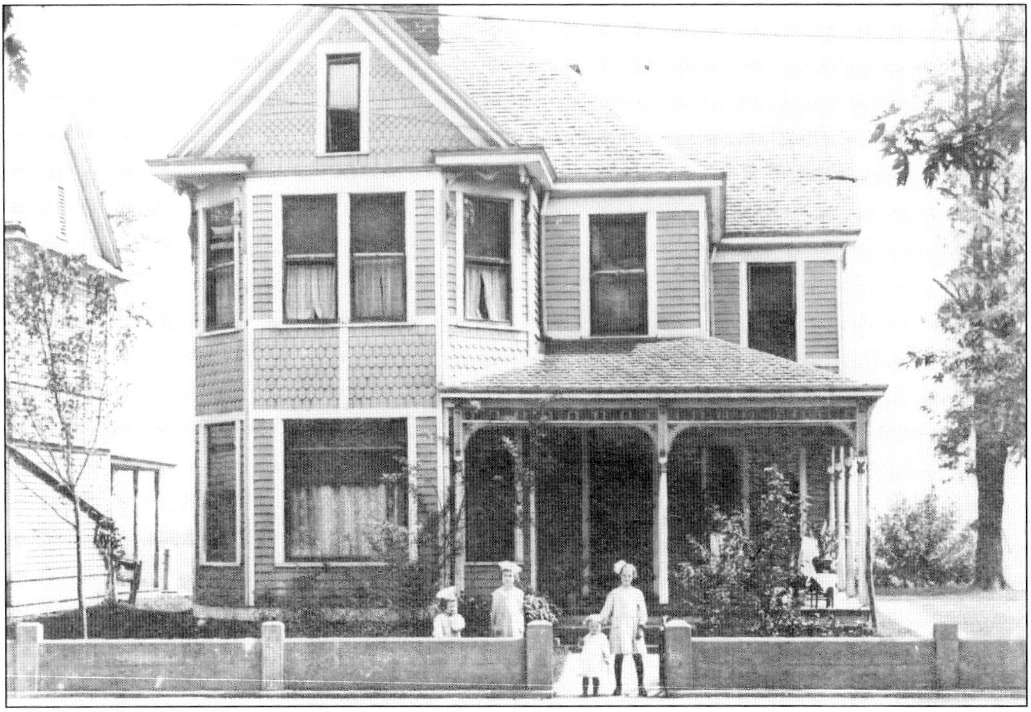

FOUR GIRLS AT PLAY. Four young girls stand side by side in their front yard in this 1910s photograph. This home was known as the Richardsons House. During this time, many homes were named after their designer or the first owner, such as the Putnam Home, the Gen. George Poage Home, and the Henry Clay Gartell Home. (Courtesy of the James C. Powers Collection.)

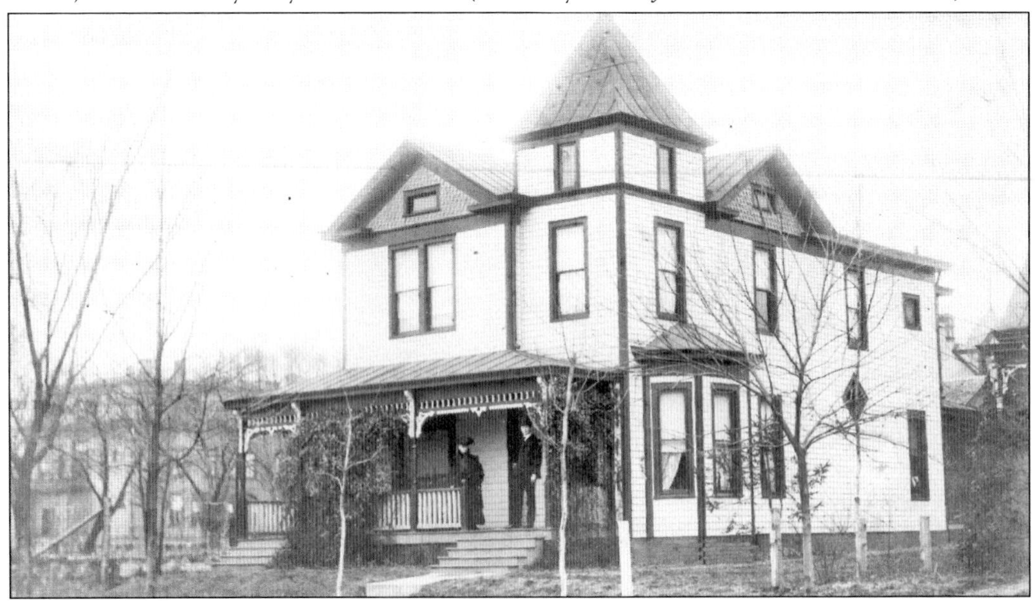

VICTORIAN STYLE. This home, photographed around 1905, was known as the Charles A. Fields Home. It still stands today on Montgomery Avenue. Ashland has quite a few homes that have survived well over a century and are beautiful. Several dozen are located in the Central Park and Bath Avenue area. (Courtesy of the James C. Powers Collection.)

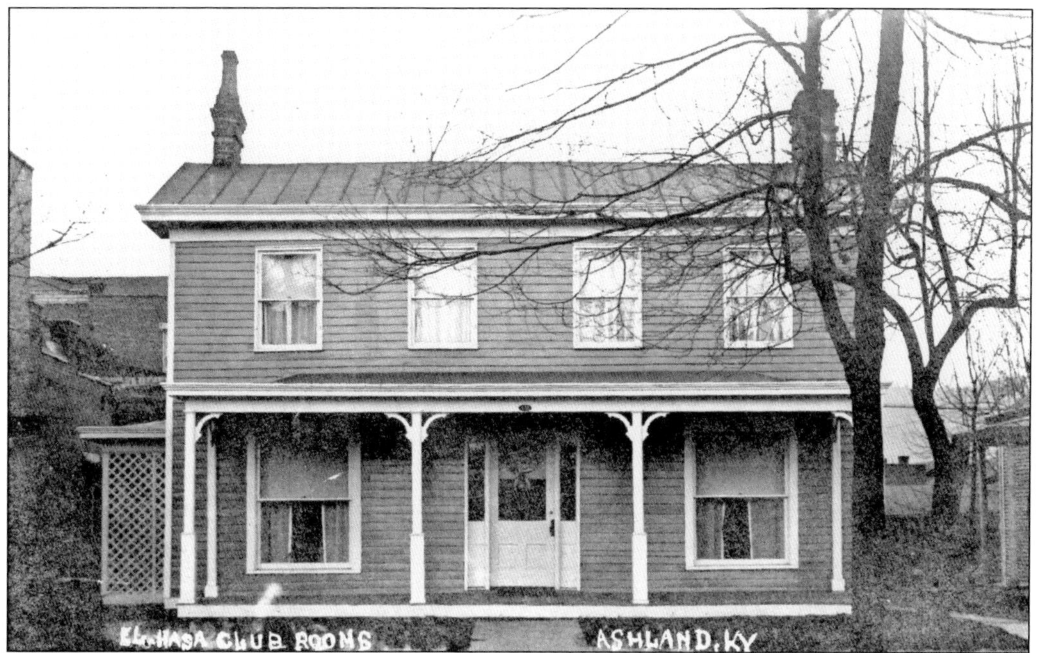

ANOTHER DOCTOR'S HOME. This home belonged to Dr. Harry S. Swope at one time and was located at 208 West Winchester Avenue. Many physicians working at nearby hospitals and private practices have bought and sold homes in Ashland. Several have purchase homes in neglected states and have had them restored better than their original state. (Courtesy of the James C. Powers Collection.)

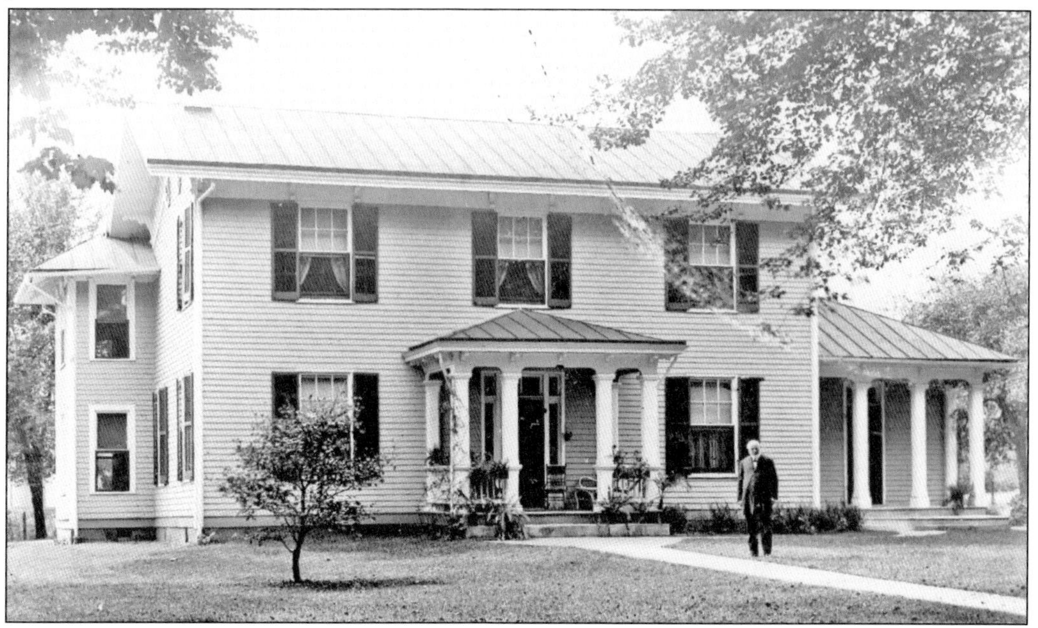

ON BATH AVENUE. This home was built in 1868 by M. T. Hilton, the same gentleman who came up with Ashland's street layout in 1854. The home was named after its longtime resident, W. C. Condit. The home stood at 1220 Bath Avenue for over a century. (Courtesy of the James C. Powers Collection.)

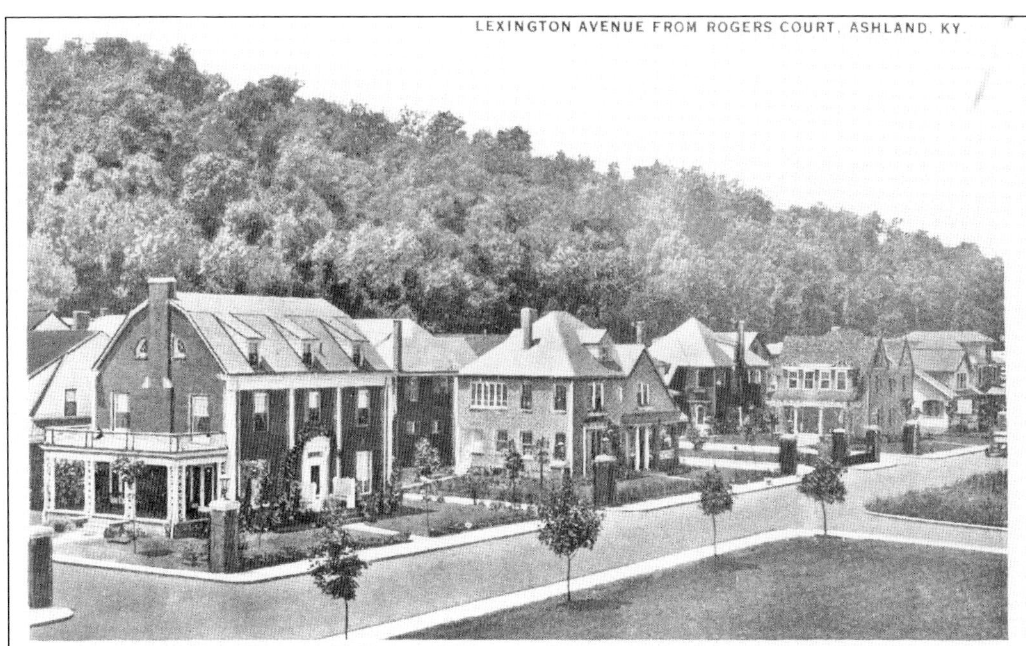

ROGERS COURT. On the right, along Lexington Avenue going east from Kings Daughters Hospital, is Rogers Court, a neighborhood of stately homes that were built in the early 1920s. This postcard dates from the 1930s and demonstrates that the homes have changed very little almost 90 years later. (Courtesy of the James C. Powers Collection.)

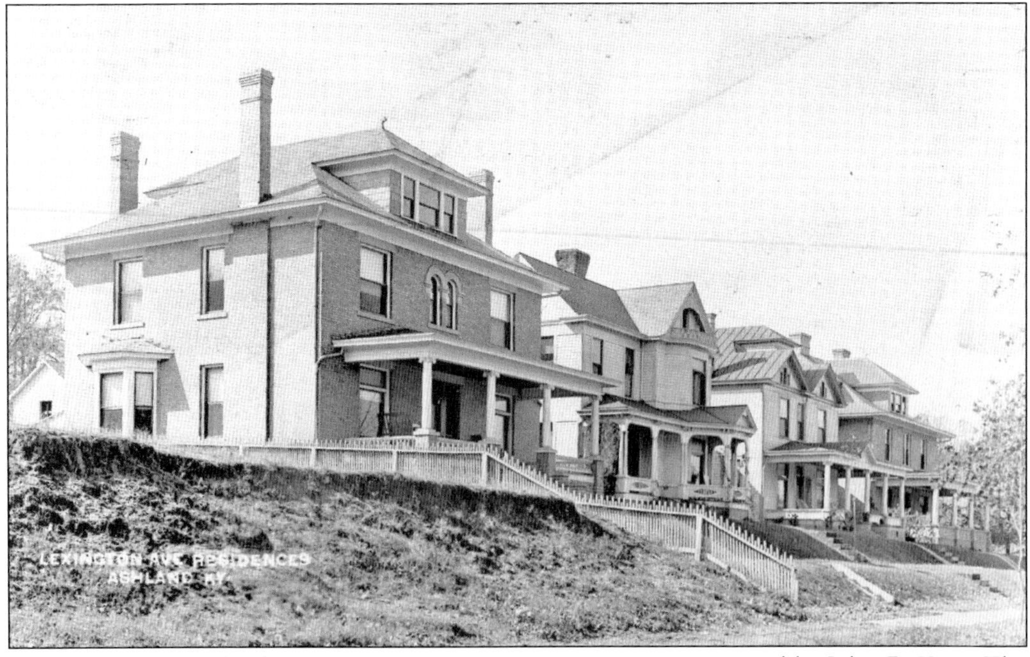

TALL CHIMNEYS. This home at 112 East Lexington Avenue was owned by John B. King. The chimneys were built higher than all parts of the roof in order to draw pressure away from the lower parts of the home. This lessened the risk or a downdraft, which would fill the home with smoke and heat. (Courtesy of the James C. Powers Collection.)

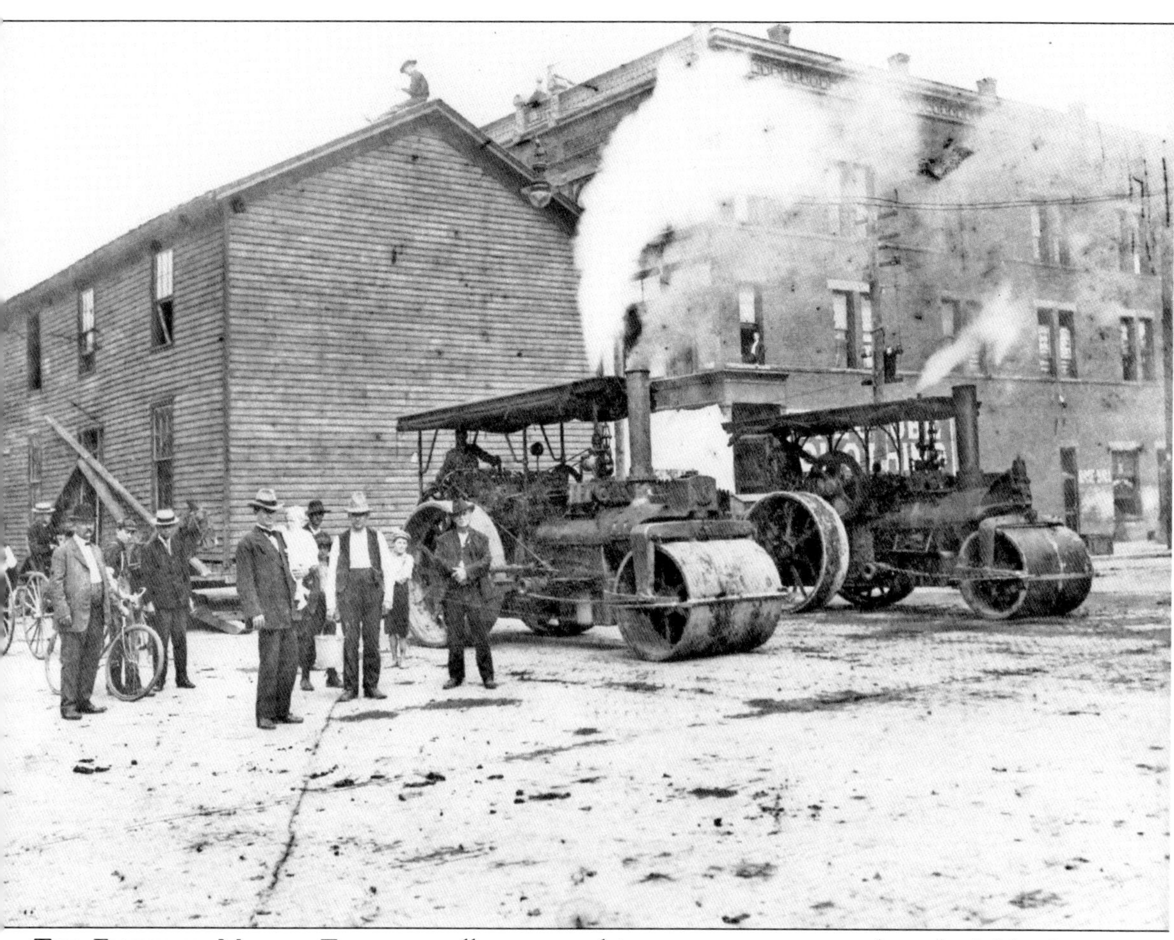

THE FIGHTING MAYOR. Two steamrollers move this two-story structure through Ashland streets around 1918 as the "Fighting Mayor" William Salisbury, his young son, and others stop to pose for this photograph. Mayor Salisbury (holding the child) was well known for buying buildings that were for sale and having them moved to parcels of land that he owned. He may have purchased water-damaged buildings after floods, moved them to his desired location, and remodeled them at a reduced rate. He was also well known for being at opposite ends with city and county commissioners and therefore received the nickname "Ashland's Fighting Mayor" in the 1920s. He owned the Crystal Ice and Cold Storage Company on Twenty-second Street and Central Avenue, which supplied ice before iceboxes became commonplace in the community. (Courtesy of the Arnold Hanners Photographic Collection, Minnie Winder Room, Boyd County Public Library.)

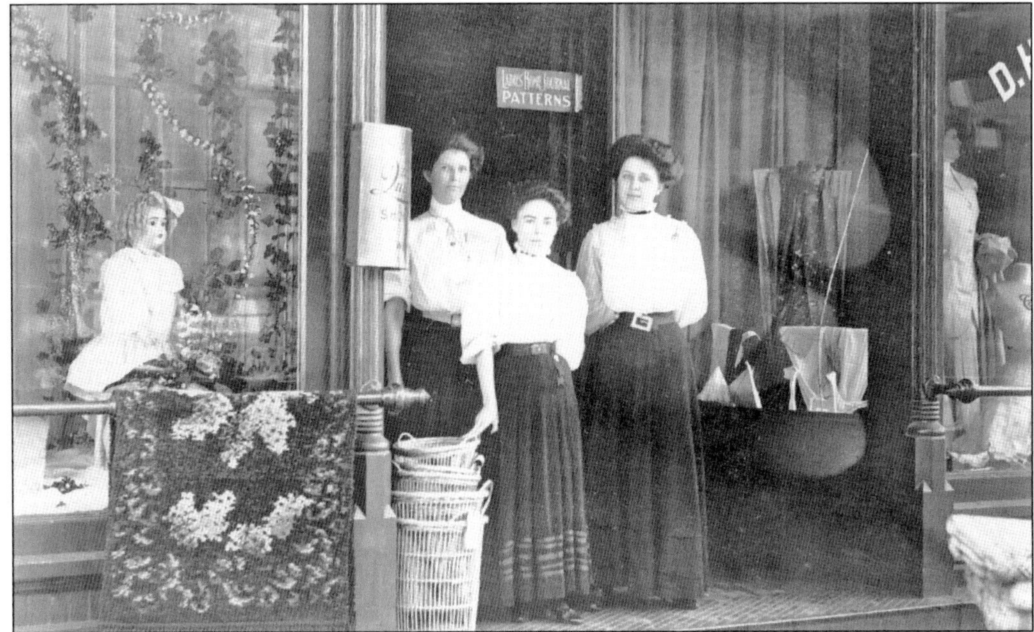

THREE SISTERS. The three Ellis sisters pose in front of an Ashland store. Leona, Lillian, and Lyda (from left to right) never married, and early on, they worked together at the W. E. Faulkner dry goods store. Eventually Lyda ran the Lyda Ellis dress shop with her sisters. When Lyda died, Lillian and Leona continued the business. (Courtesy of the James C. Powers Collection.)

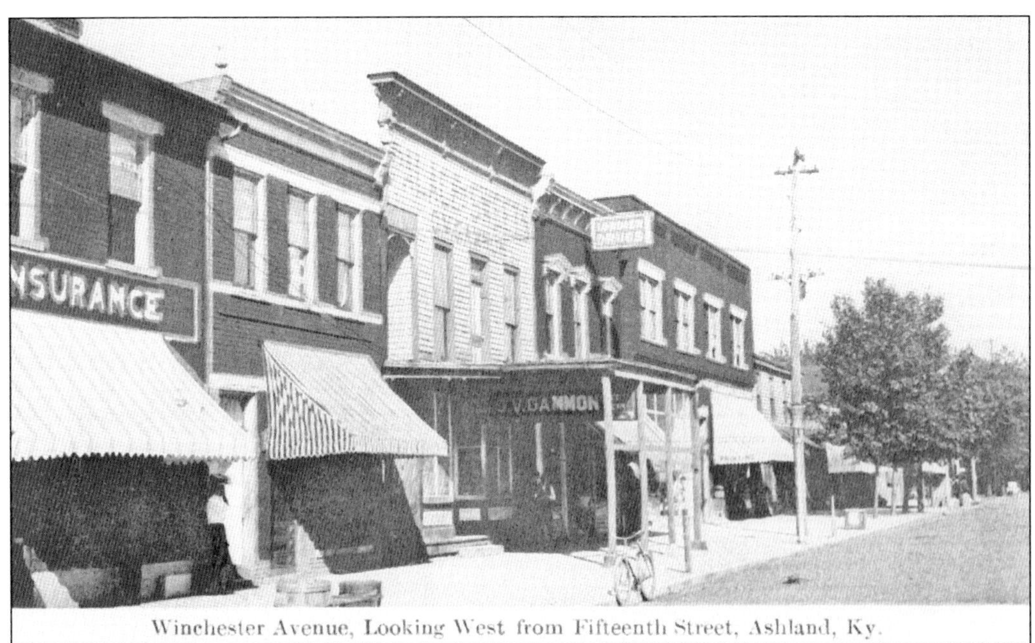

Winchester Avenue, Looking West from Fifteenth Street, Ashland, Ky.

WINCHESTER BUSINESSES. This postcard from around 1918 shows Winchester Avenue from Fifteenth Street looking west. It seems that the first structure built in Ashland was a log cabin near Broadway and Front Street. The Poage family built the first brick house near Twenty-eighth Street and Front Street. (Courtesy of the James C. Powers Collection.)

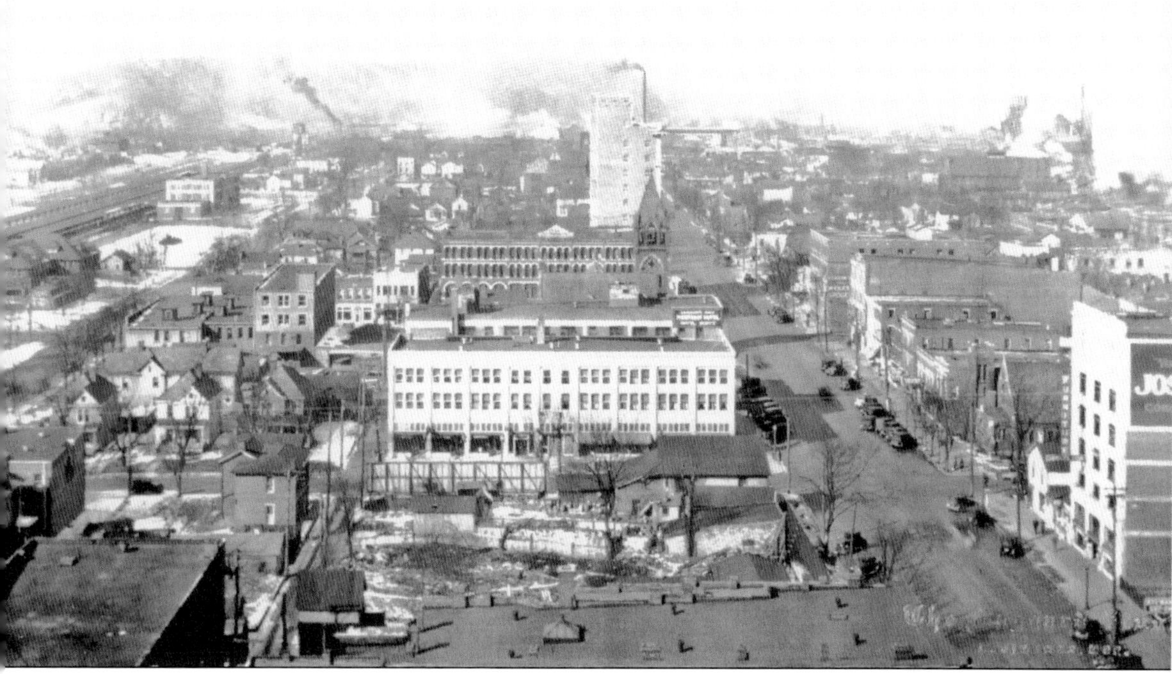

LOOKING WEST. This *c.* 1925 photograph is a view from the Ashland National Bank Building looking west. Smoke rising from several businesses is easily visible directly west, where the Ashland Town Center Mall is located today. The hill where Wal-Mart is located has been heavily logged, like many hills in the area. The C&O Railway Station is easy to spot at the left. Many passengers coming from the east passed through this station on their way to Cincinnati and north. The Ventura Hotel is the tall building straight ahead. Parts of Armco Steel can be identified in the upper right corner as Winchester Avenue stretches west past several structures that are used today. Winchester Avenue continues to be a center of community activity and has seen many types of parades and celebrations through the years. (Courtesy of the Arnold Hanners Photographic Collection, Minnie Winder Room, Boyd County Public Library.)

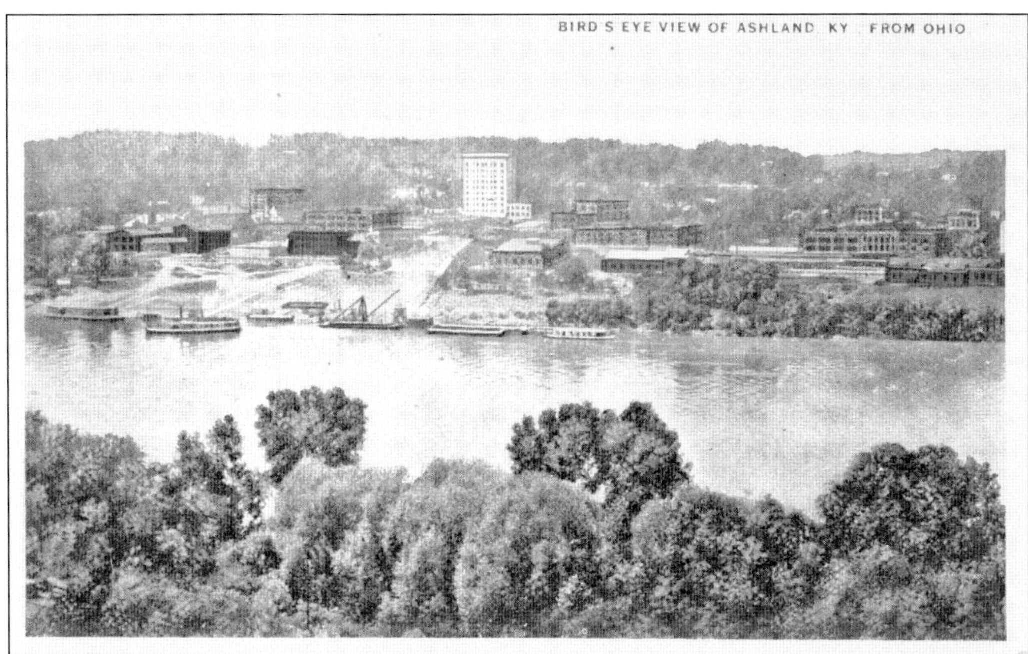

VIEW FROM OHIO. Ashland is easily recognizable in this postcard from the mid-1920s. The Ashland National Bank and the hills behind have changed little from that time until now. Discernable changes are the skyline, homes along the hills, and the addition of two bridges that cross the Ohio River into Coal Grove, Ohio. (Courtesy of the James C. Powers Collection.)

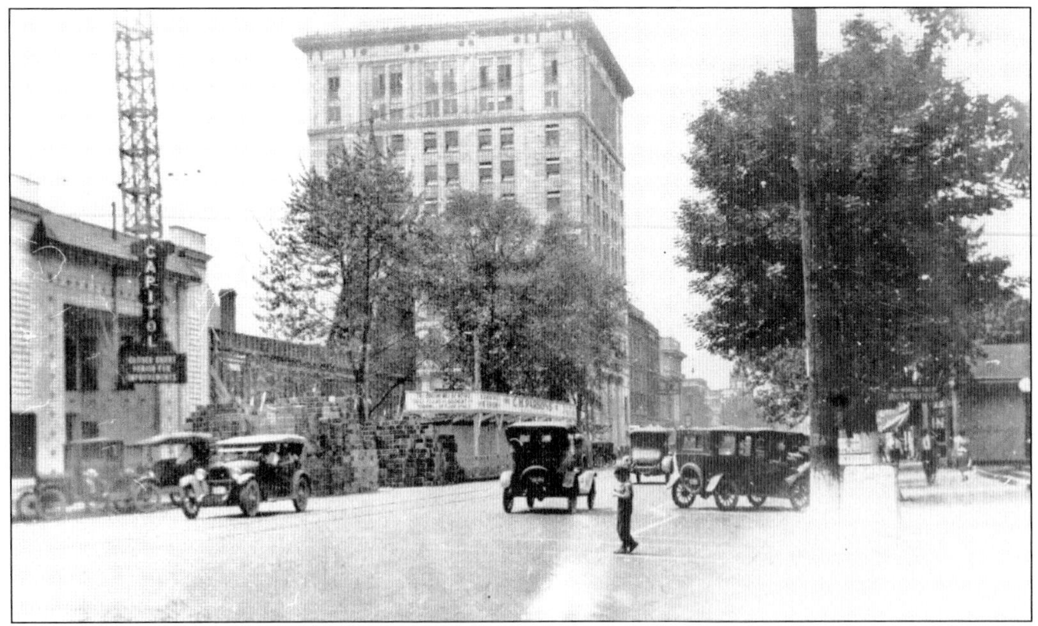

A LONE BOY. The C. H. Parsons Building is being constructed in the background of this photograph from around 1928. A lone boy crosses Winchester Avenue in front of the Capital Theater as automobiles buzz by near the 1600 block. A marquee was added to the Capital Theater sometime later. (Courtesy of the Arnold Hanners Photographic Collection, Minnie Winder Room, Boyd County Public Library.)

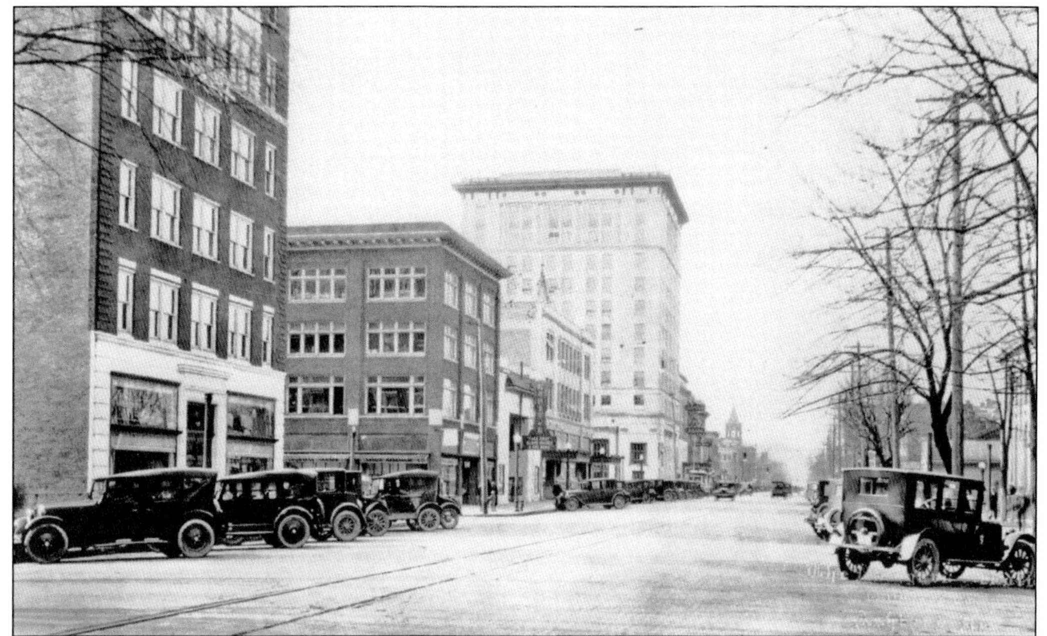

WINCHESTER BUSINESS DISTRICT. This 1930 photograph from about 25 yards east of the last photograph shows the Parsons Building completed with three stories and a basement. The post office building is to the right, and the streetcar tracks disappear into the west along the brick road. (Courtesy of the Arnold Hanners Photographic Collection, Minnie Winder Room, Boyd County Public Library.)

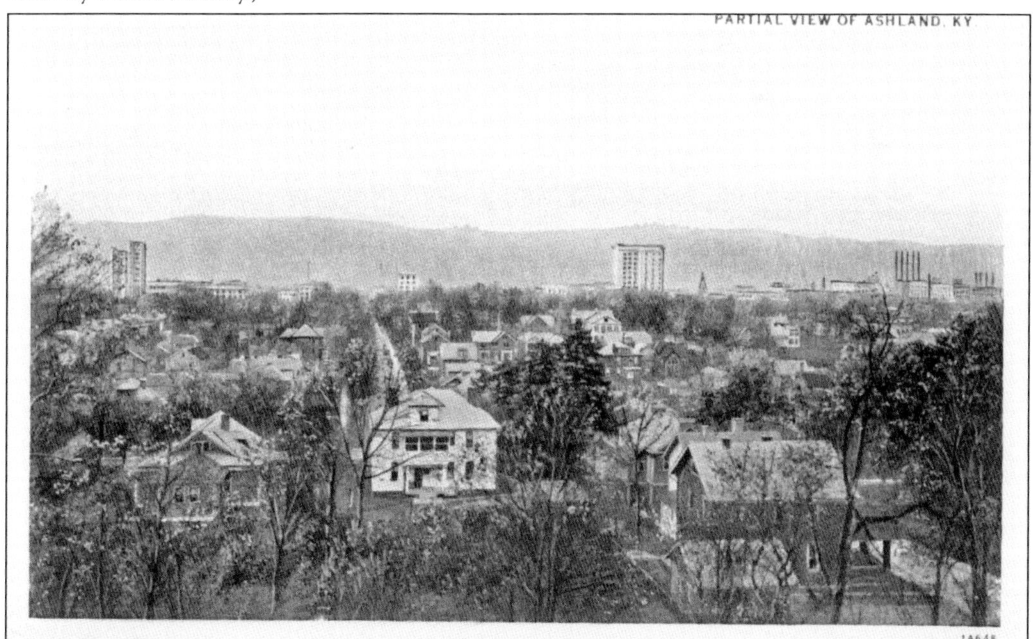

ASHLAND'S CENTER. This postcard is looking north toward Ohio from near Fourteenth Street and Lexington Avenue. Several homes in the foreground stand today as reminders of Ashland's rich past. Lifelong resident and author, James C. Powers, was born and continues to live in the area pictured here. (Courtesy of the James C. Powers Collection.)

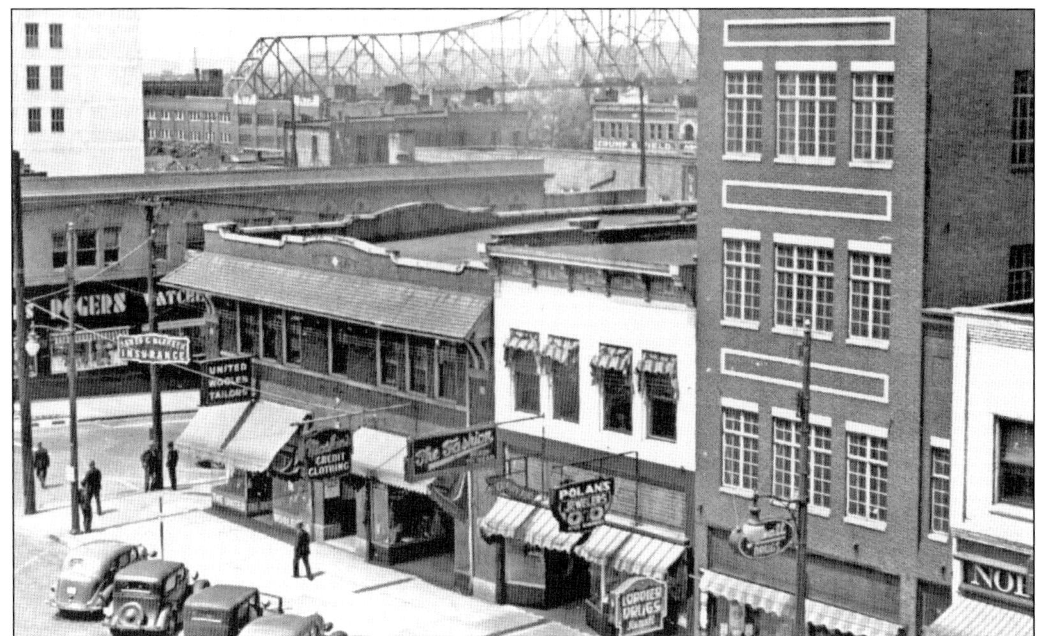

LOOKING TOWARD IRONTON, OHIO. Shown in 1940 is the Ashland Bridge looking northwest toward Ironton, Ohio. Notice the Crump and Field Building centered on Greenup Avenue. Several clothing stores are on the lower left along Winchester Avenue: United Woolen Tailors, Credit Clothing, and the Fashion Ready to Ware. (Courtesy of the Arnold Hanners Photographic Collection, Minnie Winder Room, Boyd County Public Library.)

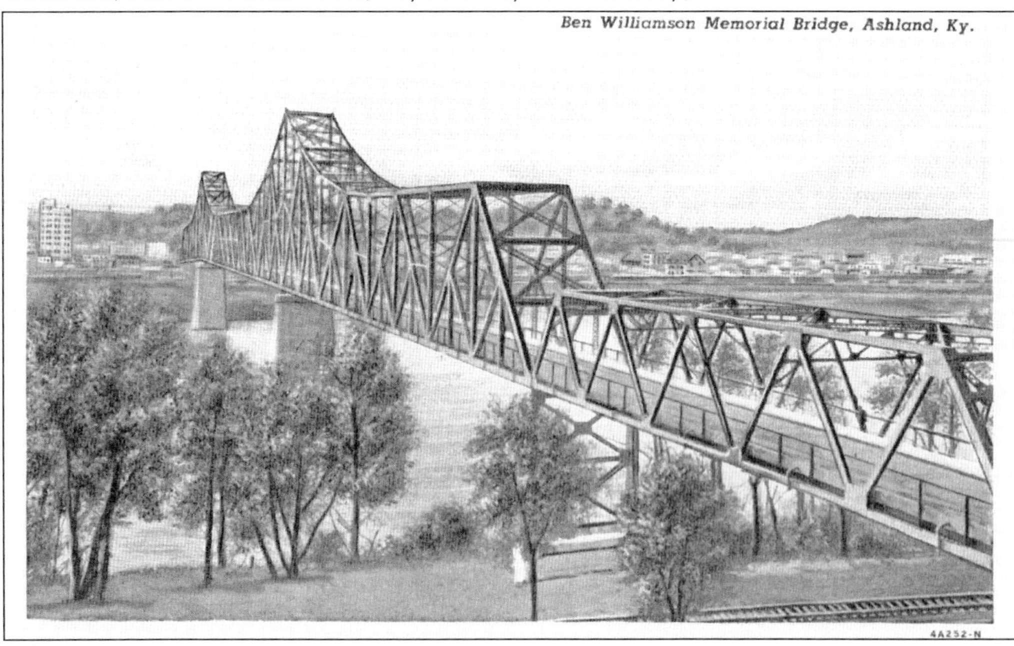

A BRIDGE INTO ASHLAND. This postcard of Ashland from Coal Grove, Ohio, features the two-lane Ben Williamson Memorial Bridge. Today the bridge has had a facelift of unique green paint and continues as a one-way, cantilever-truss bridge across the Ohio River into the city. (Courtesy of the James C. Powers Collection.)

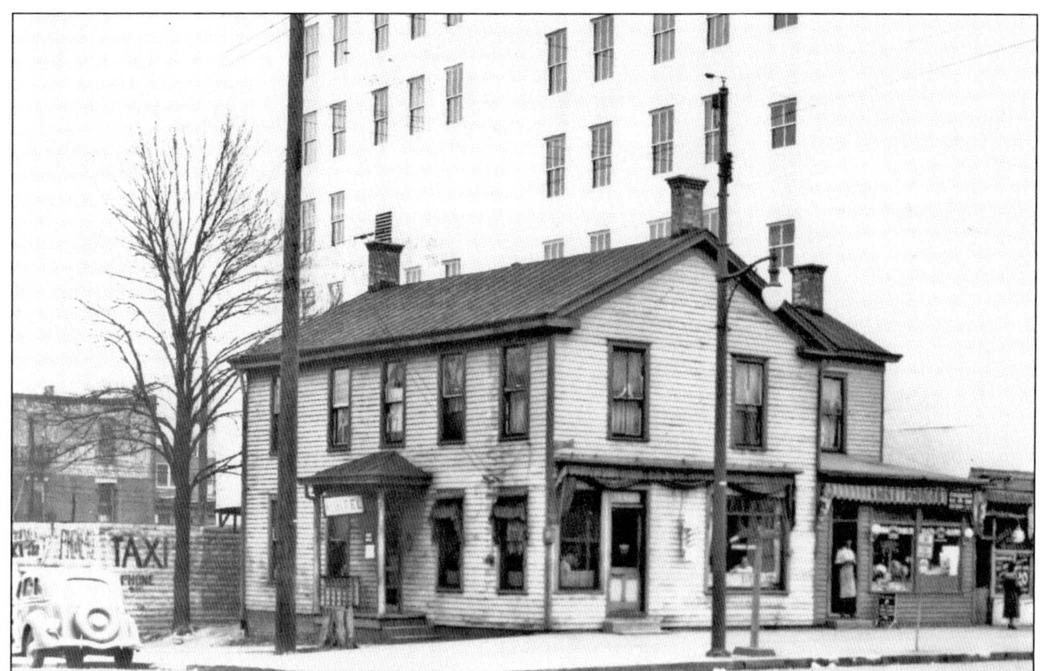

The Joseph Burdett Home. Pictured around 1940, the Joseph Burdett Home was built in 1863 on the corner of Sixteenth Street and Winchester Avenue. The home was torn down around 1951 and replaced by the Johnson Center Building, which housed the Ashland Oil Headquarters at one time. (Courtesy of the Arnold Hanners Photographic Collection, Minnie Winder Room, Boyd County Public Library.)

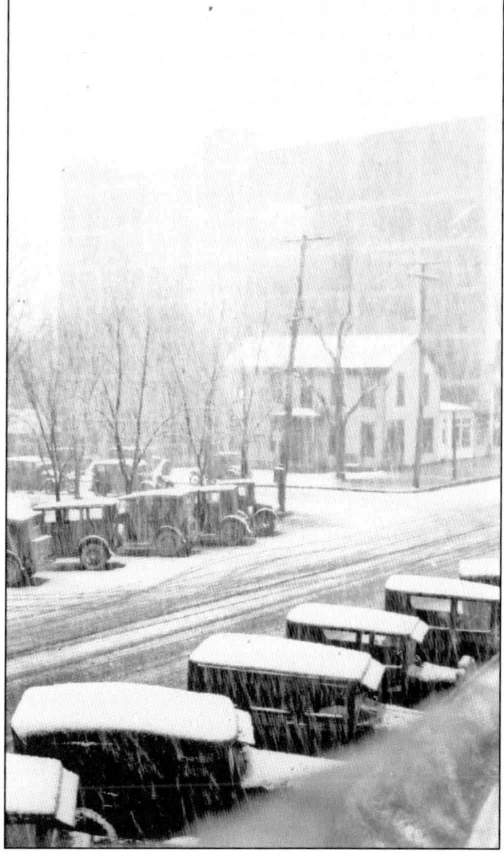

Ice Storm. This rare photograph taken during an ice storm around 1938 shows the parking spaces along Winchester Avenue filled up, and the Joseph Burdett Home stands out against the silhouette of the Haskell Building. The Joseph Burdett Home housed a hotel, a barbershop, a shine shop, and a hat shop during this time. (Courtesy of the Arnold Hanners Photographic Collection, Minnie Winder Room, Boyd County Public Library.)

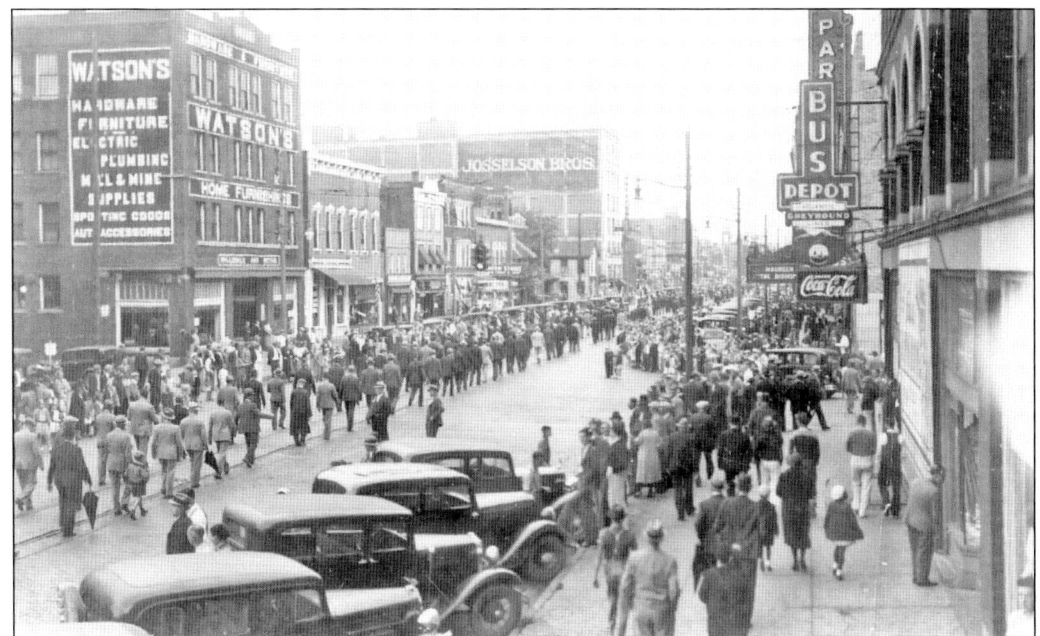

IRON MEN. In this *c.* 1935 photograph, a large two-column line of men walks east on Winchester Avenue in front of the Hotel Ventura and Greyhound Bus Depot, and across Thirteenth Street is the newly built Paramount Theater with its recognizable marquee. The Ventura is long gone, but many of the structures in this photograph stand today. (Courtesy of the Arnold Hanners Photographic Collection, Minnie Winder Room, Boyd County Public Library.)

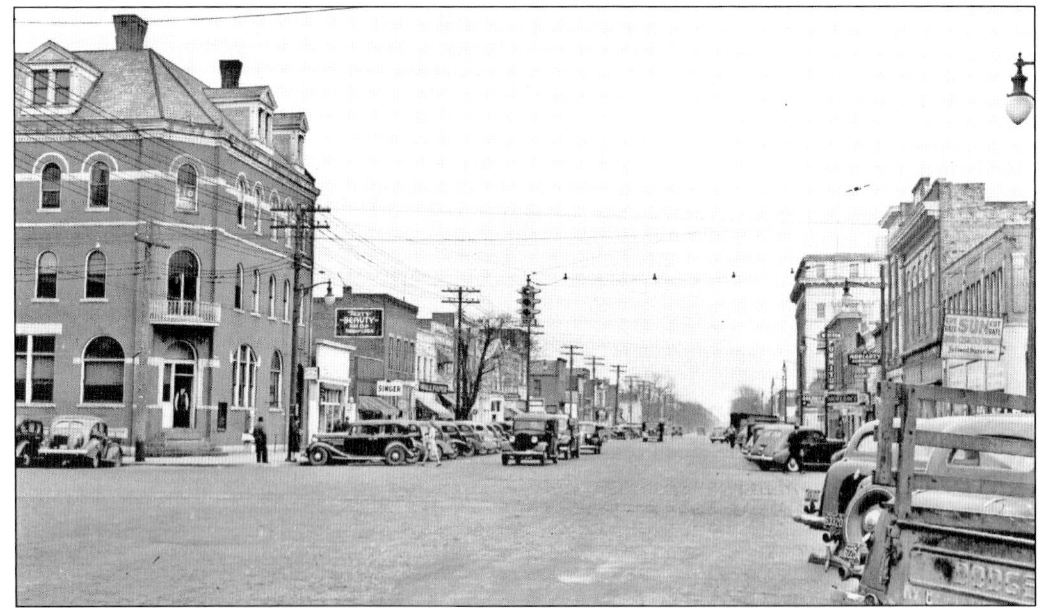

GREENUP AVENUE IN 1939. Brick paves Greenup Avenue from Sixteenth Street east in this picture from 1939. The old Beckette Block or Cole Building is across the street, and by this time, the Second National Bank has moved on a different location. A barbershop has settled into the first floor, and the five-story City Building is visible to the right. (Courtesy of the James C. Powers Collection.)

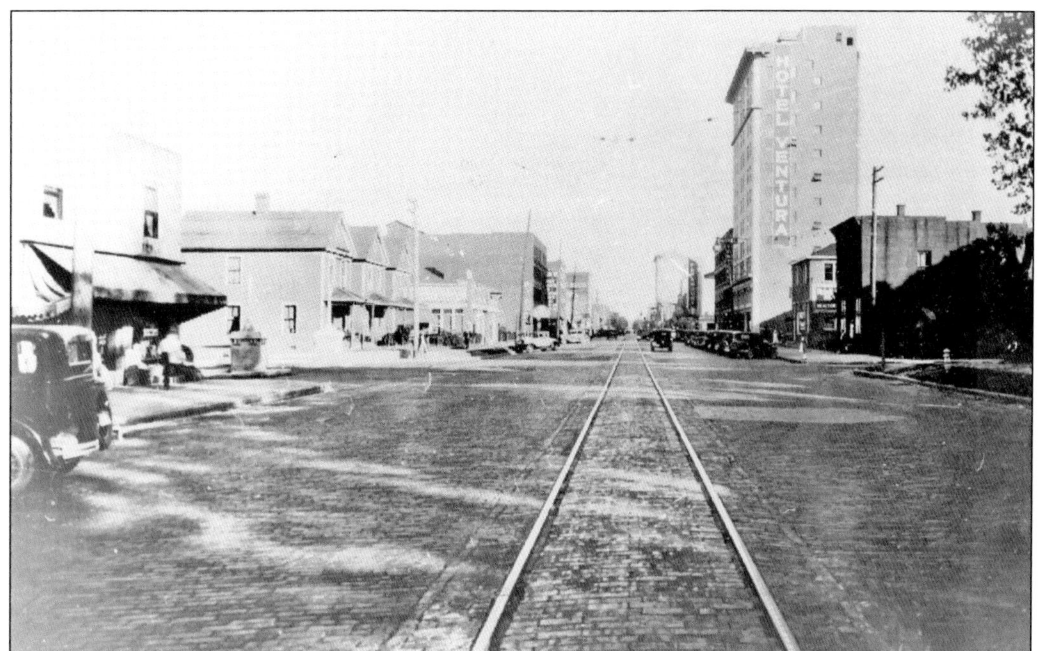

WINCHESTER EAST. The streetcar track runs east down the middle of Winchester Avenue from around where Blue Ribbon Lanes is located today. The streetcars were giving way to the city buses that began to run around this time in the early 1940s. The Hotel Ventura is to the right, as is the Paramount. (Courtesy of the James C. Powers Collection.)

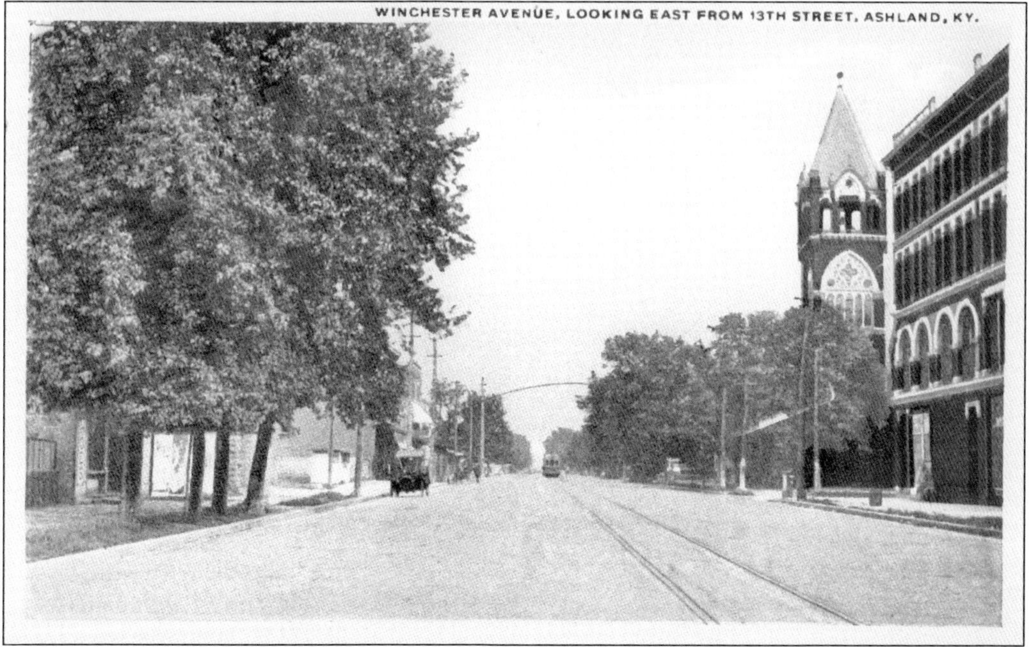

WINCHESTER EAST IN 1915. In this view, from just a street or two east, Winchester Avenue runs east with the same rails running down the middle. The Ventura is again visible, with the familiar church-bell house across Thirteenth Street where the Paramount will be located 16 years from when this picture was taken. (Courtesy of the James C. Powers Collection.)

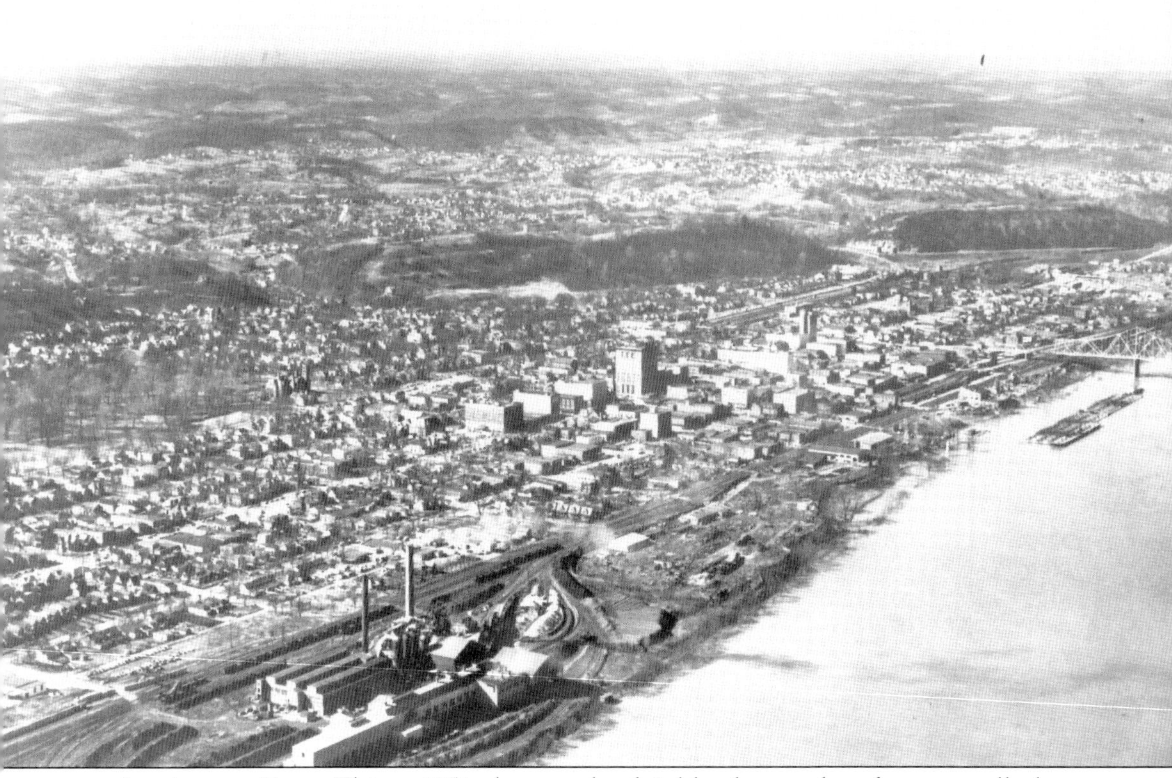

AN AERIAL VIEW. This c. 1951 photograph of Ashland was taken from a small plane over the Ohio River northeast of downtown and clearly shows the Ashland National Bank as the centerpiece to the city. The Central High School building is in the northeast corner of Central Park, and the Hotel Ventura is easily recognizable. A spectacular bird's-eye drawing of Ashland dating back to the 1880s is located at the Minnie Winder Room on the second floor of the Boyd County Public Library on Central Avenue in Ashland. Many historical structures from Ashland's early days encircle the drawing. It has been used in several historical narratives regarding Ashland, Eastern Kentucky, Western West Virginia, and Southern Ohio. The drawing was owned by a couple that married in the 1880s, thus enabling historians to accurately date the drawing. (Courtesy of the Arnold Hanners Photographic Collection, Minnie Winder Room, Boyd County Public Library.)

Two

CITY BUSINESSES

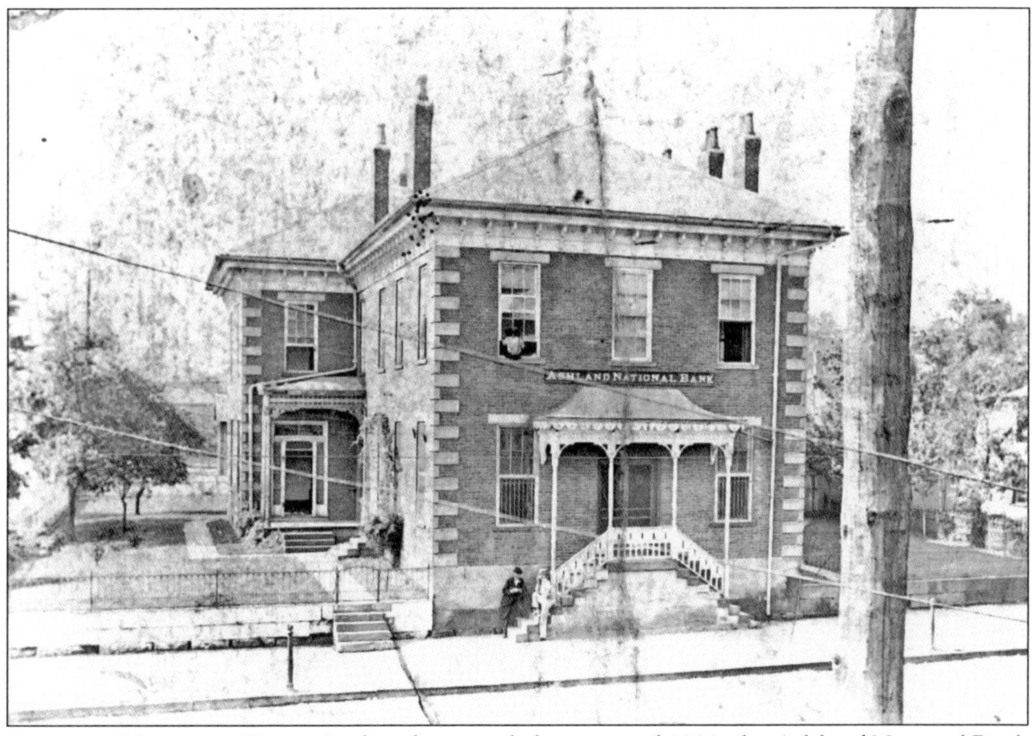

ASHLAND NATIONAL BANK. In this photograph from around 1900, the Ashland National Bank is an impressive two-story brick structure on the southeast corner of Broadway and Winchester Avenue. The 1864 building was razed in 1922 and replaced by the Second National Bank Building, which still stands today. In early 1856, Hugh and Thomas Means helped organize the Bank of Ashland. Hugh Means became the first bank president, and Thomas's son, John, served as the bank's cashier until 1869. In 1872, the Bank of Ashland closed but reopened after being reorganized as the Ashland National Bank with Hugh Means as president and John Means as vice president. Another prominent banker and businessman was A. C. Campbell. In 1866, he became a bookkeeper for the Bank of Ashland, a position he held until 1868, when he was elected as cashier. A decade later, Campbell, John Russell, and other investors organized the Catlettsburg National Bank. (Courtesy of the Arnold Hanners Photographic Collection, Minnie Winder Room, Boyd County Public Library.)

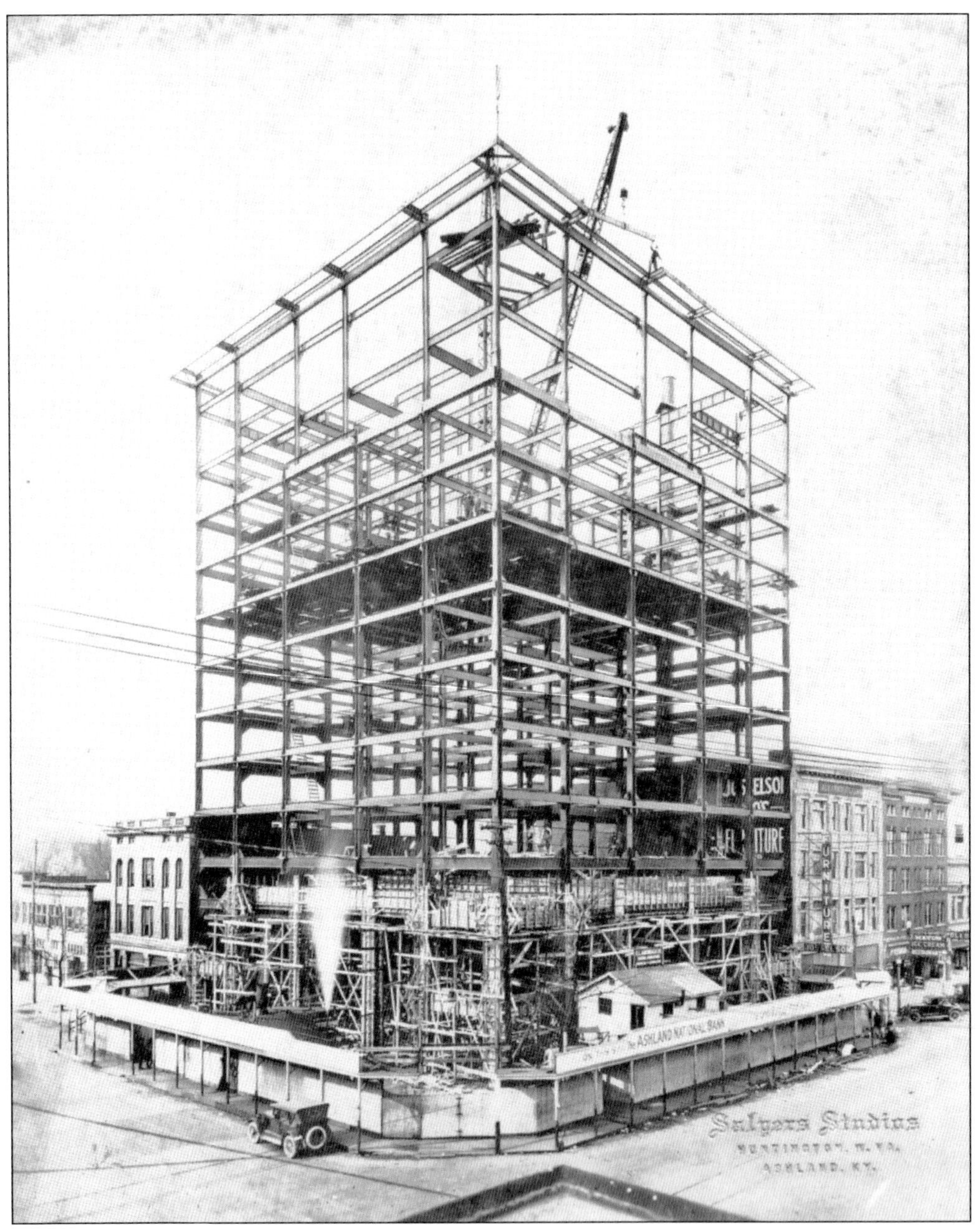

ASHLAND'S CENTERPIECE. The Ashland National Bank Building has long been considered the heart of downtown. Whether entering the city from Catlettsburg, Ironton, South Point, Cannonsburg, or Belefonte, this landmark structure is one of the first buildings visitors notice. In May 1923, construction workers are finishing placing the last piece of steel on the north side or the Winchester Avenue side of the framework. The building was designed and constructed by Schenck and Williams of Dayton, Ohio, in 1922 and has been scaled by at least by one individual, Harry Gardiner, "The Human Fly," who did it within an hour during a rainstorm several decades back in early February 1927. The building stands at a height of 116 feet with 11 stories and is currently the home of Community Trust Bank in Ashland. This structure has changed very little since 1922. (Courtesy of the Minnie Winder Room, Boyd County Public Library.)

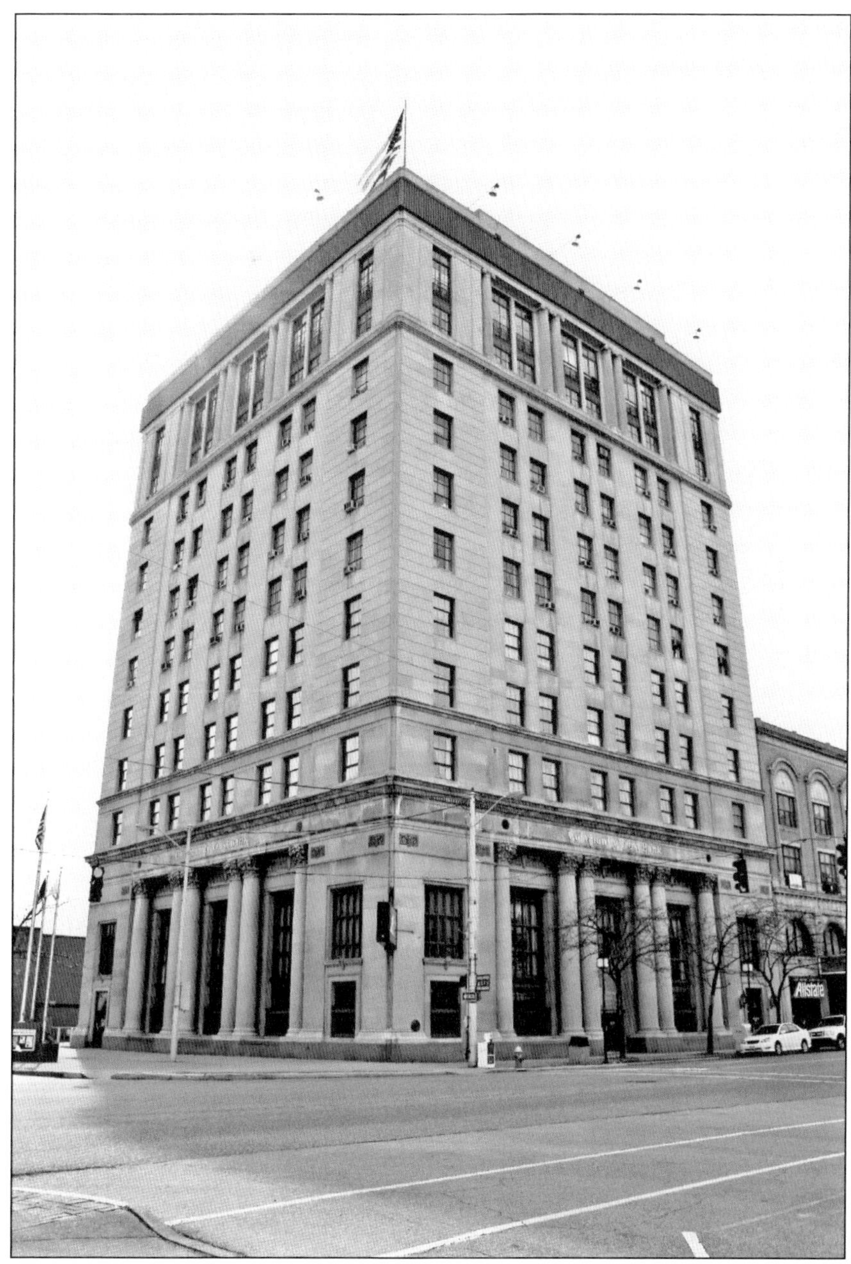

STILL STANDING TALL. The old Ashland National Bank Building continues to impress area residents with its noble facade. Lights installed around the rim of the top illuminate the building during the night and highlight the skyline, especially from the Ohio side of the river. The streets at the base of the 116-foot structure were Winchester Avenue and Sixteenth Street when constructed. In the late 1980s, the name of this intersection was changed to Judd Plaza in honor of Ashland natives and country music legends the Judds. Plans are underway to renovate the area with a larger stage, tables, and a clock at the bottom of the old Ashland National Bank Building, now the Community Trust Bank. The improvements are sure to make the plaza an even larger draw than it is now. Community events and many other functions are certain to be centered at this grand building. (Photograph by Terry L. Baldridge.)

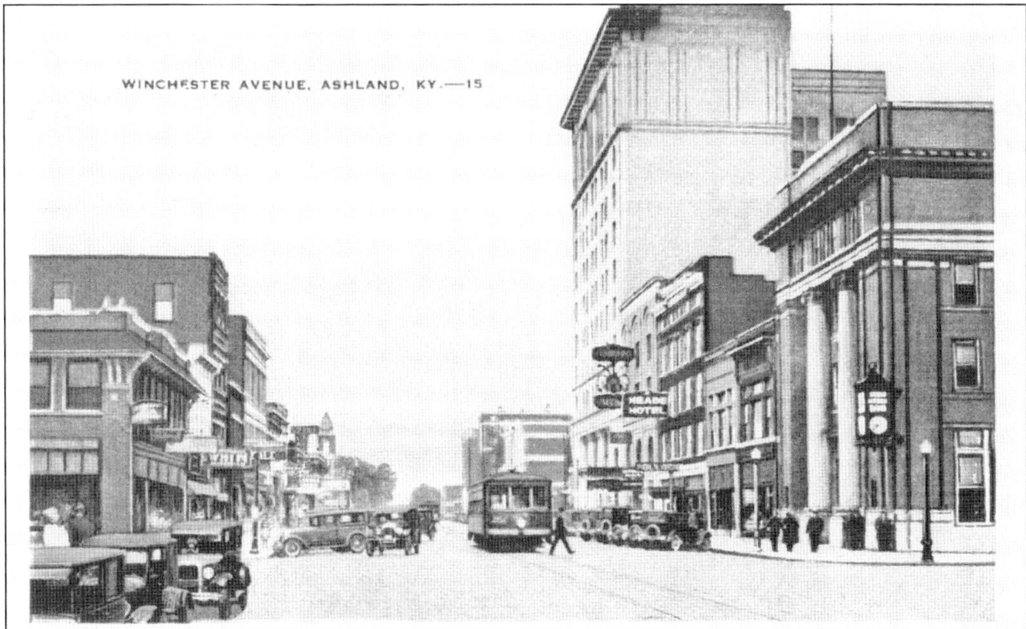

AN EASTWARD VIEW. In this eastward view from around Fifteenth Street and Winchester Avenue in the 1930s, several businesses lead up to the Ashland National Bank Building on the right. Automobiles are parked diagonally from the direction of the street in the background, and several are parked parallel on the left. (Courtesy of the James C. Powers Collection.)

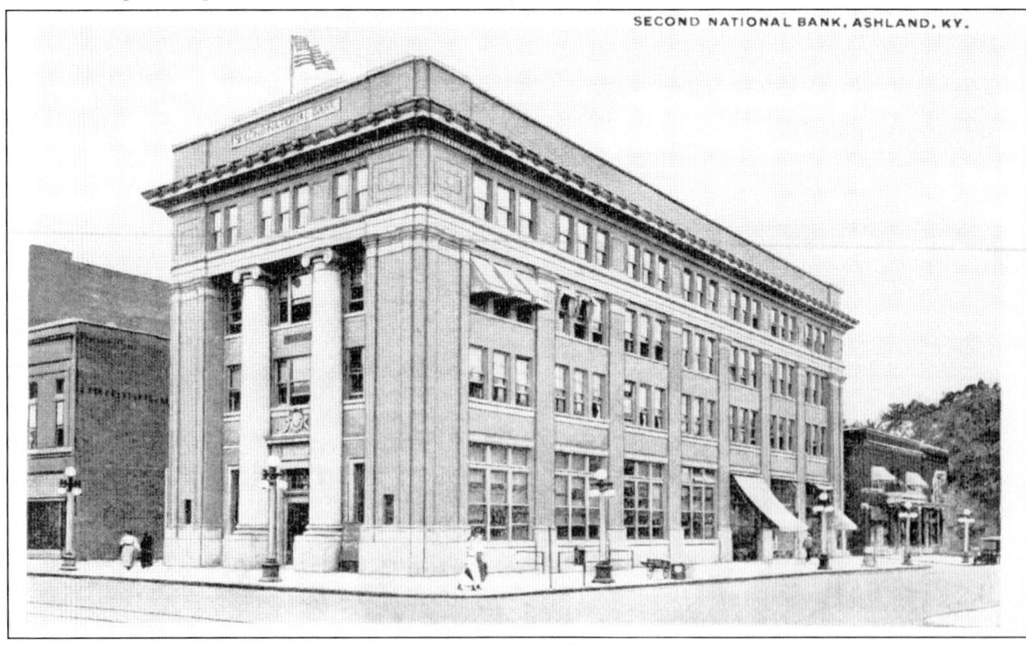

TWO-COLUMNED ENTRANCE. The Ashland Second National Bank takes center stage in this postcard from around 1930. The structure's design hints at architecture of the time period, with some Greek Revival in the columns and the top of the building. The structure stands today at the southeast corner of Winchester Avenue and Fifteenth Street. (Courtesy of the James C. Powers Collection.)

A STREETCAR STOP. Streetcars routinely stopped at the Ashland National Bank Building at the corner of Sixteenth Street going east on Winchester Avenue. Besides the Ashland National Bank, many other businesses were in the area along Sixteenth Street on Greenup Avenue to the north and Carter Avenue to the south. (Courtesy of the Terry L. Baldridge Collection.)

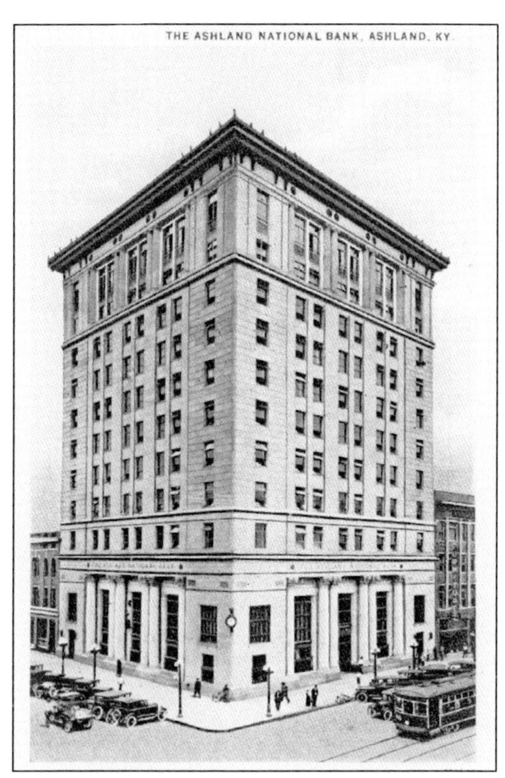

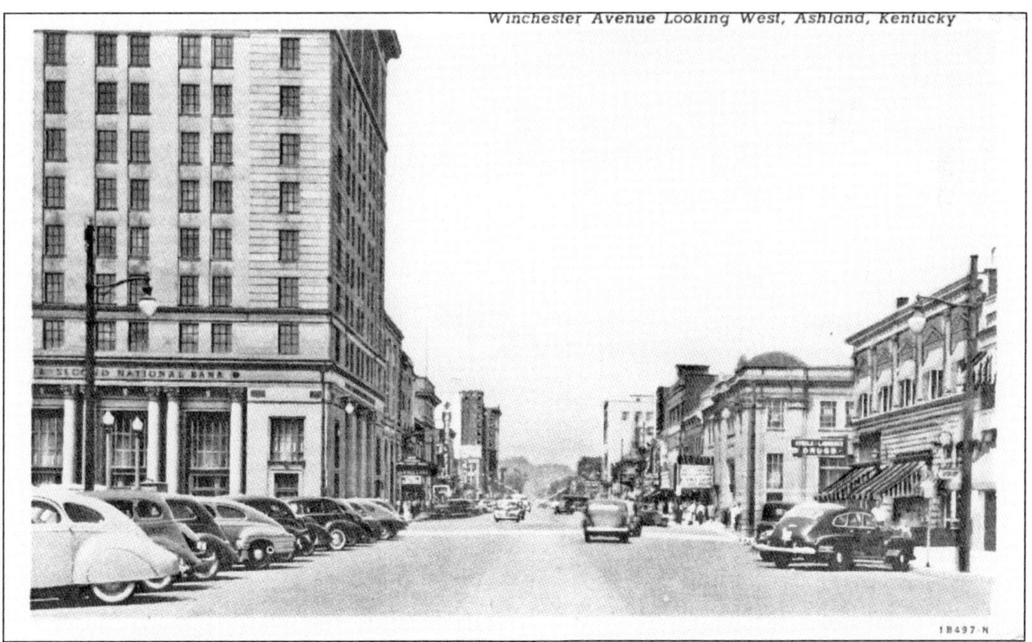

BUSINESS DISTRICT. This postcard from the early 1950s shows a view from Fifteenth Street looking west through the business district of Winchester Avenue toward Sixteenth Street and beyond. The drugstore, Third National Bank, and a theater are on the left. The Ashland National Bank and businesses are along the right. The streetcar rails have long since been taken up. (Courtesy of the James C. Powers Collection.)

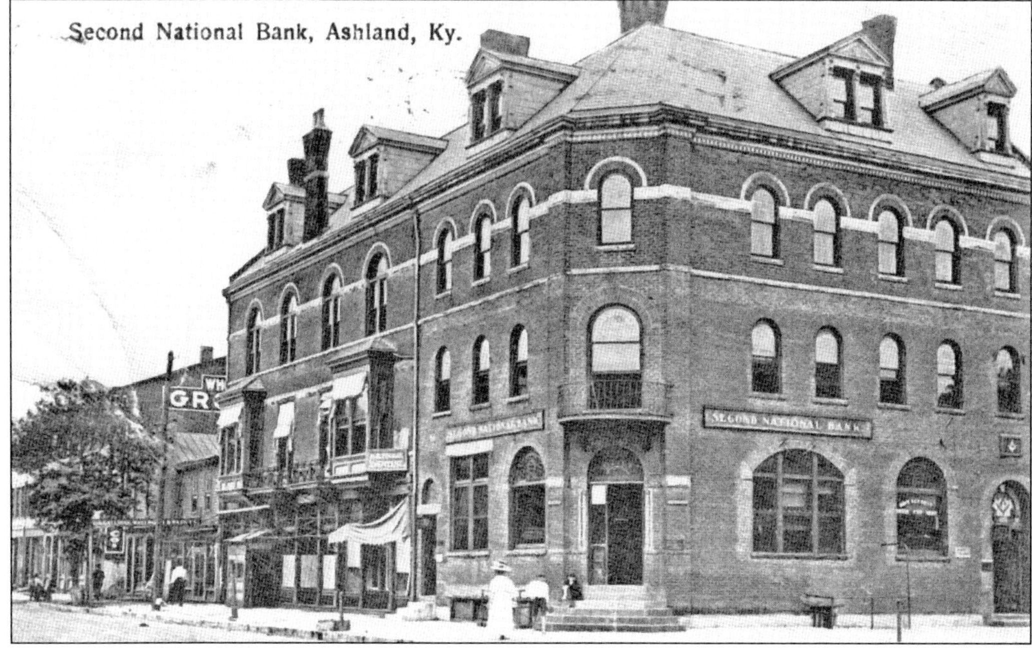

Boys on the Corner. Two boys are interacting outside the steps of the Second National Bank; perhaps their apartments are on the upper floors. This photograph was taken at the middle of Greenup Avenue and Sixteenth Street looking north. A dentist and a paint store are to the left of the corner entrance. (Courtesy of the James C. Powers Collection.)

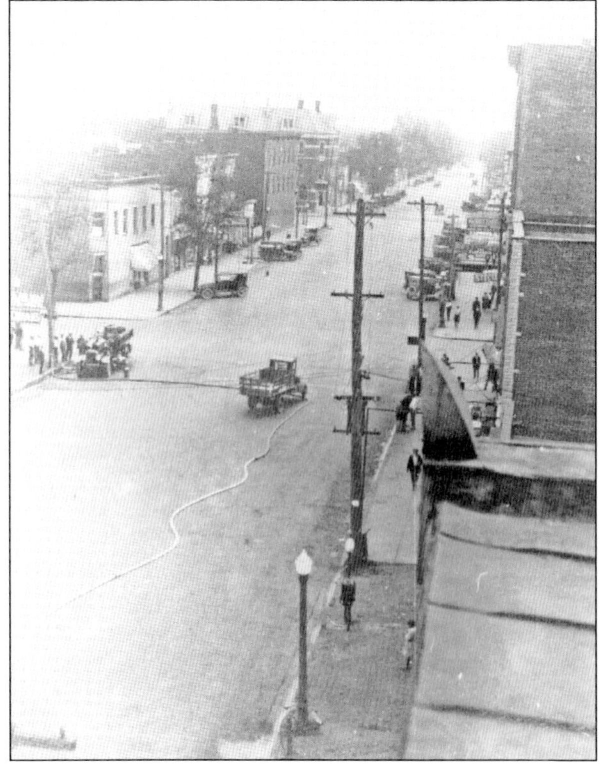

A Fire Drill. This photograph taken from a third-story window or roof shows a fire truck on the northwest corner of Greenup Avenue and Seventeenth Street. No smoke can be seen, which indicates that some sort of a fire drill or test is going on during a less busy time. (Courtesy of the Arnold Hanners Photographic Collection, Minnie Winder Room, Boyd County Public Library.)

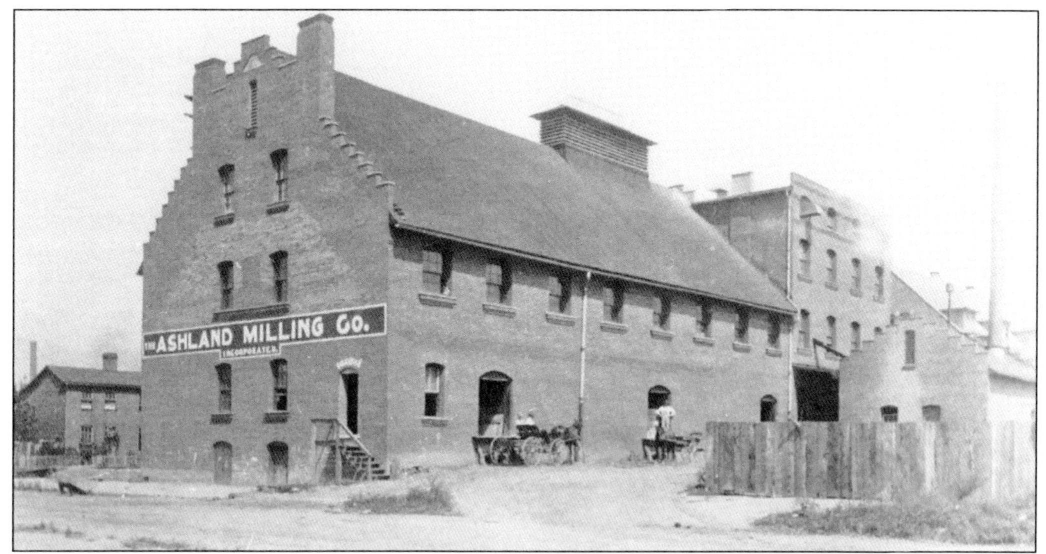

ASHLAND MILLING COMPANY. The unique Ashland Milling Company building is pictured around 1895. Many farmers from eastern Kentucky and southern Ohio made routine trips to this location to purchase feed for livestock, have their corn ground, and purchase tools and hardware for their farms. (Courtesy of the Arnold Hanners Photographic Collection, Minnie Winder Room, Boyd County Public Library.)

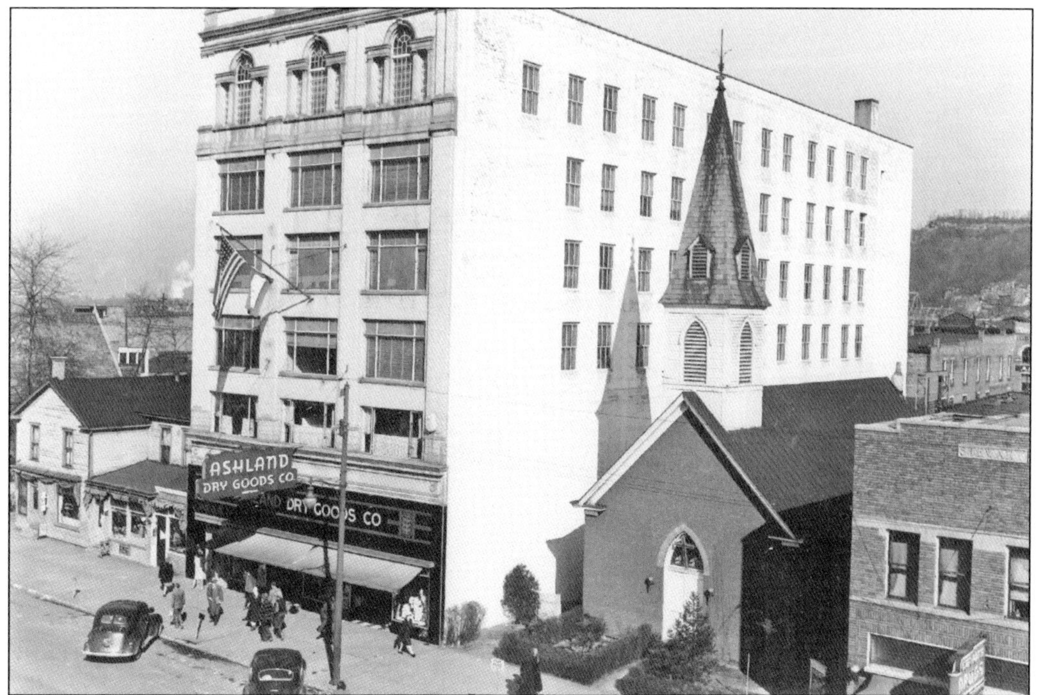

DRY GOODS. The old Josselson Building stands six stories tall at 1406 Winchester Avenue around 1945. The first floor contained the Ashland Dry Goods store, which sold specialties and novelty items for several decades. A drugstore is in the first floor of the Stewart Building to the lower right. (Courtesy of the Arnold Hanners Photographic Collection, Minnie Winder Room, Boyd County Public Library.)

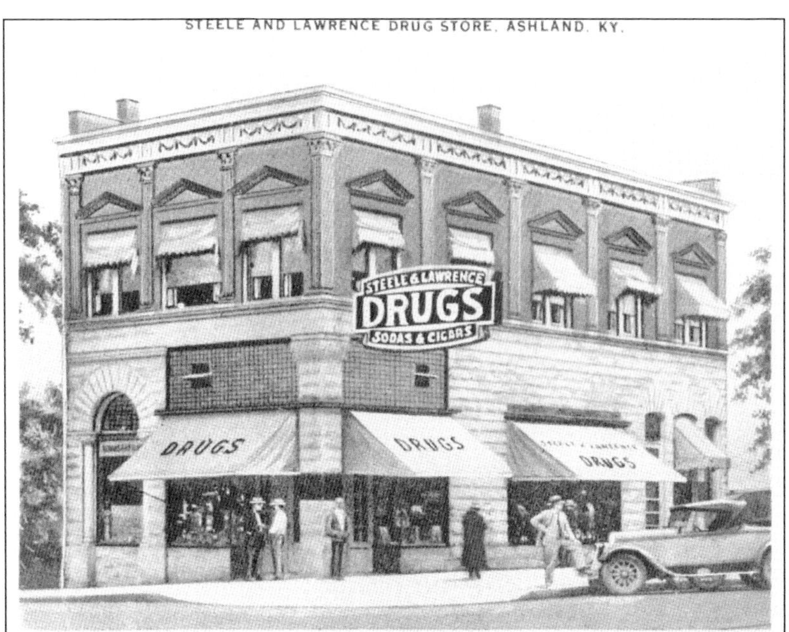

DRUGS AND SODAS. Operating out of the northeast corner of Winchester and Sixteenth Street was the drugstore, Steele and Lawrence Sodas and Cigars. The store did business at that location for many years despite competition from other drugstores and one large flood in 1937. (Courtesy of the James C. Powers Collection.)

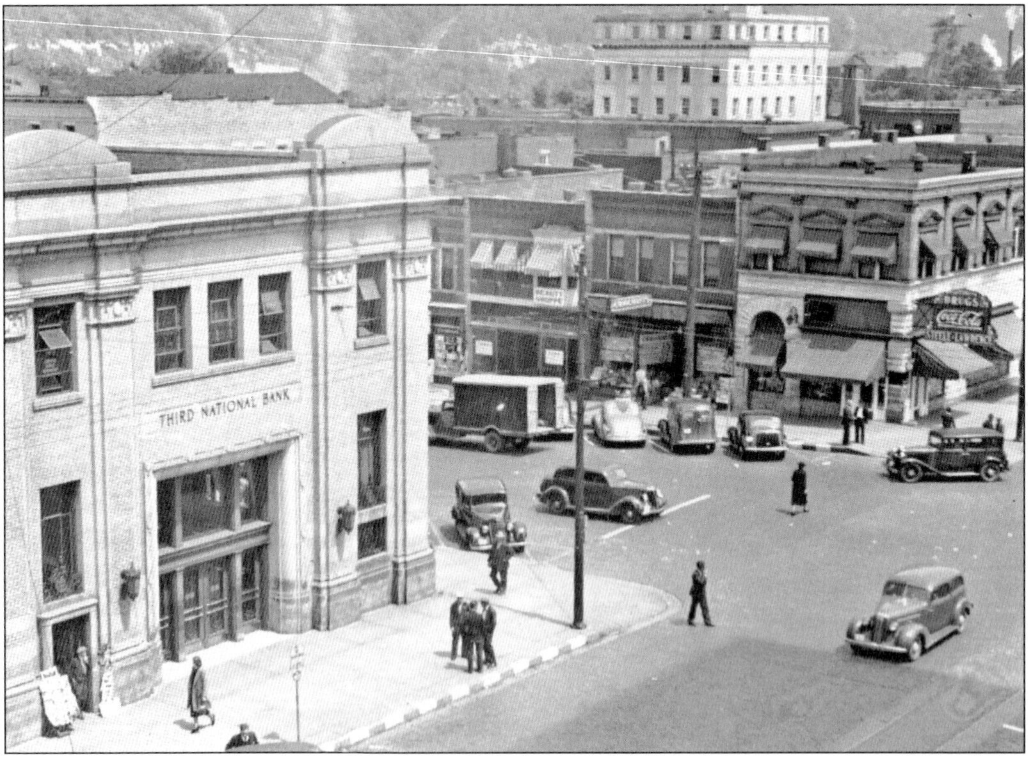

THIRD NATIONAL BANK. The Third National Bank Building was constructed on the northwest corner of Winchester and Sixteenth Street around 1929. The bank began in 1916 as the Ashland Day and Night Bank and changed its name in 1922. Notice the Steele and Lawrence drugstore on the lower right. (Courtesy of the Arnold Hanners Photographic Collection, Minnie Winder Room, Boyd County Public Library.)

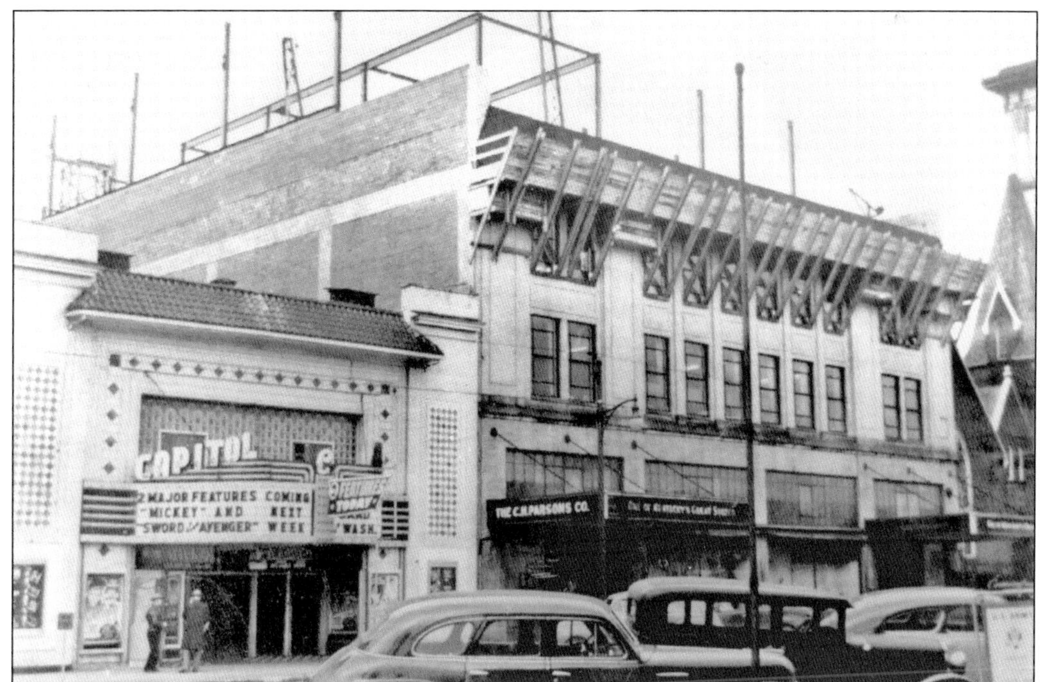

ADDING SPACE. In 1948, the C. H. Parsons Company began to add fourth and fifth floors to their company on Winchester Avenue near Sixteenth Street. The Capital Theater is next door, and the marquee advertises two major features of the time. Today the Highland Museum and Discovery Center is nearby and has many interesting exhibits. (Courtesy of the Arnold Hanners Photographic Collection, Minnie Winder Room, Boyd County Public Library.)

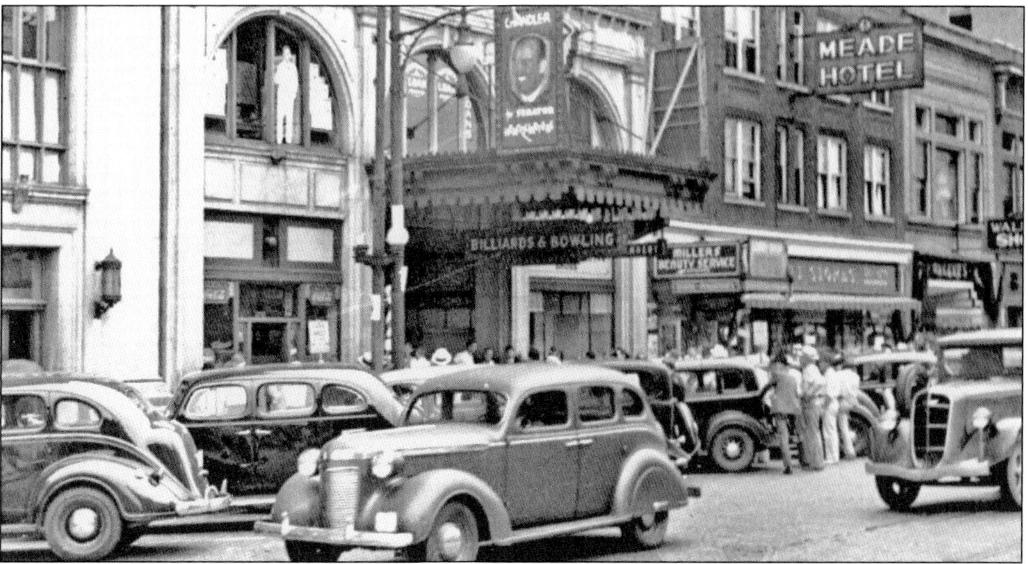

CHANDLER FOR SENATOR. Sen. Albert B. "Happy" Chandler is running for re-election in the early 1940s from his Ashland headquarters located between the Meade Hotel and the Ashland National Bank Building on Winchester Avenue. Chandler served as Kentucky's governor, a senator, and as commissioner of baseball. He was elected to the Baseball Hall of Fame in 1982. (Courtesy of the Arnold Hanners Photographic Collection, Minnie Winder Room, Boyd County Public Library.)

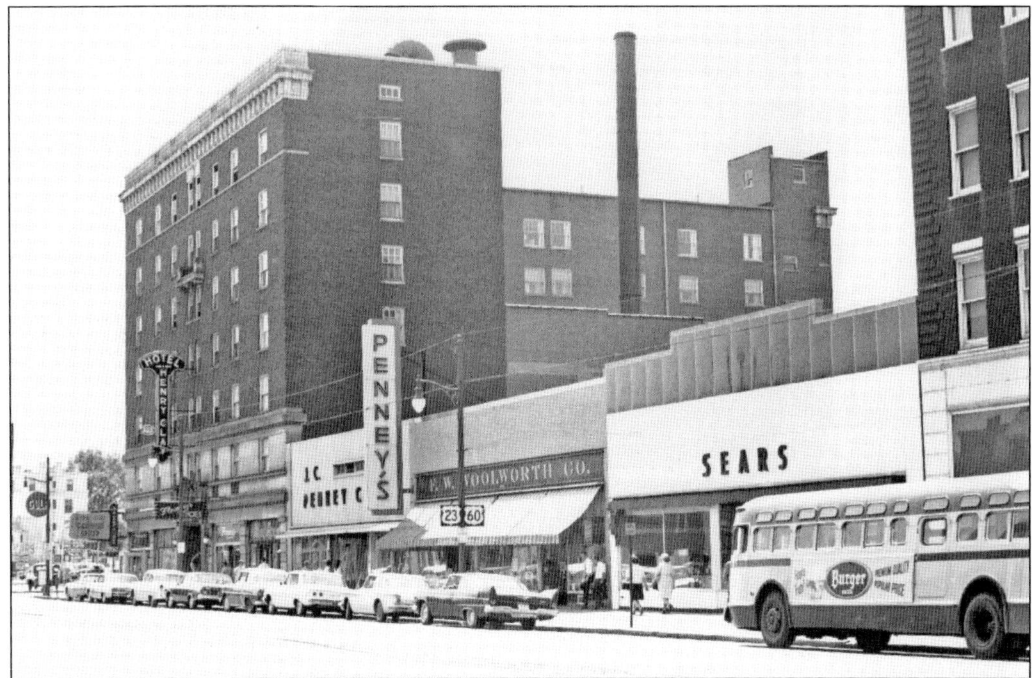

The Henry Clay. The impressive Henry Clay Hotel is seen in this view looking east on Winchester Avenue, as well as the J. C. Penney Company, F. W. Woolworth Company, Sears, and an Ashland city bus. A coffeehouse and Fleming's Shoes were in the first-story portion of the Henry Clay. (Courtesy of the James C. Powers Collection.)

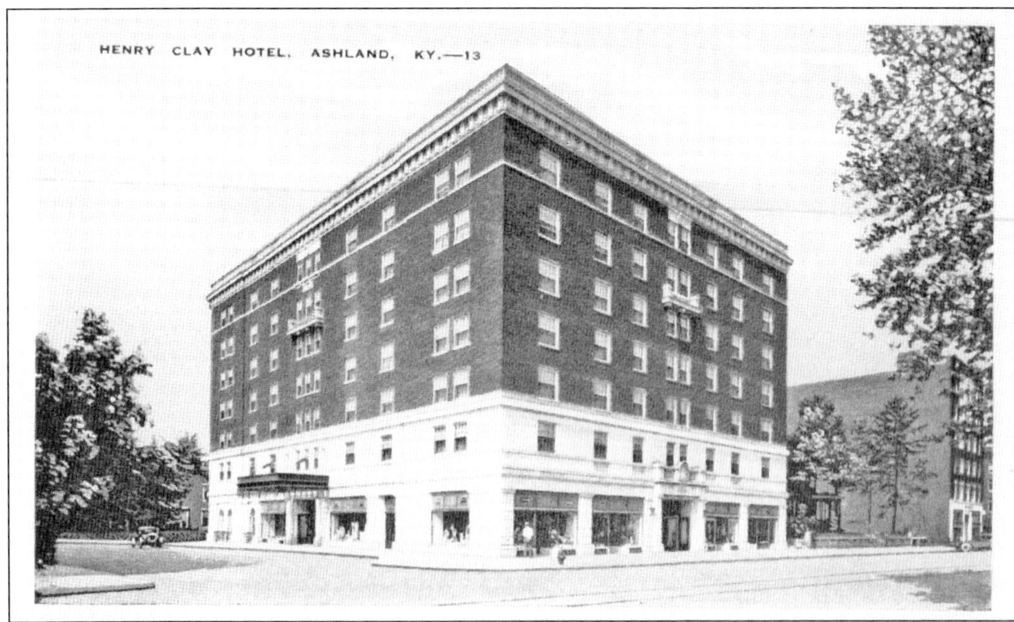

A New Hotel. This postcard illustration from around 1928 shows the newly completed seven-story Henry Clay Hotel, which still stands today. The structure was a mix of several styles, as was the custom during the Depression era. Notice that several shops are visible on the first story of the building. (Courtesy of the James C. Powers Collection.)

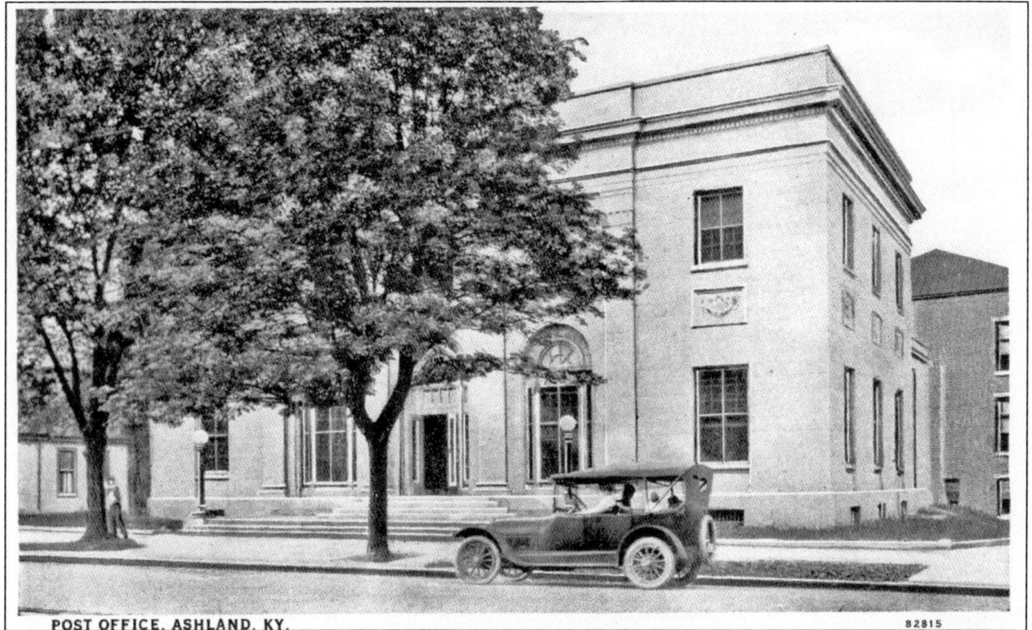

POST OFFICE. The old Ashland Post Office building on Winchester Avenue served the city for nearly 60 years and was designed in the popular classical style of the period. The first post office of Ashland dates to the time of the Poage Settlement and was one of the first post offices in eastern Kentucky. (Courtesy of the James C. Powers Collection.)

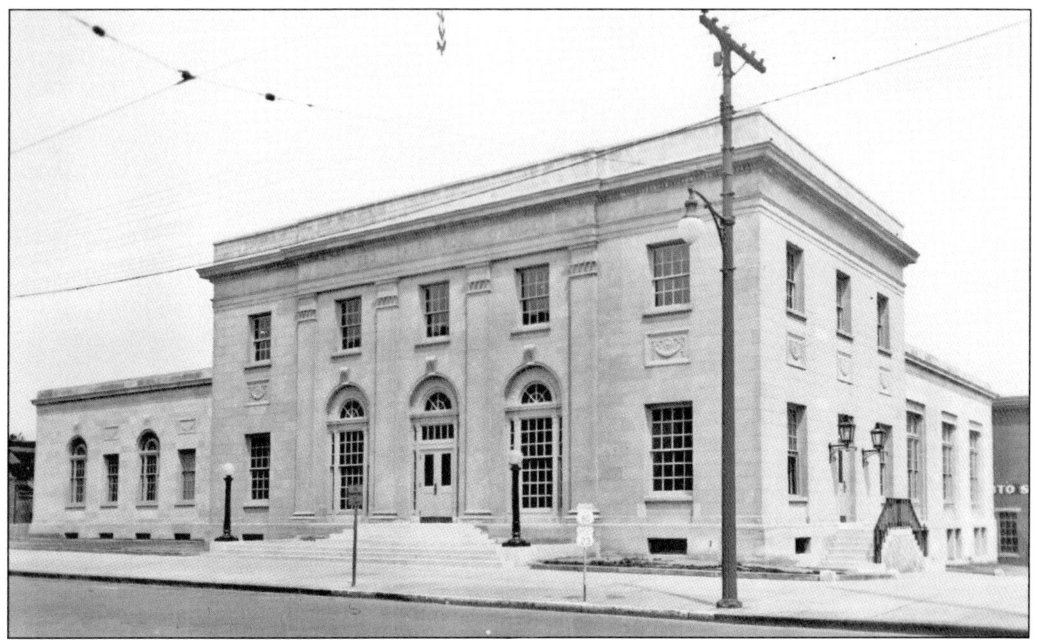

THE JESSE STUART FOUNDATION. The western addition of the Ashland Post Office was built not long before this photograph was taken in the 1930s. Today the building houses the Jesse Stuart Foundation on Winchester Avenue. The foundation promotes the literary works of Kentucky author Jesse Stuart, as well as other Appalachian works. (Courtesy of the Arnold Hanners Photographic Collection, Minnie Winder Room, Boyd County Public Library.)

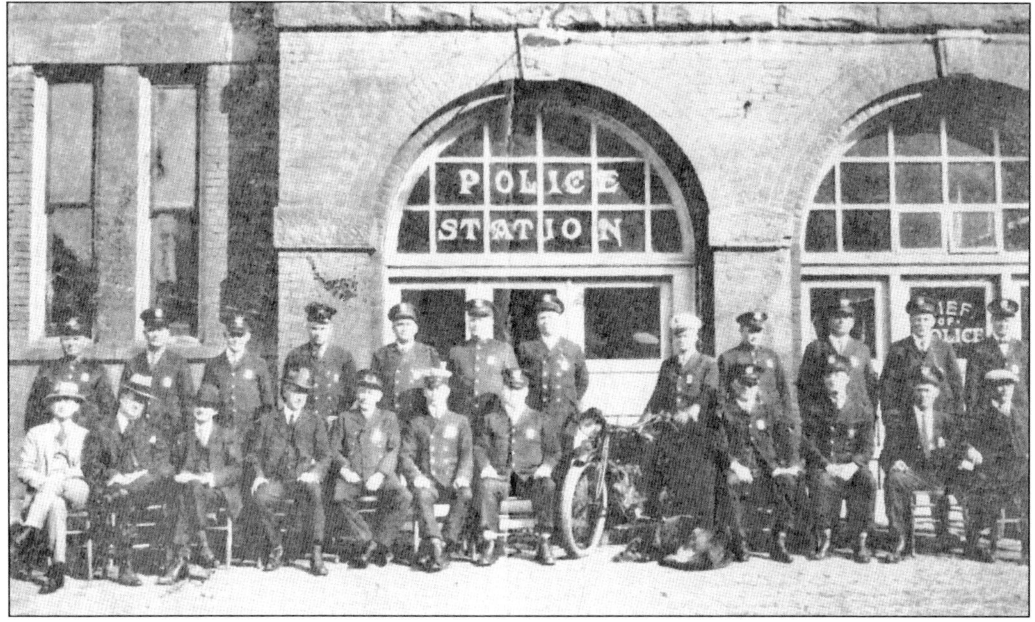

ASHLAND POLICE. Ashland police officers pose for this 1910s photograph with their motorbike front and center. The police and fire departments and city hall worked out of the same central building along Seventeenth Street and Greenup Avenue. For well over a century and a half, the citizens of Ashland have been well protected by this dedicated force. (Courtesy of the Arnold Hanners Photographic Collection, Minnie Winder Room, Boyd County Public Library.)

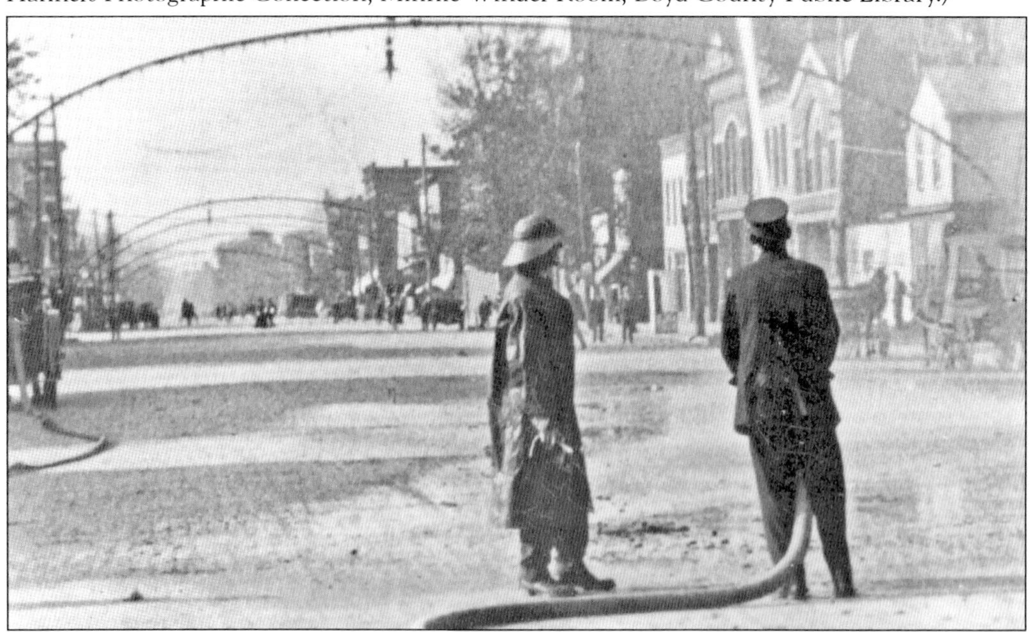

WATER HOSE. wTwo firemen test a water hose as people in the background pause to watch. This *c.* 1911 photograph was taken on Greenup Avenue looking west from Seventeenth Street. Fires during this time were a very real threat, and regular testing of equipment was a must. (Courtesy of the Arnold Hanners Photographic Collection, Minnie Winder Room, Boyd County Public Library.)

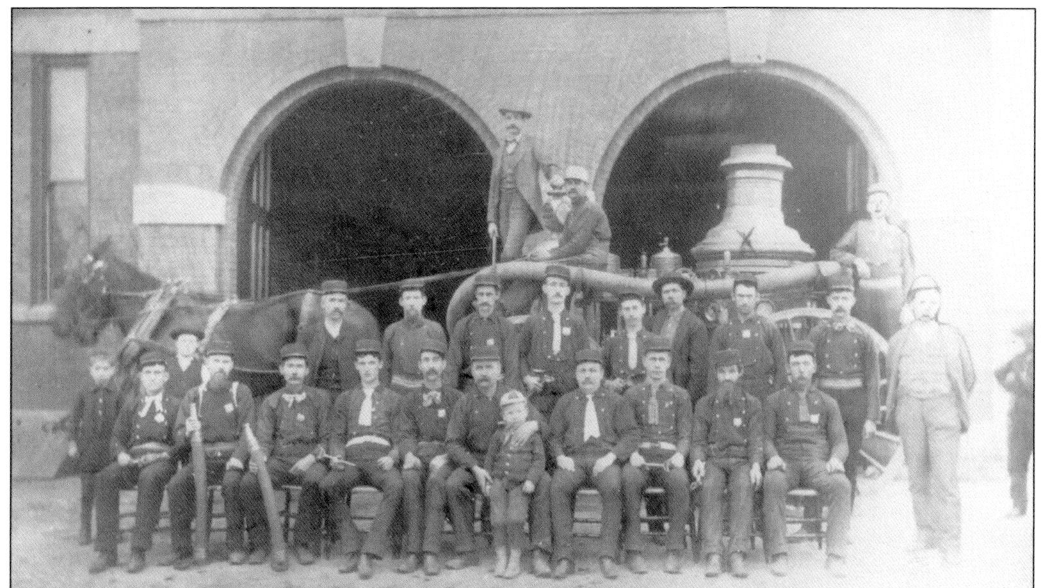

Ashland Firemen. The Ashland Volunteer Fire Department poses with its wagon and horses for a photograph in 1889. The station was located in the large city building on Greenup Avenue and Seventeenth Street, where the police station is located today. Note several young future firemen posing with the group. (Courtesy of the Arnold Hanners Photographic Collection, Minnie Winder Room, Boyd County Public Library.)

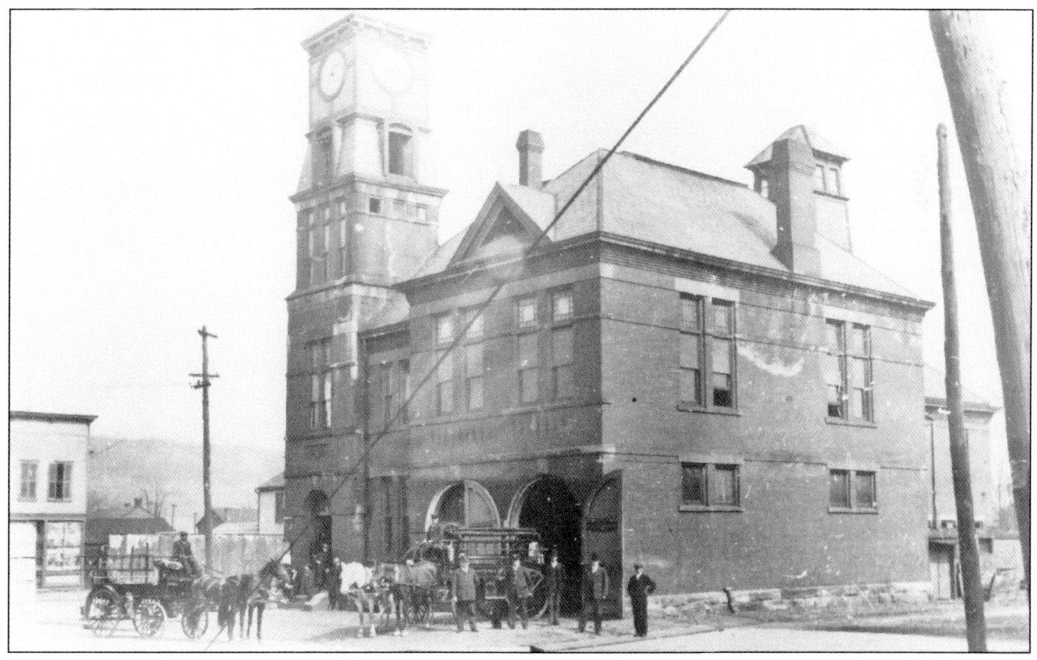

City Hall. Several firemen, a wagon, and horses pose for this early 1900s photograph during late fall or early spring. The building was a beautiful two-story structure that contained a lookout nest to the east and a clock tower. Many people would set their pocket watches to this clock. (Courtesy of the Arnold Hanners Photographic Collection, Minnie Winder Room, Boyd County Public Library.)

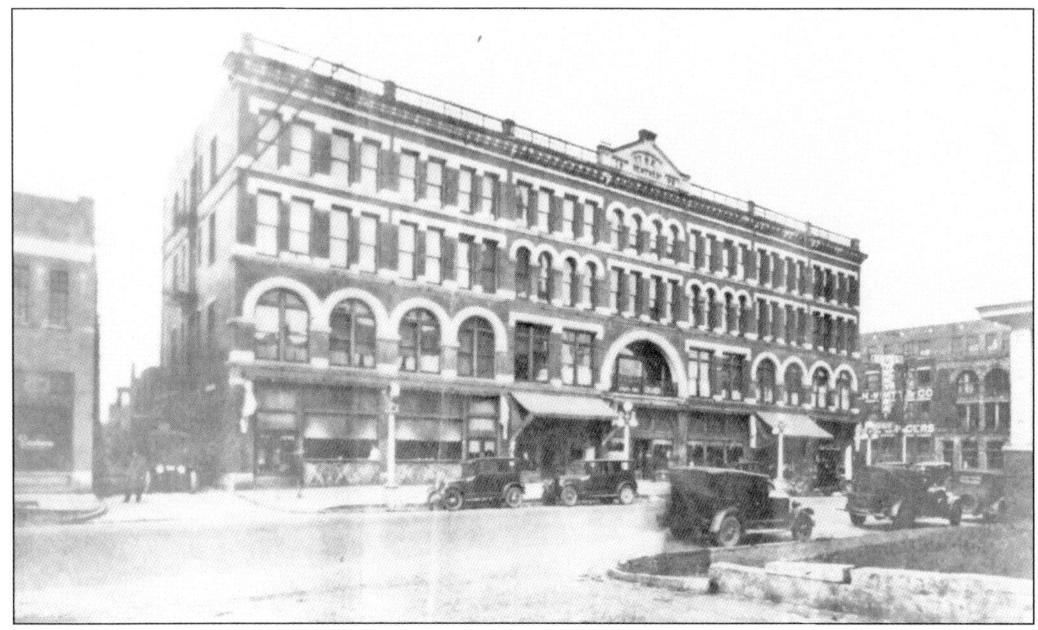

HOTEL VENTURA . The Hotel Ventura building highlighted Ashland's cityscape for many years. Like many hotels of the day, the first floor contained several privately owned shops, a bus station, and a restaurant. The front of the building faced east at the southwest corner of Thirteenth Street and Winchester Avenue. (Courtesy of the Arnold Hanners Photographic Collection, Minnie Winder Room, Boyd County Public Library.)

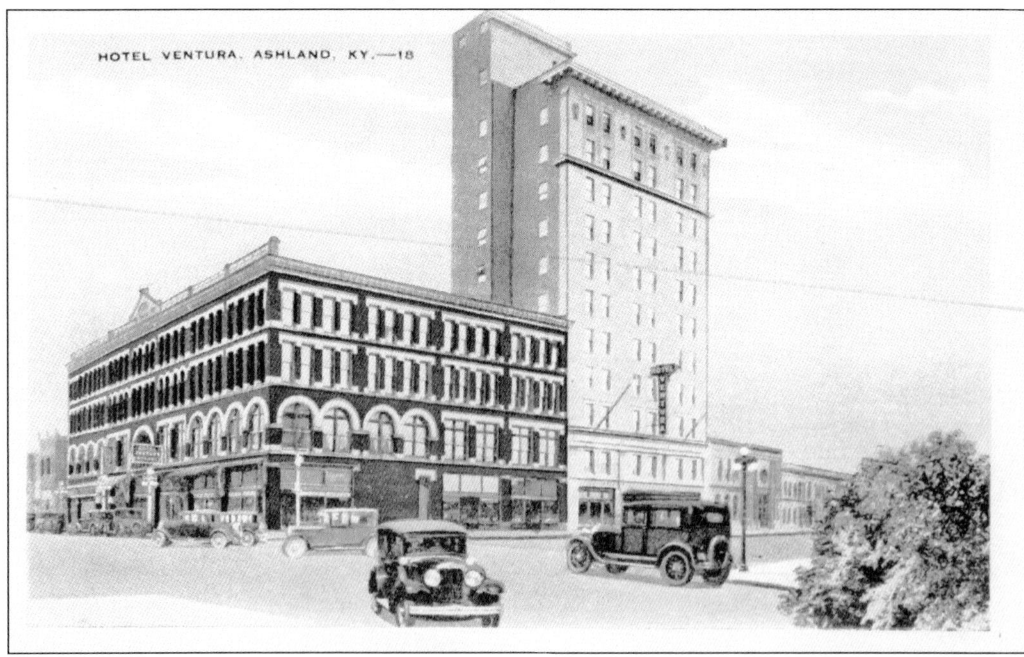

HOTEL VENTURA. In this postcard view of the Hotel Ventura in the mid-1930s, the 11-story addition to the west of the main structure is impressive. This view comes from Thirteenth Street looking southwest. Today a Burger King and Starbucks coffee shop occupy this location. (Courtesy of the James C. Powers Collection.)

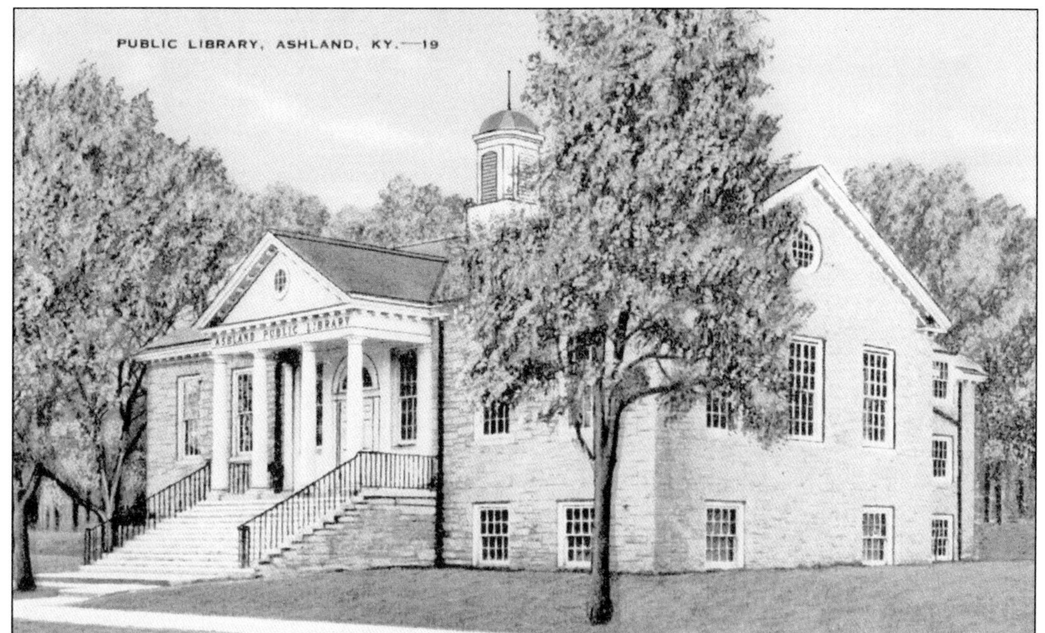

ASHLAND LIBRARY. Like many towns in the area, Ashland has a very useful library that utilizes technology to provide information. The building that replaced this fine structure can be found on the northwest corner of Central Park at 1740 Central Avenue. This library has one of the finest genealogy rooms in the area. (Courtesy of the James C. Powers Collection.)

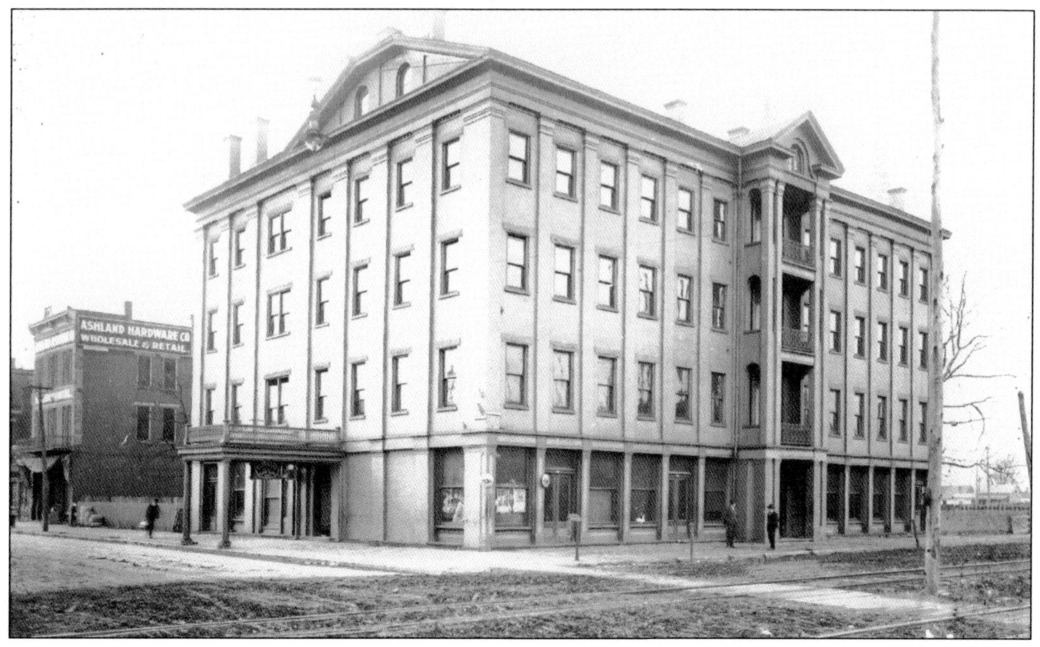

HOTEL ON FRONT STREET. The Aldine Hotel was a classical four-story structure with 50 rooms that faced north on Front Street and Fifteenth Street. It was completed in 1855 by the Kentucky Iron, Coal, and Manufacturing Company and used as a government hospital during the Civil War. (Courtesy of the Arnold Hanners Photographic collection, Minnie Winder Room, Boyd County Public Library.)

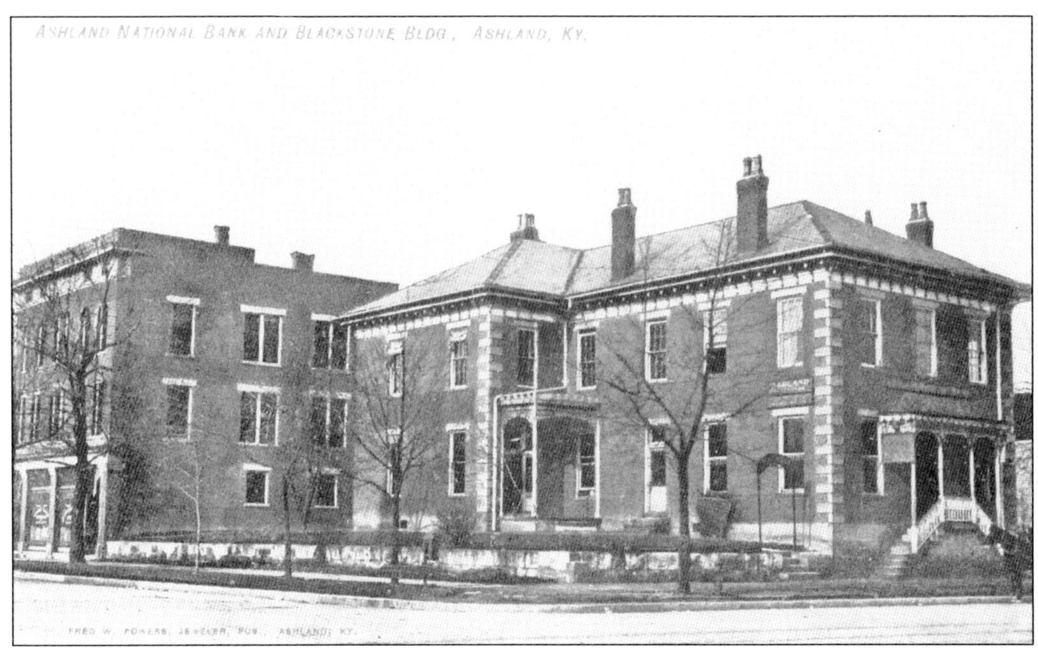

BLACKSTONE BUILDING. This photograph, which was produced around the beginning of the 20th century by Fred Powers, shows the old Blackstone Building and the Ashland National Bank Building. The buildings were located on the corner of Broadway or Sixteenth Street and Winchester Avenue and were razed and replaced in 1922. (Courtesy of the Arnold Hanners Photographic Collection, Minnie Winder Room, Boyd County Public Library.)

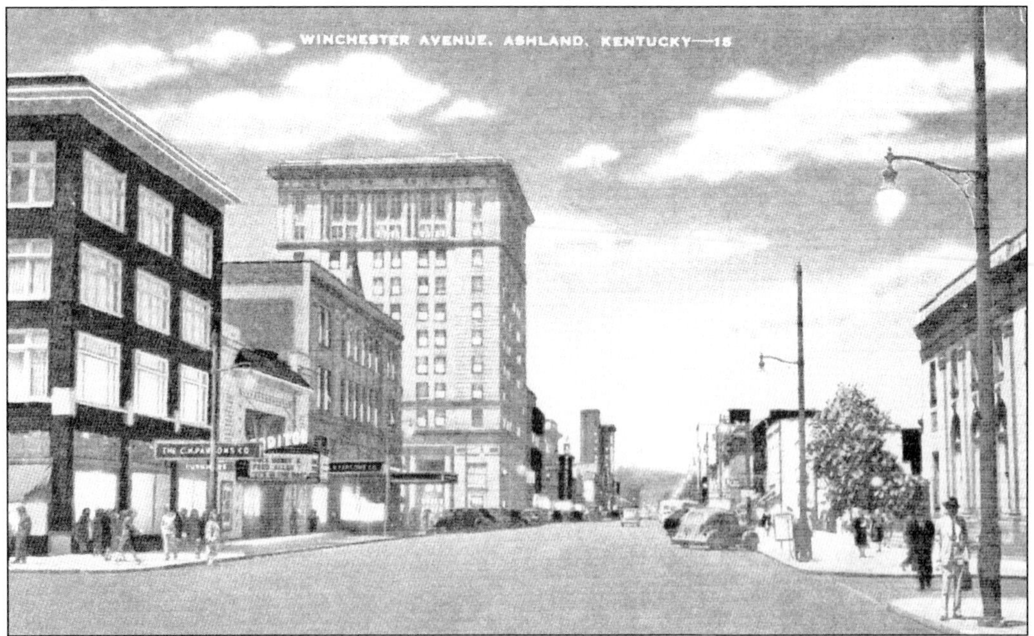

RARE NIGHT SCENE. This postcard from the 1930s is a rare night scene of the Ashland business district looking west on Winchester Avenue from around Seventeenth Street. The streets are almost clear of people and vehicles, and almost all of the businesses are dark along the quiet bricked streets. (Courtesy of the James C. Powers Collection.)

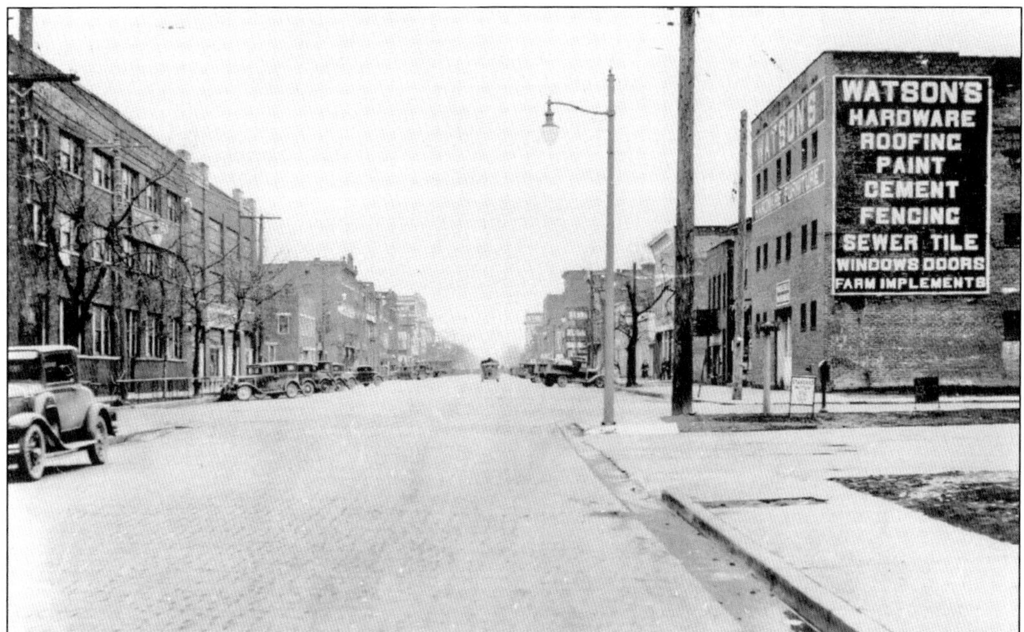

A BUSY DAY. This photograph from the mid-1930s was snapped on a very busy weekday. Vehicles are parked along Greenup Avenue looking east until they run out of the shot. This photograph was taken around the intersection of Thirteenth Street and Greenup Avenue, or from where the green bridge, the Ben Williamson Memorial Bridge, crossing into Ohio is. (Courtesy of the Arnold Hanners Photographic Collection, Minnie Winder Room, Boyd County Public Library.)

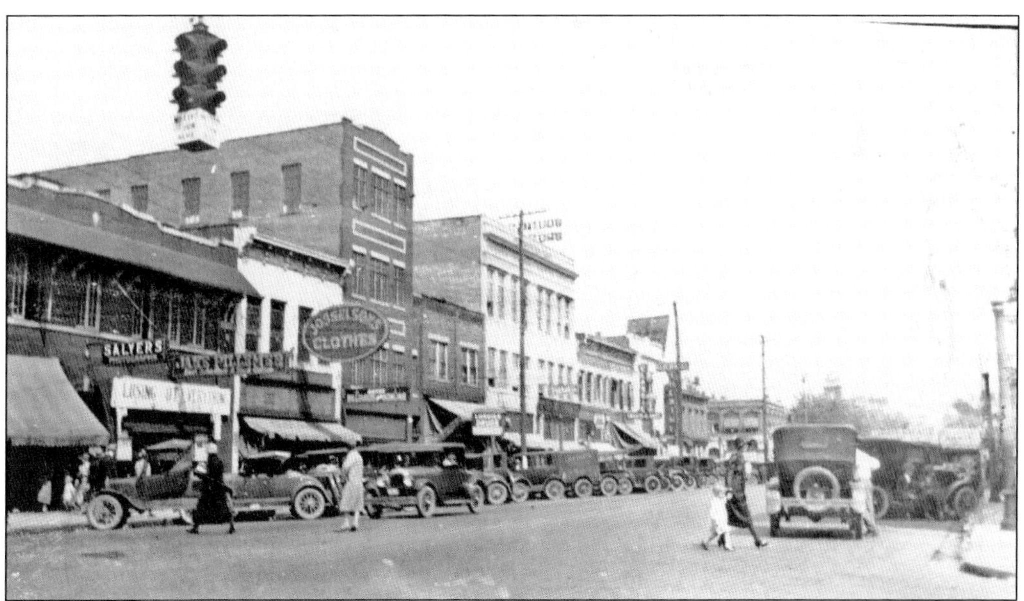

TIME TO WALK. A young mother walks her child across Winchester Avenue around 1935 amid a busy time in downtown. Salyers Photography, Josselsons Clothes, and a drugstore are located next to a place to bowl. The old half-circle streetlights were long gone by the time this photograph was taken and replaced by the more reliable traditional lamps on the right. (Courtesy of the Arnold Hanners Photographic Collection, Minnie Winder Room, Boyd County Public Library.)

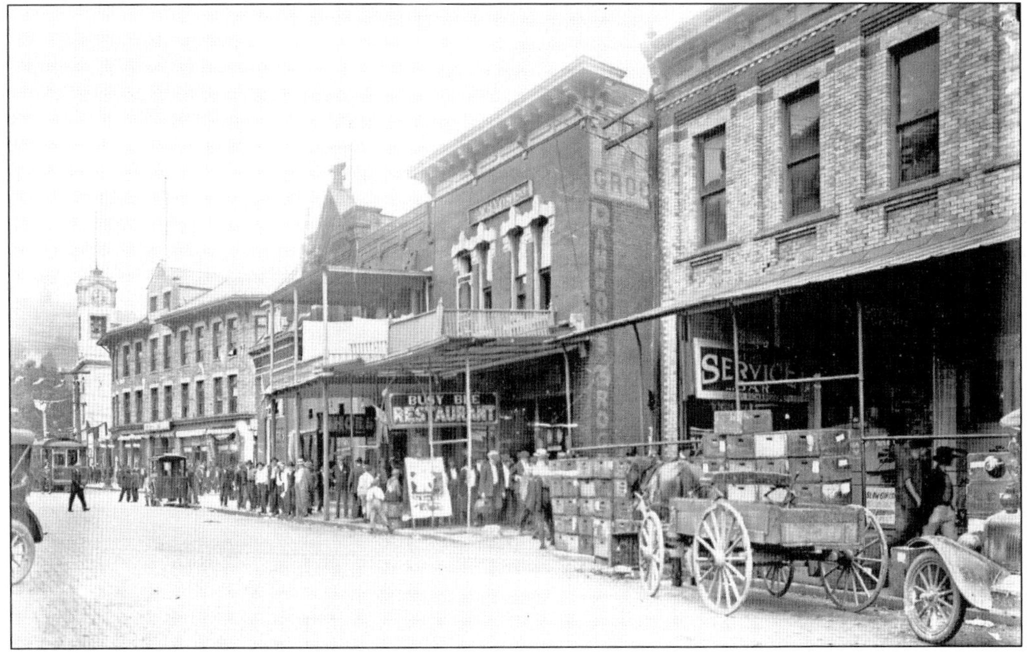

County Seat. Catlettsburg is the county seat of Boyd County, Kentucky. The city is located several miles east of Ashland on the banks of the Ohio and Big Sandy Rivers. Many of the same individuals who worked to make Ashland into a city also worked to create this beautiful town. (Courtesy of the James C. Powers Collection.)

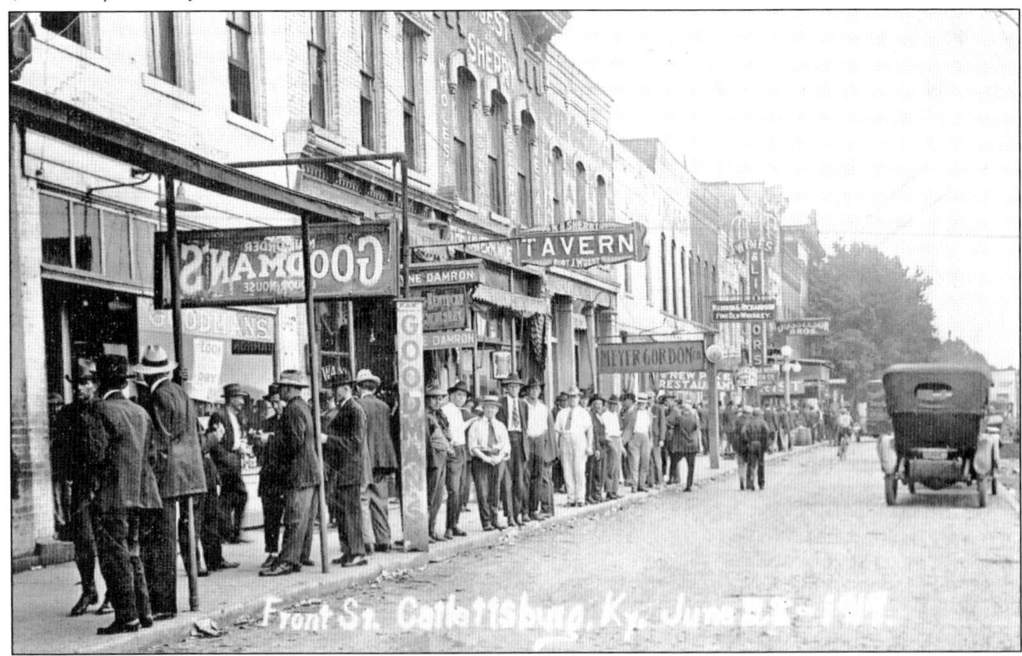

Catlettsburg Businesses. Being busy is the order of the day in this photograph taken on Catlettsburg's Front Street on June 28, 1919. Men are busy telling stories, having a few drinks, and posing for a rare picture. Front Street was lined with many businesses that sold Kentucky whiskey, wine, and beer. (Courtesy of the James C. Powers Collection.)

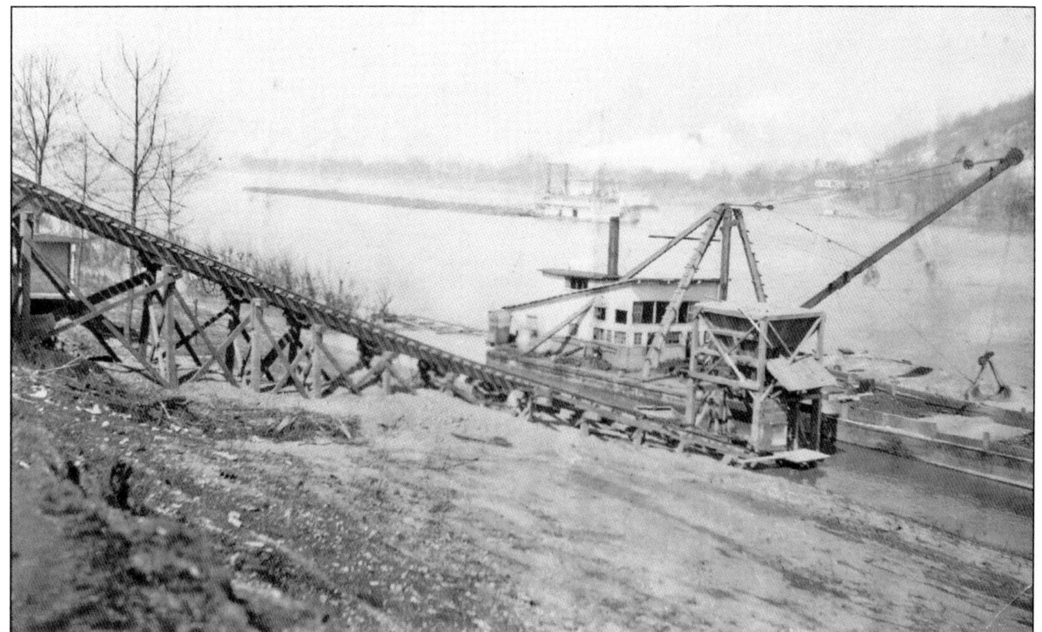

River Delivery. Many businesses along the Ohio River received shipments and deliveries via the river. Barges loaded with coal or timber often would make a run to and from Ashland. This steam shovel barge is unloading coal onto a shoot, underneath which a coal car is waiting to be filled and brought up the steep bank. (Courtesy of the Arnold Hanners Photographic Collection, Minnie Winder Room, Boyd County Public Library.)

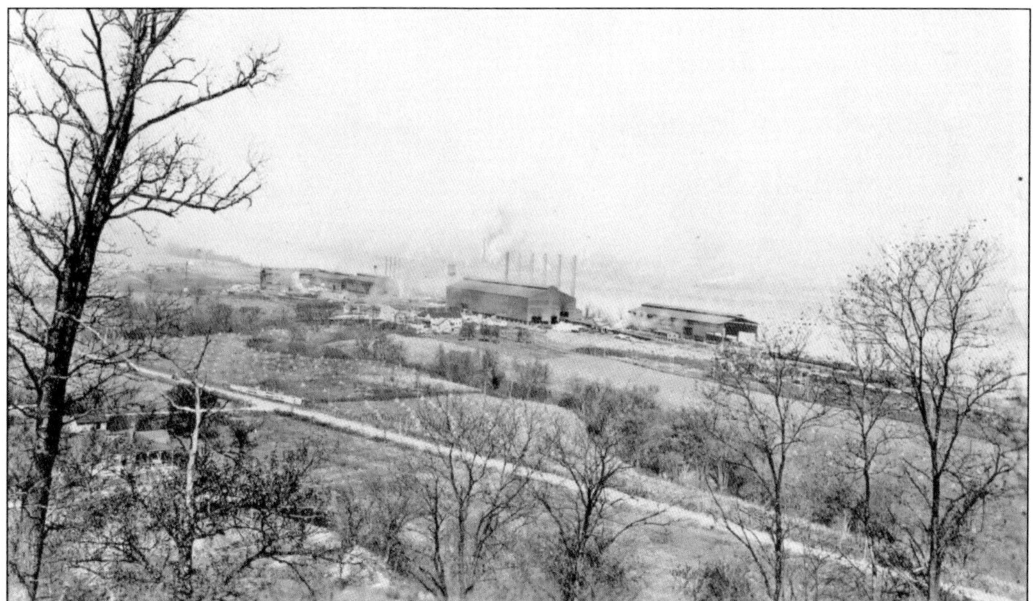

Before Armco. Shown in the photograph from around 1920, the Ashland Iron and Mining Company was west of Ashland. Ashland had long since been a central location of the pig iron industry, and over time, many took advantage of the city's ties with iron, coal, and the Ohio River. (Courtesy of the Arnold Hanners Photographic Collection, Minnie Winder Room, Boyd County Public Library.)

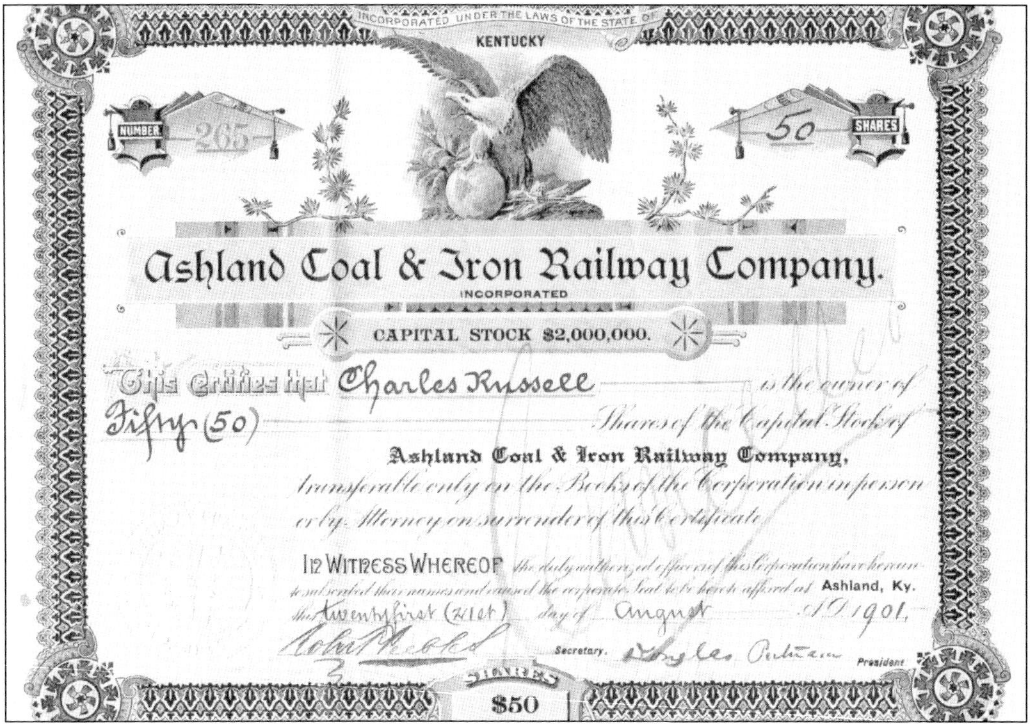

INCORPORATED UNDER THE LAWS OF THE STATE OF KENTUCKY

NUMBER 265 | 50 SHARES

Ashland Coal & Iron Railway Company.

INCORPORATED

CAPITAL STOCK $2,000,000.

This Certifies that Charles Russell is the owner of Fifty (50) Shares of the Capital Stock of

Ashland Coal & Iron Railway Company,

transferable only on the Books of the Corporation in person or by Attorney on surrender of this Certificate.

In Witness Whereof the duly authorized officers of this Corporation have hereunto subscribed their names and caused the corporate Seal to be hereto affixed at Ashland, Ky. the Twentyfirst (21st) day of August A.D. 1901.

Secretary. President.

SHARES $50

FIFTY SHARES OF STOCK. This Ashland Coal and Iron Railway Company stock was worth 50 shares at $50 a share. Stock like this was offered to the public when companies began to incur losses. Eventually assets of this company, along with other privately owned iron businesses, were sold out. (Courtesy of the Terry L. Baldridge Collection.)

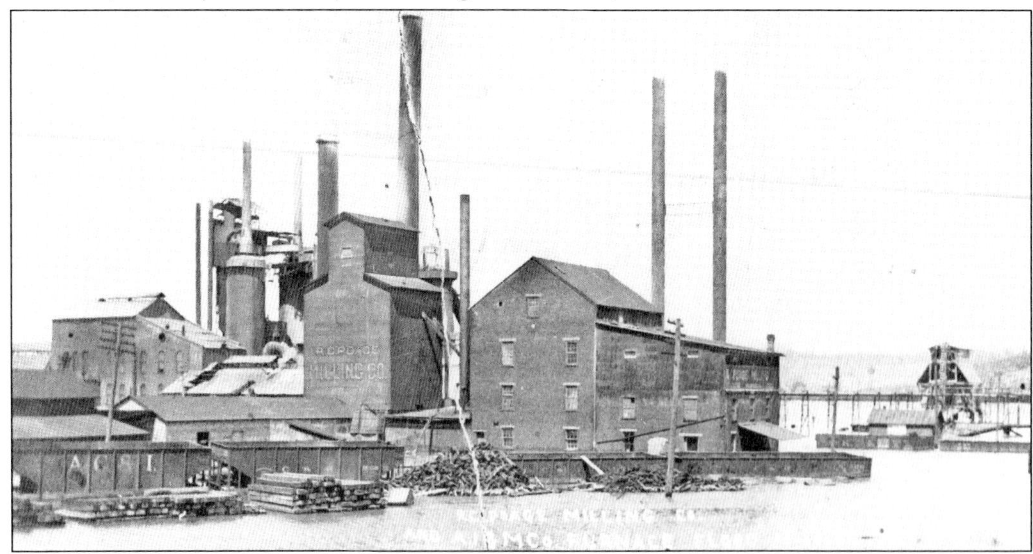

ASHLAND COAL AND IRON. Many railroads throughout the country owned plants and businesses from which they could cheaply haul their goods. The Ashland Coal and Iron plant in Ashland was no exception. The company owned coal mines, timber rights, and barges on the Ohio River. (Courtesy of the Arnold Hanners Photographic Collection, Minnie Winder Room, Boyd County Public Library.)

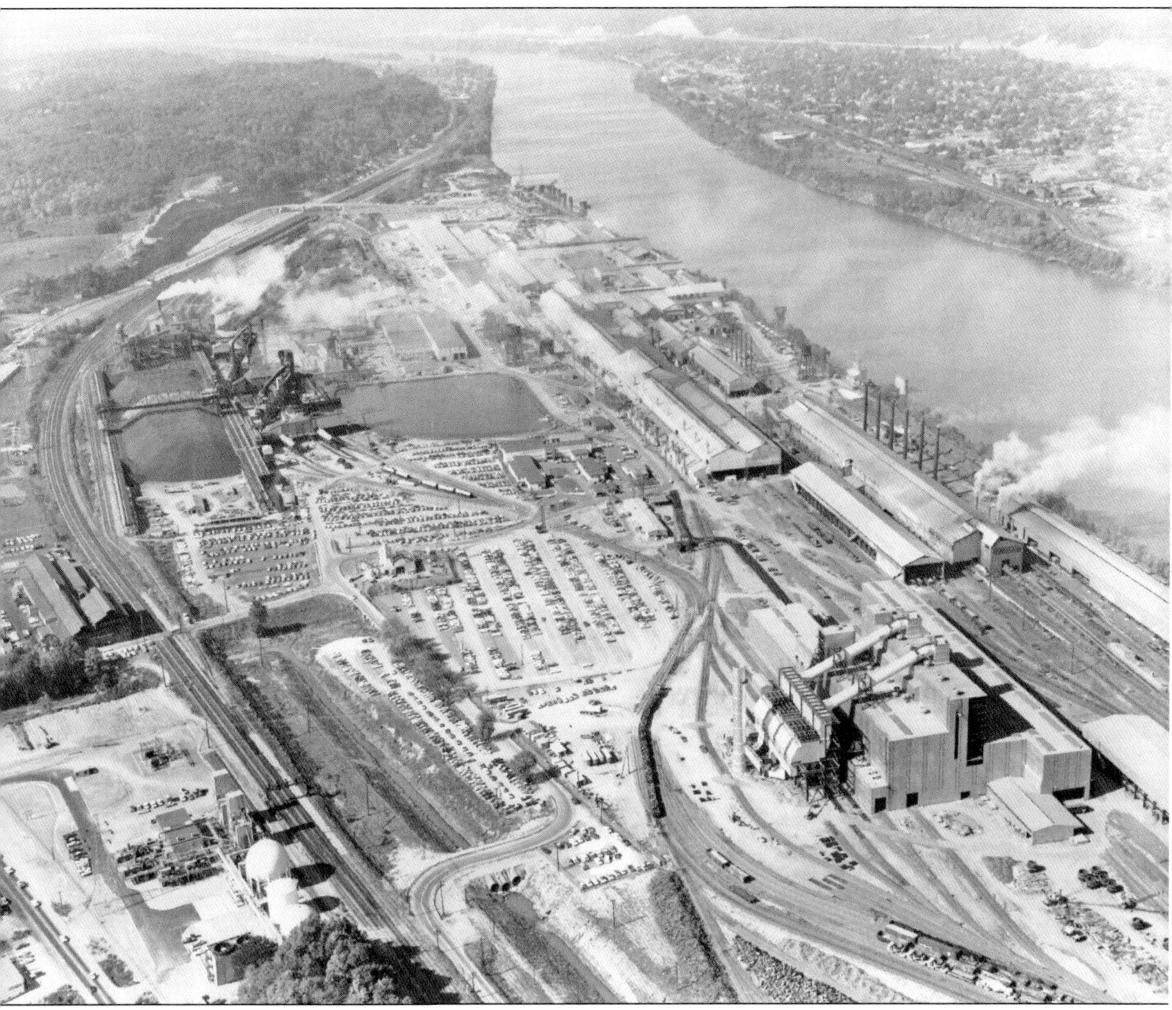

American Rolling Mill Company Steel. This aerial photograph of Armco from the late 1960s show a much larger steel manufacturing complex than that of today. The Armco plant was constructed in 1920, and by 1922, the company had purchased all remaining privately owned steel companies and assets in the area. The company was the first steel plant in the United States to produce steel sheets using the continuous rolling method. The city of Ashland began to experience tremendous growth because of Armco Steel. The population doubled in just a five-year period during the 1920s, and other businesses began to take root in the area. The plant during this time had almost 4,000 employees, and the suburban areas around Ashland began to grow, facilitating the annexation of these areas into Ashland. Like many companies during this time, Armco sponsored several sports teams that proved very successful on a national scale. (Courtesy of the Arnold Hanners Photographic Collection, Minnie Winder Room, Boyd County Public Library.)

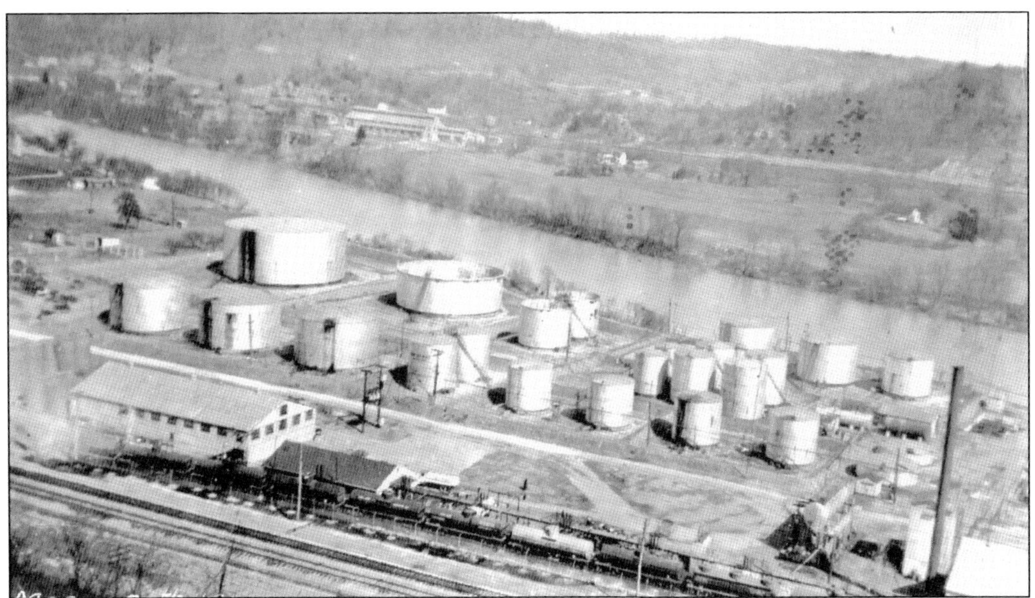

Along the Big Sandy River. The Big Sandy River and West Virginia can both be seen in this photograph of the Ashland Oil and Refining Company in 1930. When Ashland Oil incorporated in 1924, it became Ashland's second largest employer next to Armco. (Courtesy of the Arnold Hanners Photographic Collection, Minnie Winder Room, Boyd County Public Library.)

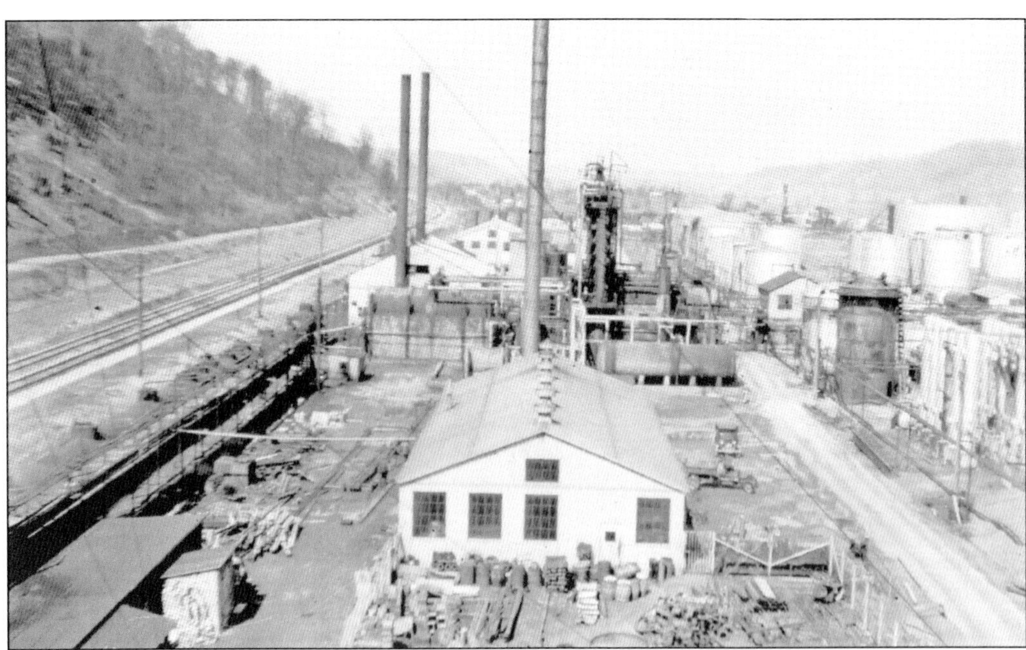

The Catlettsburg Refinery. The company invested over the years in various enterprises throughout the tri-state area and country. This enabled the company to grow rapidly during its long history. Ashland Oil supported and sponsored many school activities throughout Kentucky, Ohio, and West Virginia. The refinery continues operating today under the Marathon Oil Corporation. (Courtesy of the Arnold Hanners Photographic Collection, Minnie Winder Room, Boyd County Public Library.)

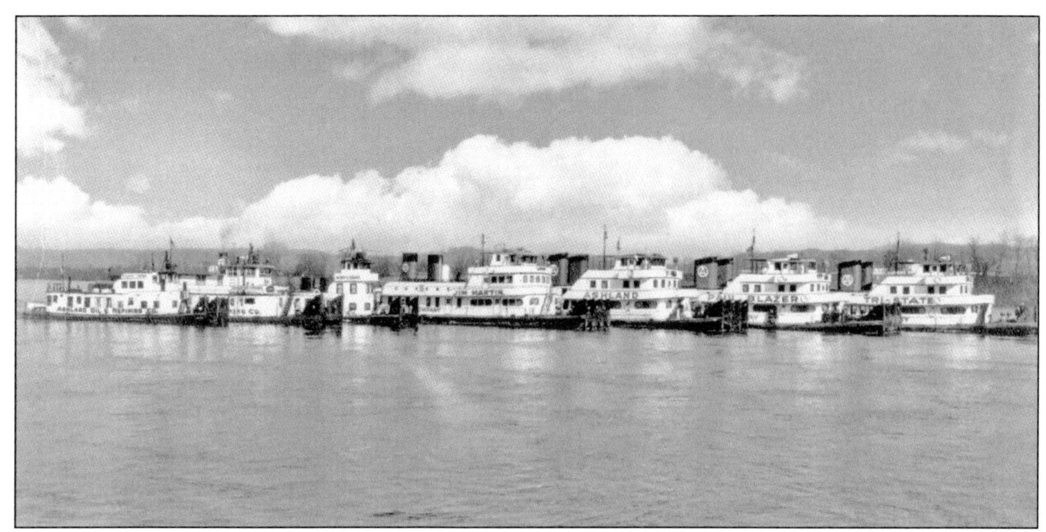

A FLEET OF BOATS. Ashland Oil owned several barges that transported fuel and coal along the rivers at a great savings. Boats pictured here are, from left to right, unidentified, the *Senator Combs*, *Jim Martin*, *Ashland*, *Paul Blazer*, and *Tri-State*. These and other boats made regular deliveries over the Ohio River. (Courtesy of the Arnold Hanners Photographic Collection, Minnie Winder Room, Boyd County Public Library.)

ASHLAND PRODUCTS. Throughout the years, Ashland Oil produced products that were easily recognizable throughout the Ashland area as well as the county. Ashland Old Gold and Ashland Penn oil products are on this advertisement. More recently, Ashland Oil's Valvoline brand has become one of the standard oil products. (Courtesy of the Terry L. Baldridge Collection.)

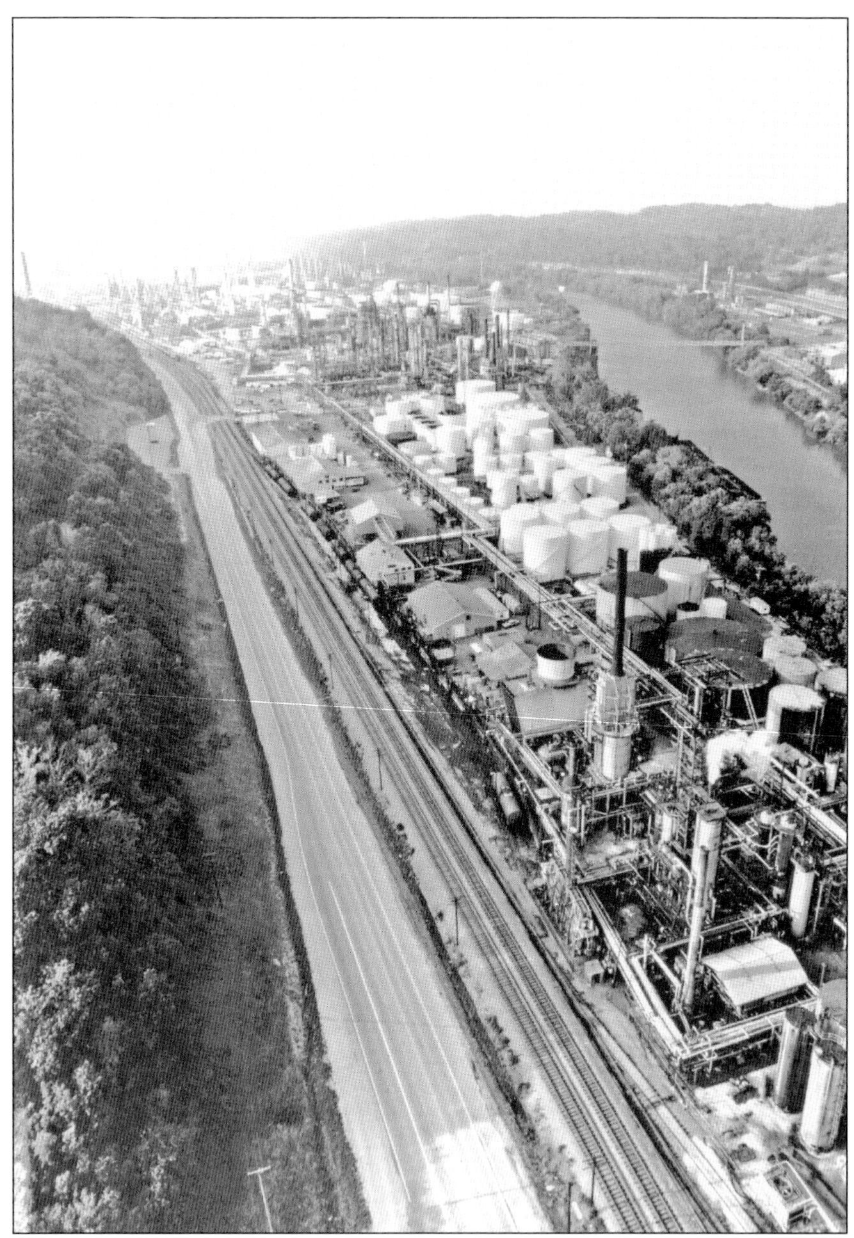

ASHLAND OIL, INC. This more recent photograph of the refinery near Catlettsburg shows the original property in the foreground, once called the Tri-State Refining Company and headed at one time under the Swiss Oil Company out of Lexington. From the beginning in 1924 under the hand of Paul Blazer, Ashland Oil expanded this refinery and their business holdings in and around the Ashland area. The company quickly put behind its humble beginnings as a 1,000-barrel-a-day, 25-employee oil company and expanded through mergers and acquisitions into a worldwide Fortune 500 company. The company purchased the old O. F. L. Beckette home on Fourteenth Street and Winchester Avenue and built their headquarters. When growth continued, Ashland Oil constructed their headquarters in Russell, Kentucky. Today the refinery is owned and operated by Marathon Oil. (Courtesy of the Arnold Hanners Photographic Collection, Minnie Winder Room, Boyd County Public Library.)

Three

FLOODWATERS

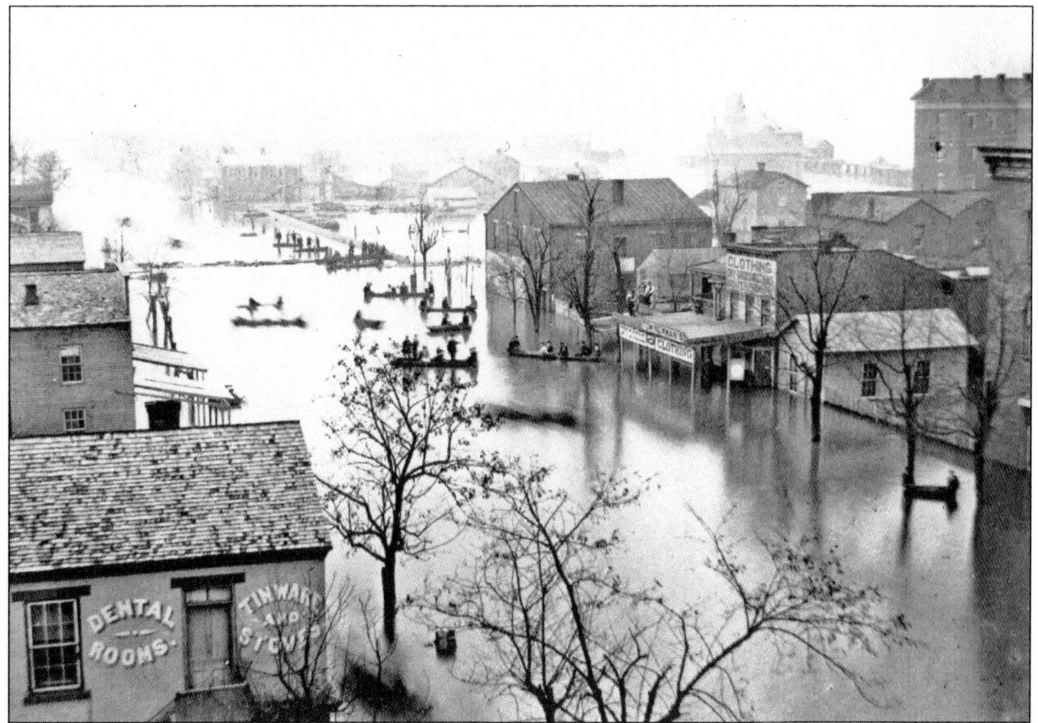

THE 1884 FLOOD. This photograph from Greenup Avenue looking west near Sixteenth Street shows just how high the Ohio River reached in 1884. The rear portion of the Aldine Hotel is seen on the upper right, and the Union Depot is the large structure to the right of center. The photograph shows 4 feet of water in Tom Newman's Dry Goods Store. Rainfall during the month of February 1884 was well above normal for the Ohio Valley. Many towns along the Ohio River were almost completely submerged, including Ashland. Reports from the time say that only two dozen homes remained above the flooding in and around Catlettsburg. After this time, the focus was put on constructing brick structures rather than wood. Very few wooden structures that were constructed near the Ohio River survive today. (Courtesy of the Arnold Hanners Photographic Collection, Minnie Winder Room, Boyd County Public Library.)

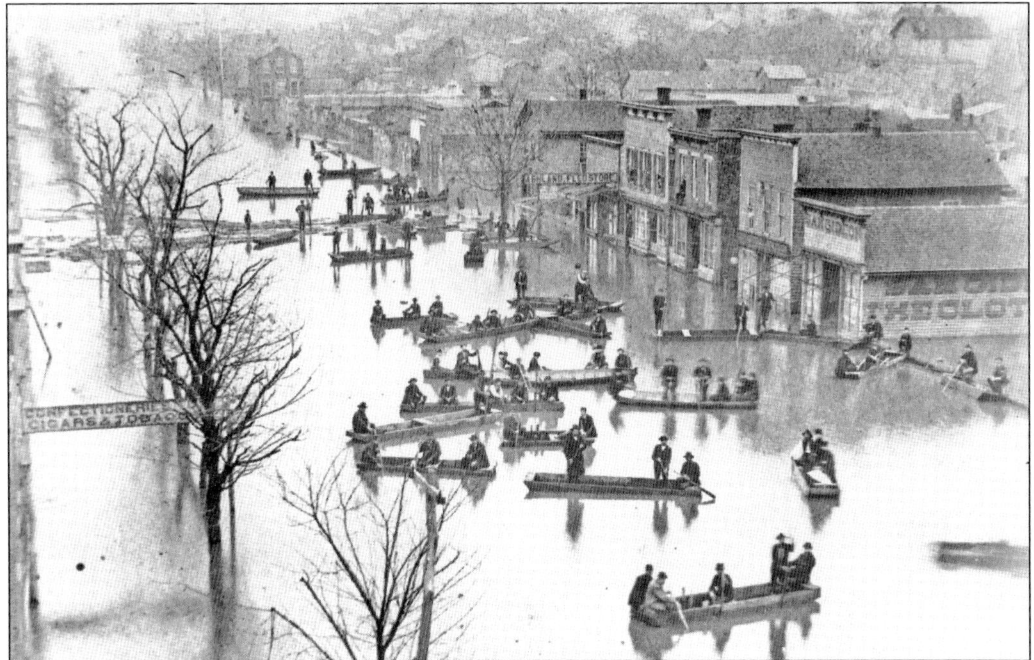

MEN IN BOATS. It would seem that the only flourishing business in the area during the flooding of 1884 was the boat business. A lone, seated woman looks to the camera near the center of this photograph taken of Greenup Avenue eastward. The curious and those ready to assist line up as though caught in traffic. (Courtesy of the Arnold Hanners Photographic Collection, Minnie Winder Room, Boyd County Public Library.)

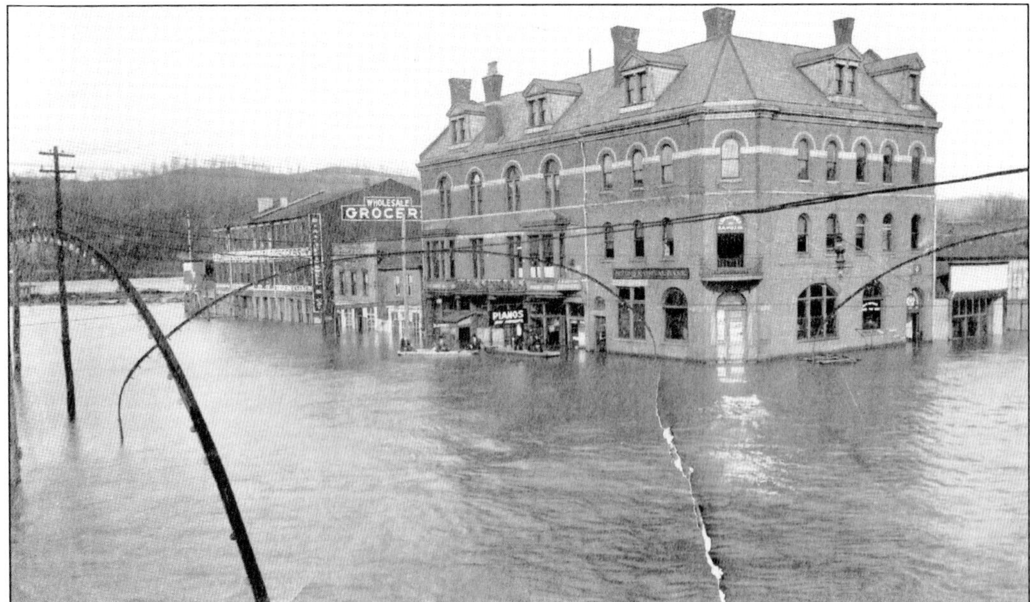

THE 1913 FLOOD. During January 1913, the total rainfall for the area was almost 11.5 inches, three times the normal amount for this time. The result was a flood even greater than that of 1884. This picture looks past the Second National Bank on the right and at the swollen Ohio River to the left. (Courtesy of the James C. Powers Collection.)

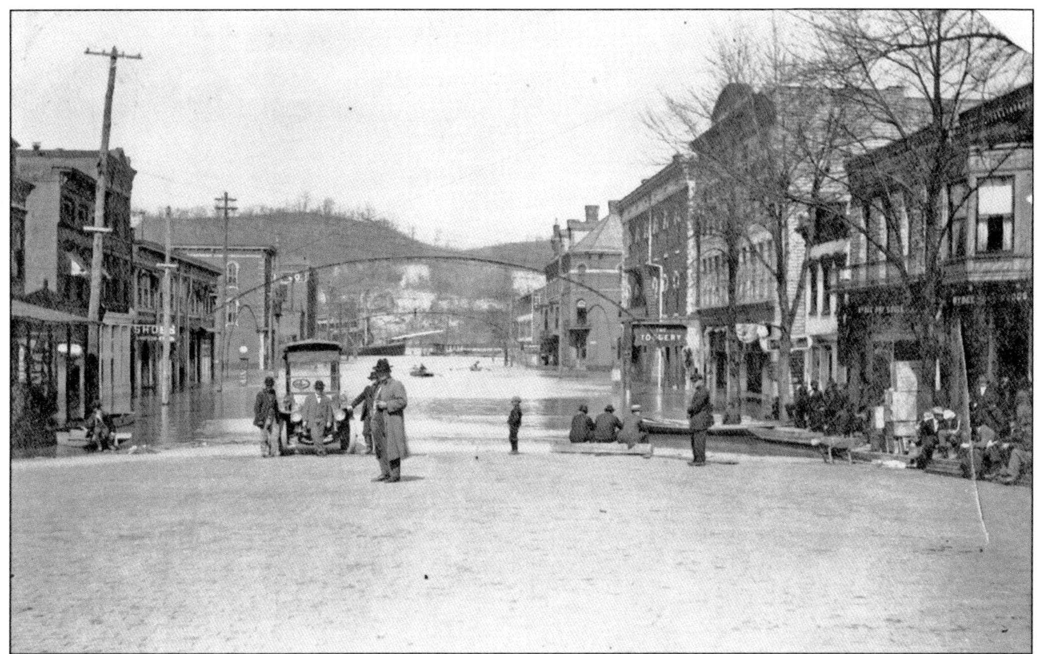

FLOOD ON SIXTEENTH STREET. The Second National Bank is in the rear to the right, and the Ohio River is in the background. The rare automobile is no doubt being used to pull boats out of the floodwaters. A little boy in the photograph seems more interested in the automobile than the waters. (Courtesy of the James C. Powers Collection.)

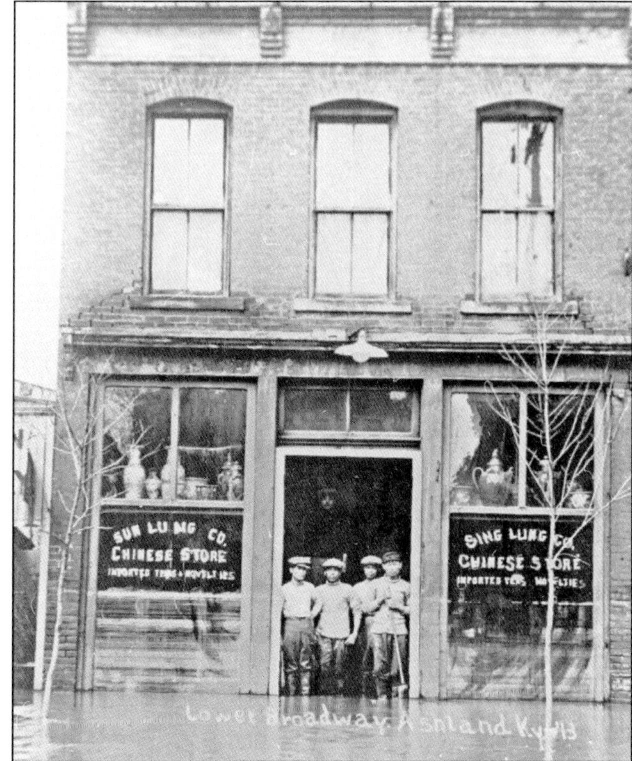

BROADWAY FLOODING. Sun and Sing Lung Company is being cleaned up and readied for a drier time. These four men have much to clean up in their Chinese store, as the waters have receded several feet by the time this photograph was taken. Notice the mud and watermarks just below the shoulders of the men. (Courtesy of the James C. Powers Collection.)

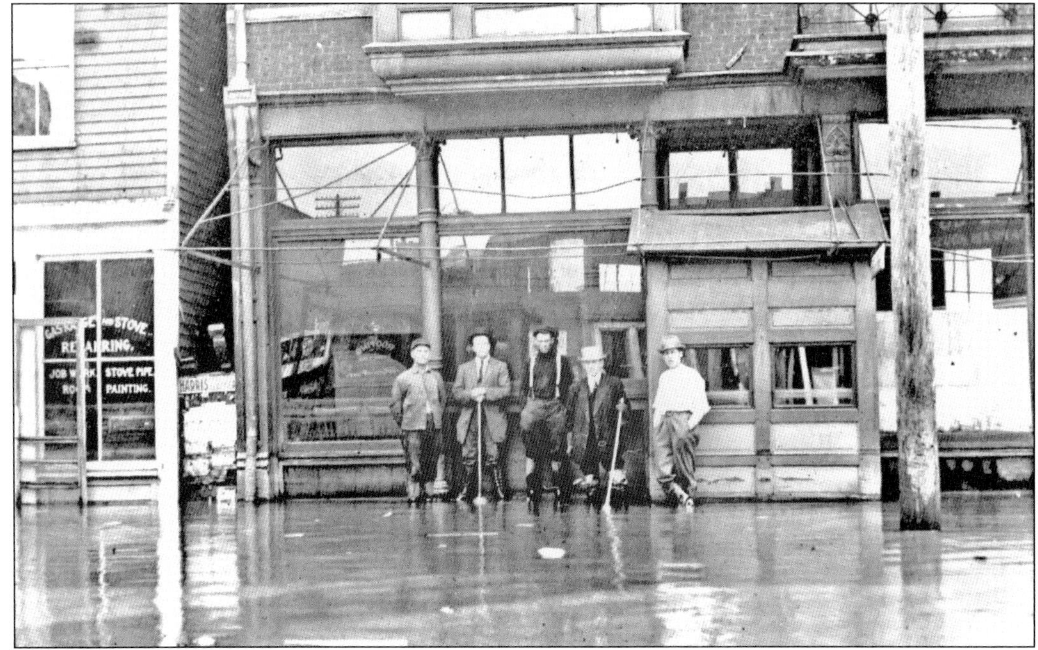

POSING IN WATER. These five men take a break from cleaning up their businesses along Sixteenth Street to pose for this picture. The stove repairing and painting shop to the left must be taken care of as quick as possible. January in Ashland can quickly turn cold. (Courtesy of the James C. Powers Collection.)

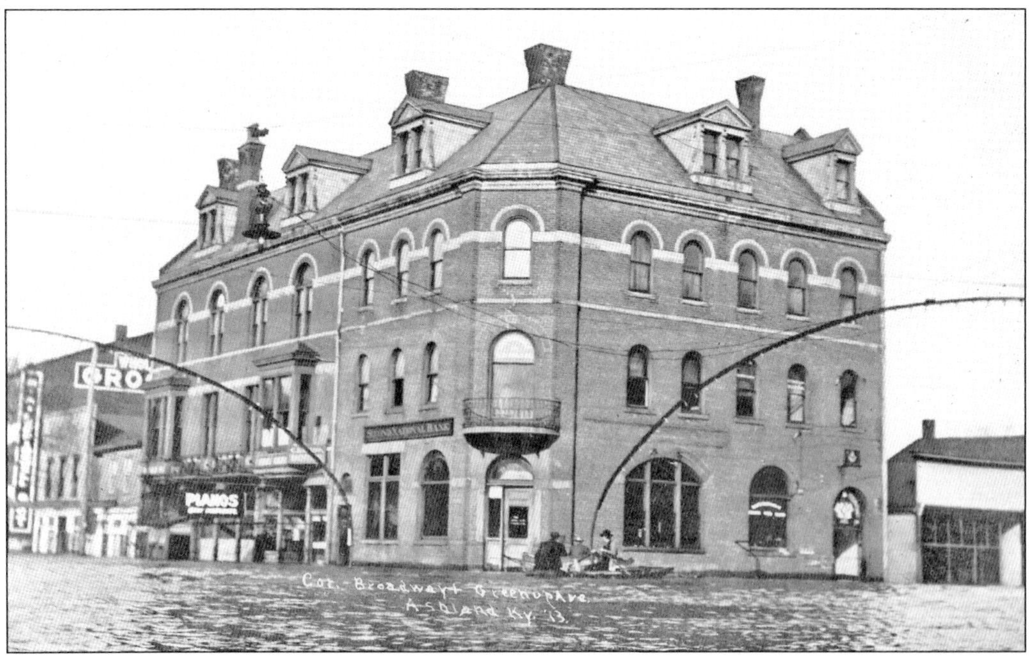

BANK BUILDING. It is unknown what the men in this photograph outside of the Second Nation Bank are up to. If they are customers, they'll have to wait at least a couple of more feet before the bank is open for business. Other cities along the river fared much worse regarding the loss of property. (Courtesy of the James C. Powers Collection.)

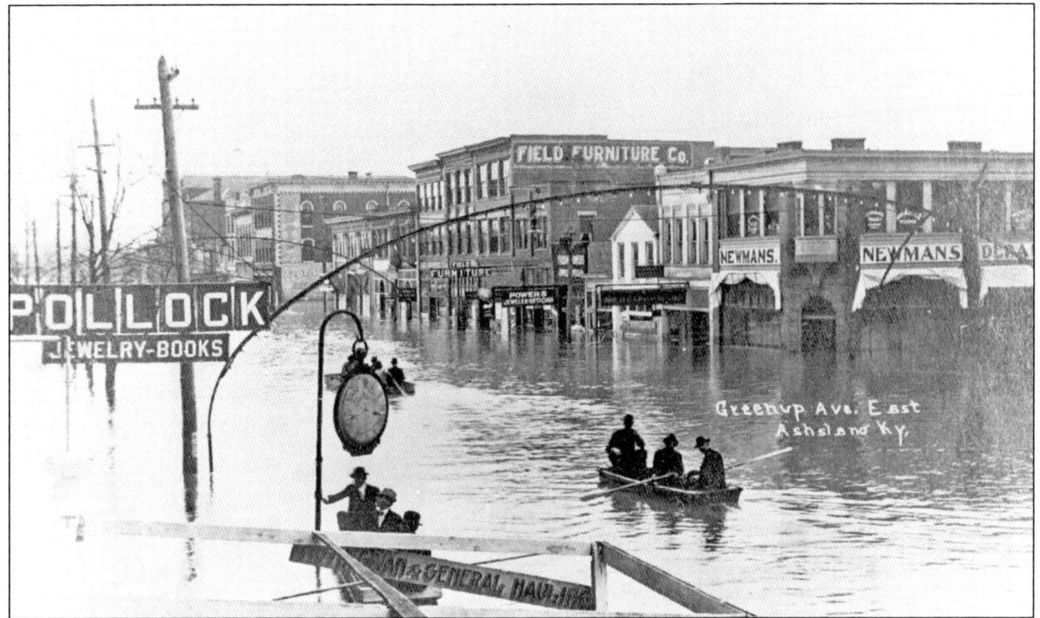

EAST GREENUP RIVER. Greenup Avenue running east looks more like a river than a business district during the flood of 1913. Business owners and the curious alike investigate the damage done during the first significant flooding for them since 1884. Notice the old Star's Fashion Building in the background. (Courtesy of the James C. Powers Collection.)

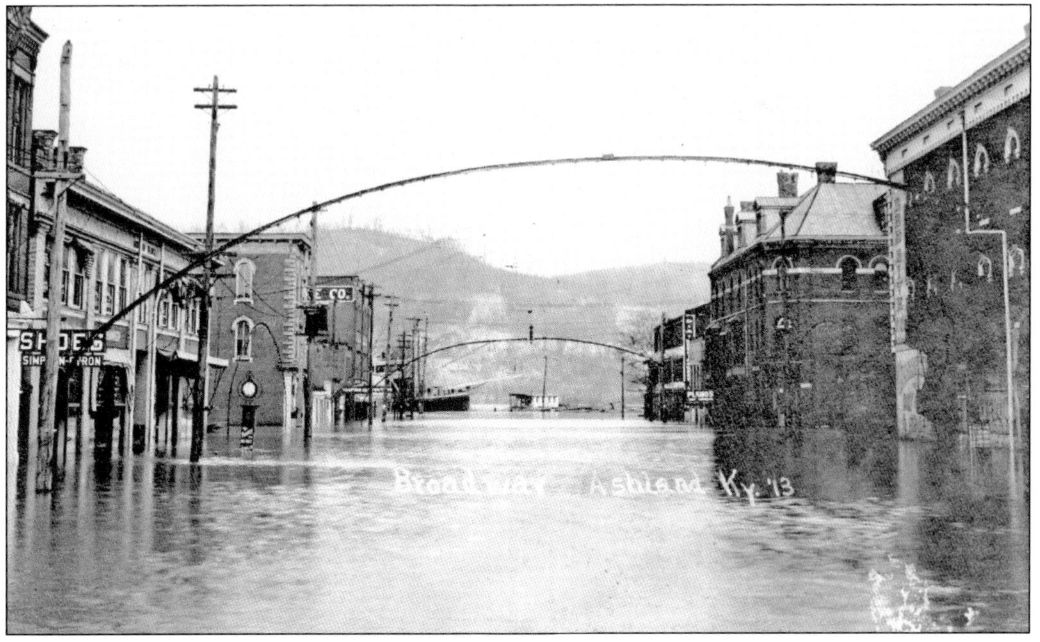

LOOKING NORTH. In another view north on Sixteenth Street, the height of the flooding is obvious by the shorter distance between the half-circle streetlights and the space between them and the water. Ohio is in the background, as are a barge and riverboat. This 1913 flood photograph is very rare in that it doesn't have people pictured in it. (Courtesy of the James C. Powers Collection.)

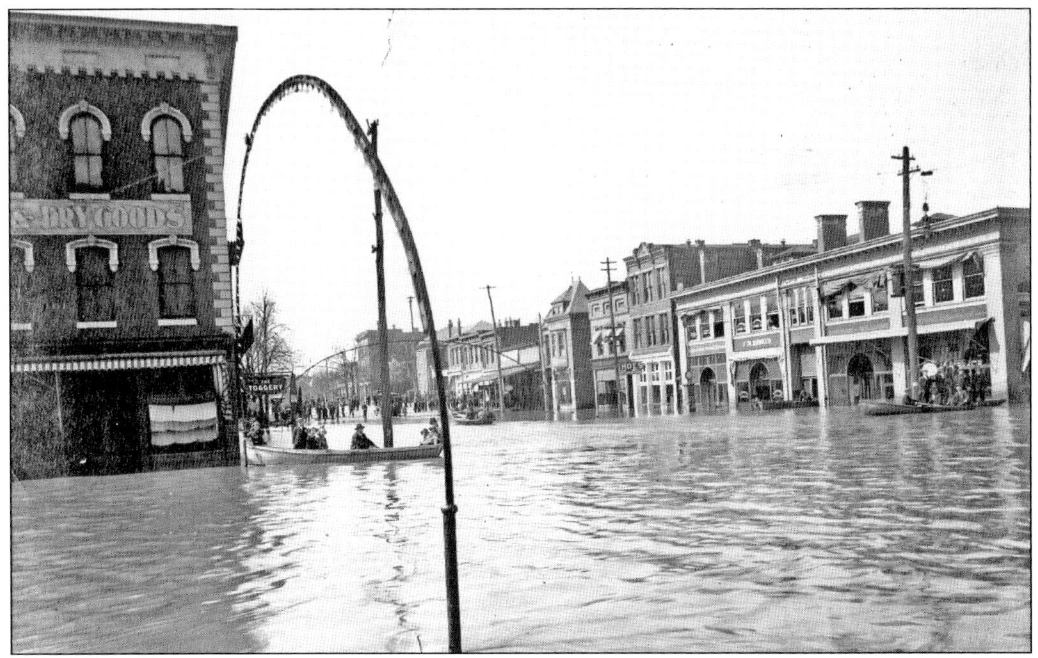

A Boating Family. This photograph was taken from near the familiar corner doorway of the Second National Bank at Sixteenth Street and Greenup Avenue. Several children are in the boat on the opposite side of the avenue under the Toggery sign. A great crowd is gathered on the steep side of Sixteenth Street in the background. (Courtesy of the James C. Powers Collection.)

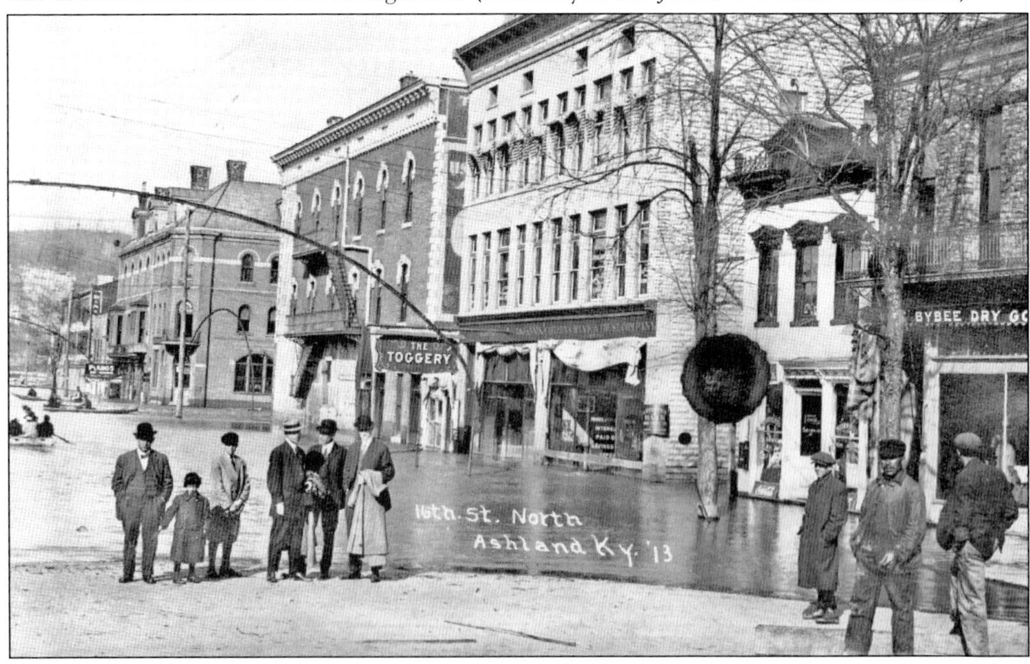

Levels Dropping. Cincinnati reached its crest stage on January 15, 1913, at 62.2 feet. Almost $200,000 in damages was reported in Cincinnati, the equivalent of several million dollars in damages today. Louisville report even higher loses in property and nearby crop storage areas. (Courtesy of the James C. Powers Collection.)

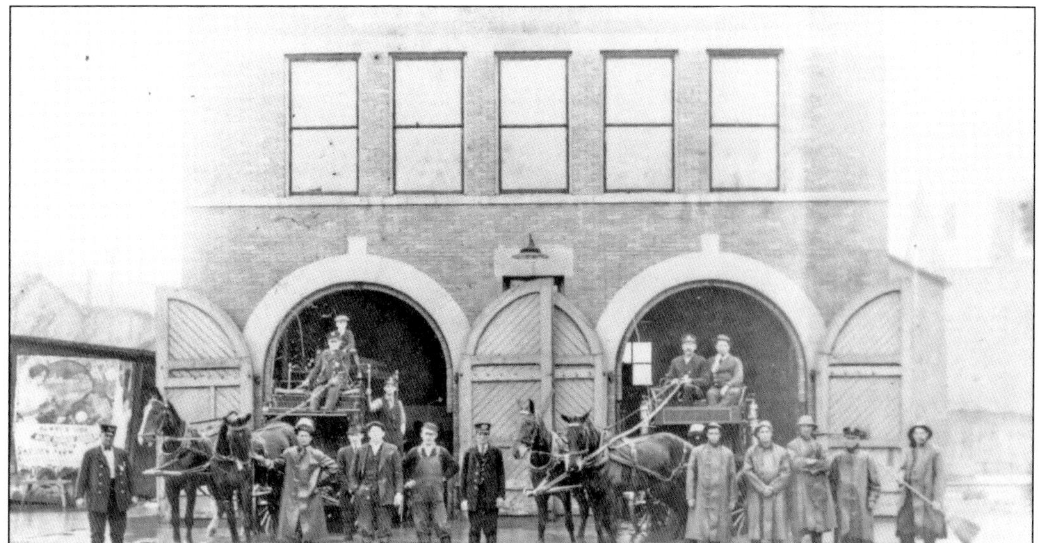

KNEE DEEP. The Ashland Fire Department on Seventeenth Street and Greenup Avenue is knee deep in water as the Ohio River makes a visit in January 1913. Water is not in short supply, as firemen, horses, and pumping wagons pose for this photograph in front of the damp and smelly city hall building. (Courtesy of the Arnold Hanners Photographic Collection, Minnie Winder Room, Boyd County Public Library.)

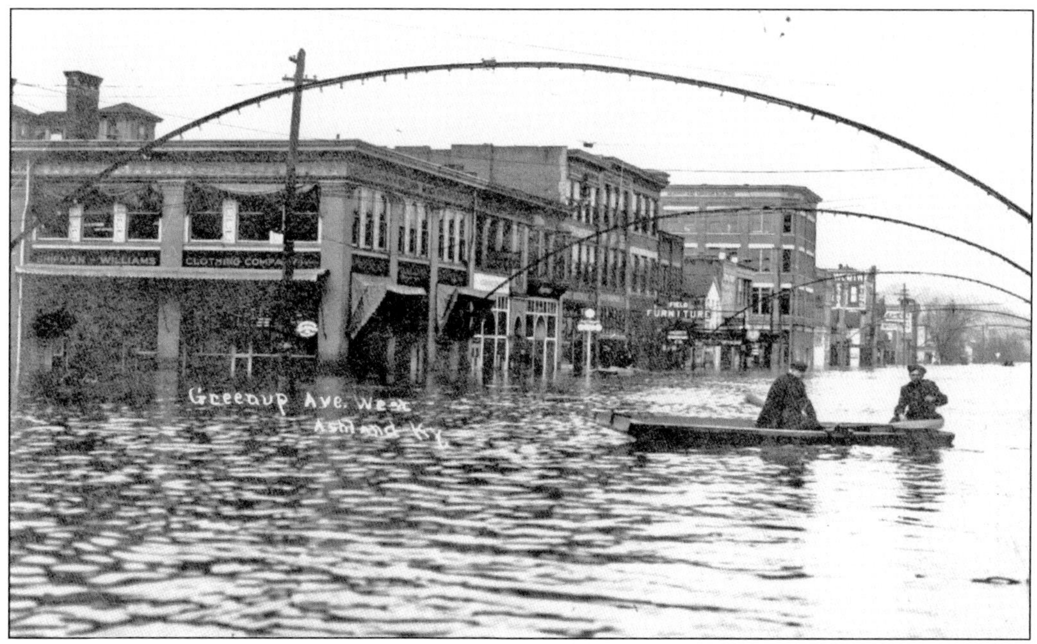

EARLY ON. This photograph was taken early on in the January 1913 flooding, as indicated by the water level in the businesses along Greenup Avenue. Shaiman Williams Clothing Company is seen in the immediate background. The four-story Murphy and Abrams Building along Greenup Avenue has water in it as well. (Courtesy of the James C. Powers Collection.)

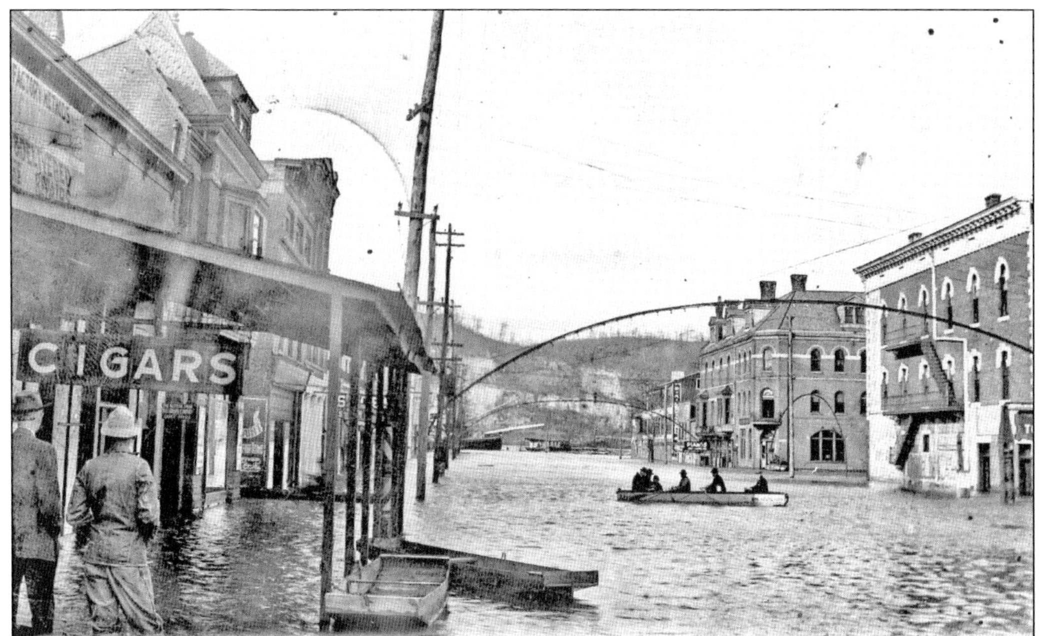

NO CIGAR. Two men inspect the cigar store on the west side of Sixteenth Street near Greenup Avenue. A business selling pianos is clearly seen near the Second National Bank or Coles Building in the distance. No doubt very few pianos—or any luxury items—sold during this difficult time. (Courtesy of the Arnold Hanners Photographic Collection, Minnie Winder Room, Boyd County Public Library.)

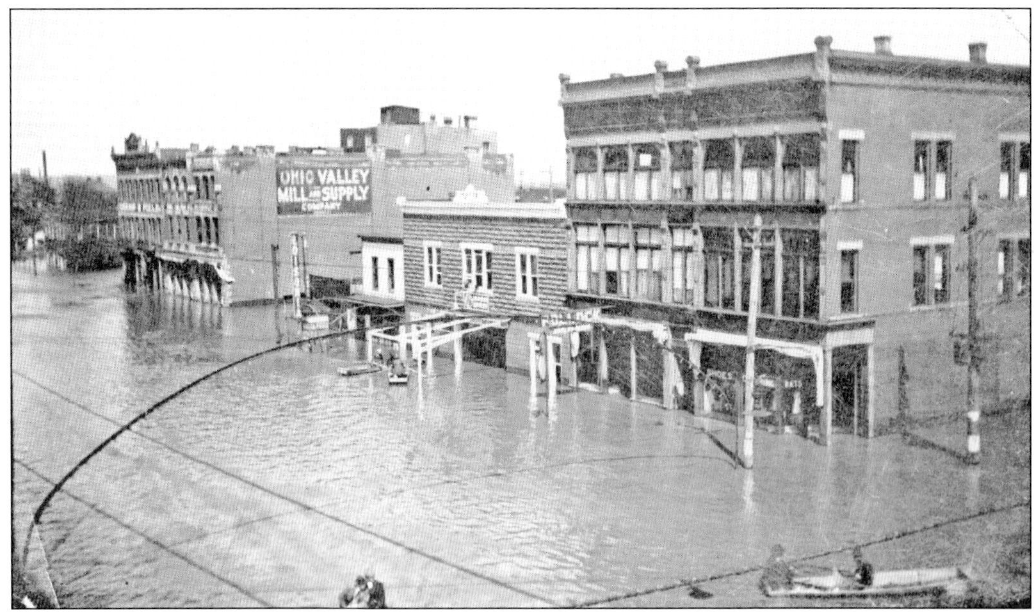

CRUMP AND FIELD. The Crump and Field Building is to the left, with the familiar crown accent on top. This beautiful building is on the north side of Greenup Avenue at the eastern corner of Fourteenth Street. The Edisonia Theater is located just left of the Taylor Building. (Courtesy of the Arnold Hanners Photographic Collection, Minnie Winder Room, Boyd County Public Library.)

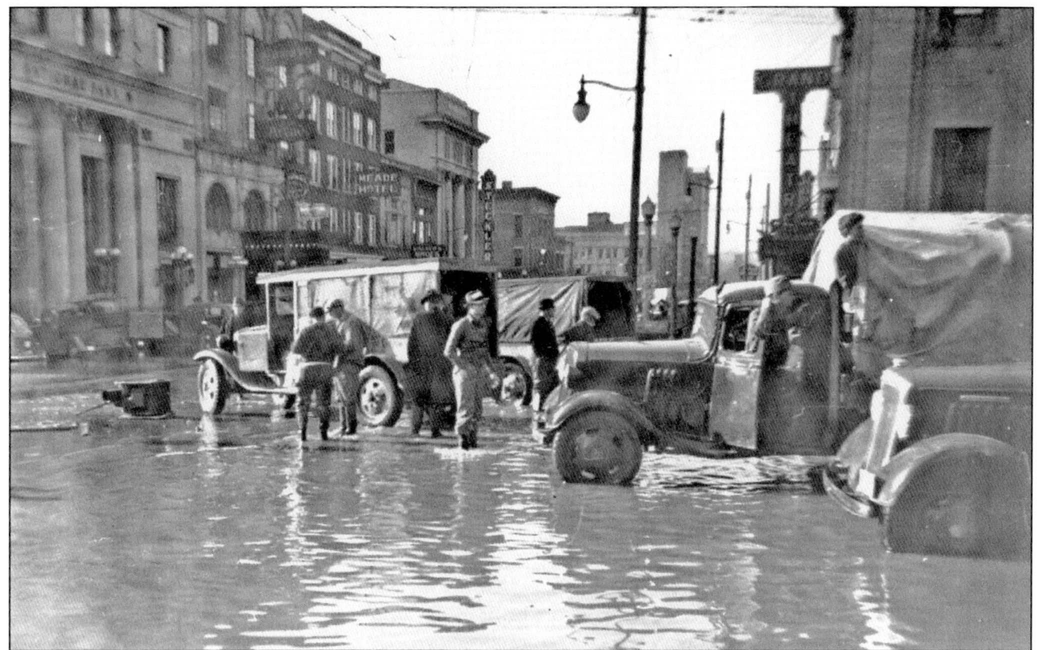

The Great Flood of 1937. The 1937 flood dwarfed all previously known floods that struck Ashland and the Ohio Valley as far back as the time of Daniel Boone. Four times the normal precipitation of January triggered this massive flood. The photograph verifies that the waters reached Winchester Avenue near today's Judd Plaza. (Courtesy of the Arnold Hanners Photographic Collection, Minnie Winder Room, Boyd County Public Library.)

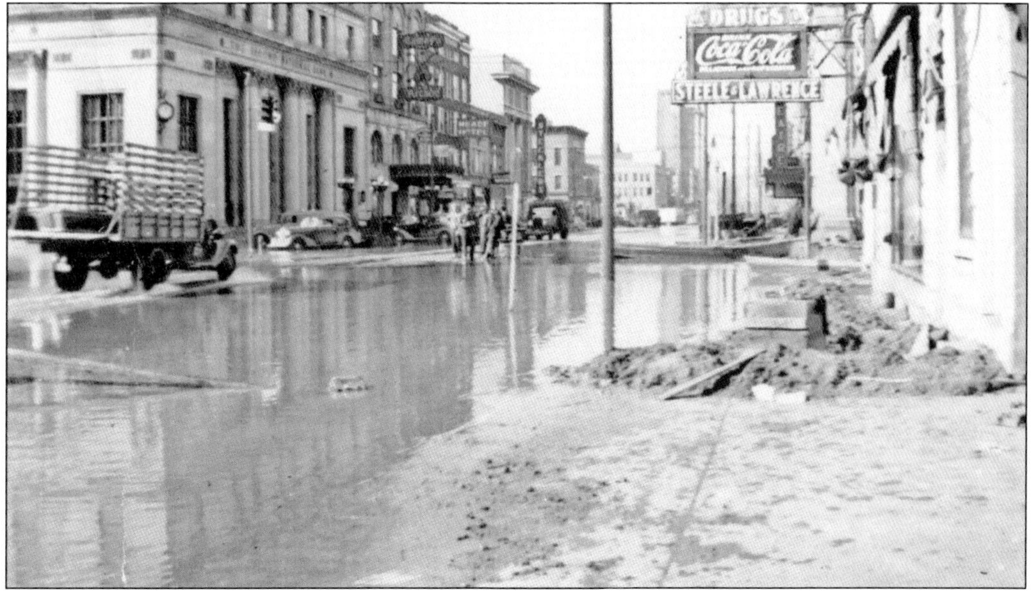

Water Near the Bank. This picture shows the floodwaters so high that a boat could be docked in the middle of Sixteenth Street and Winchester Avenue. The base of the Ashland National Bank can been seen, as can the Meade Hotel, Hotel Ventura in the distance, and the Steele and Lawrence drugstore. (Courtesy of the Arnold Hanners Photographic Collection, Minnie Winder Room, Boyd County Public Library.)

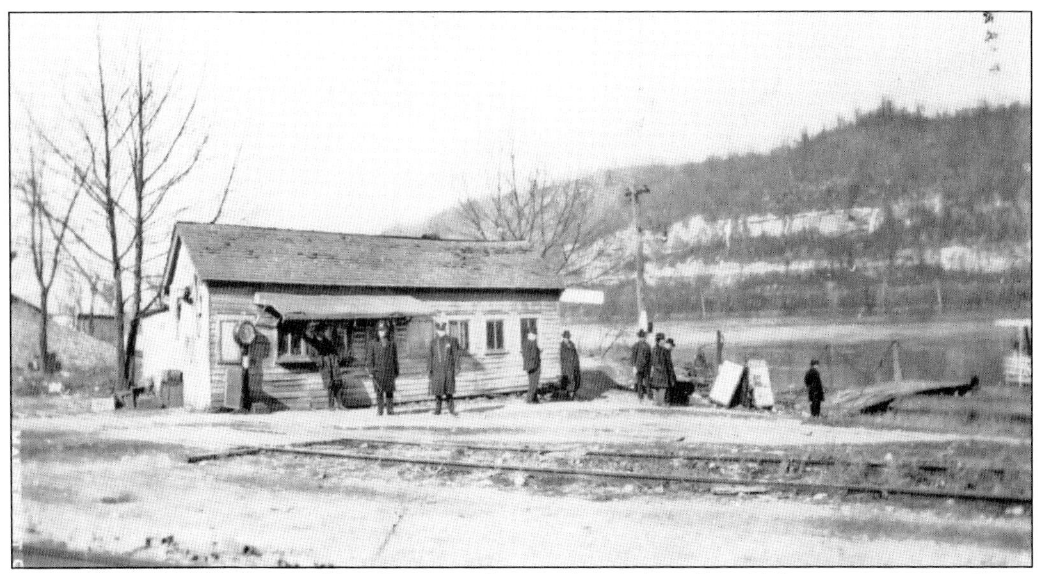

FRONT STREET VIEW. The Ohio River is about 7 feet below the old ferry station near Front Street. Buildings near the river during the flood of 1937 were almost totally wiped away. Two Ashland police officers and others pose for the camera around 1920. (Courtesy of the Arnold Hanners Photographic Collection, Minnie Winder Room, Boyd County Public Library.)

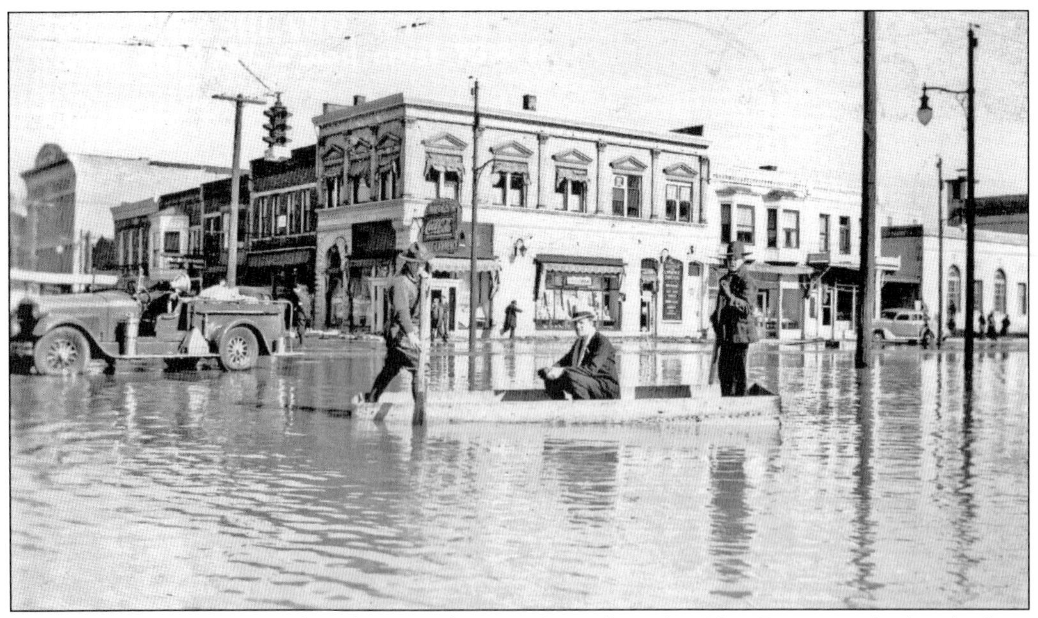

THREE MEN IN A BOAT. This photograph was taken when the Ohio River reached its highest level ever in Ashland. The picture shows the water up to the intersection of Sixteenth Street and Winchester Avenue, which provided for a rare Winchester Avenue boat ride for these three young men. (Courtesy of the Arnold Hanners Photographic Collection, Minnie Winder Room, Boyd County Public Library.)

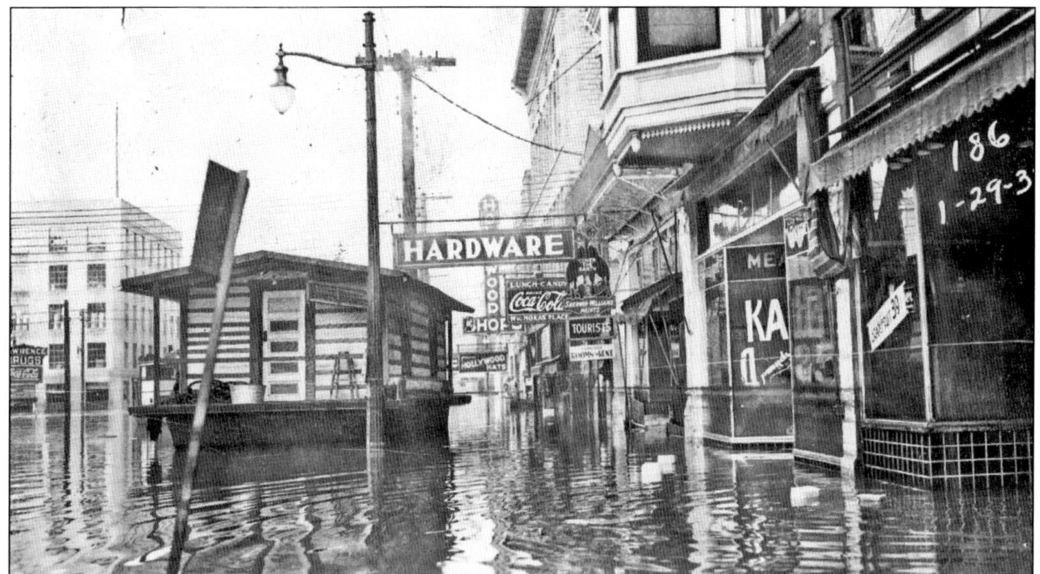

NO HOLLYWOOD. The Hollywood Shops and Hollywood Hats signs stand out as the river around them engulfs the businesses along Sixteenth Street between Greenup Avenue and Winchester Avenue. A flatboat has been brought in to store supplies to protect inventory from certain ruination. (Courtesy of the Arnold Hanners Photographic Collection, Minnie Winder Room, Boyd County Public Library.)

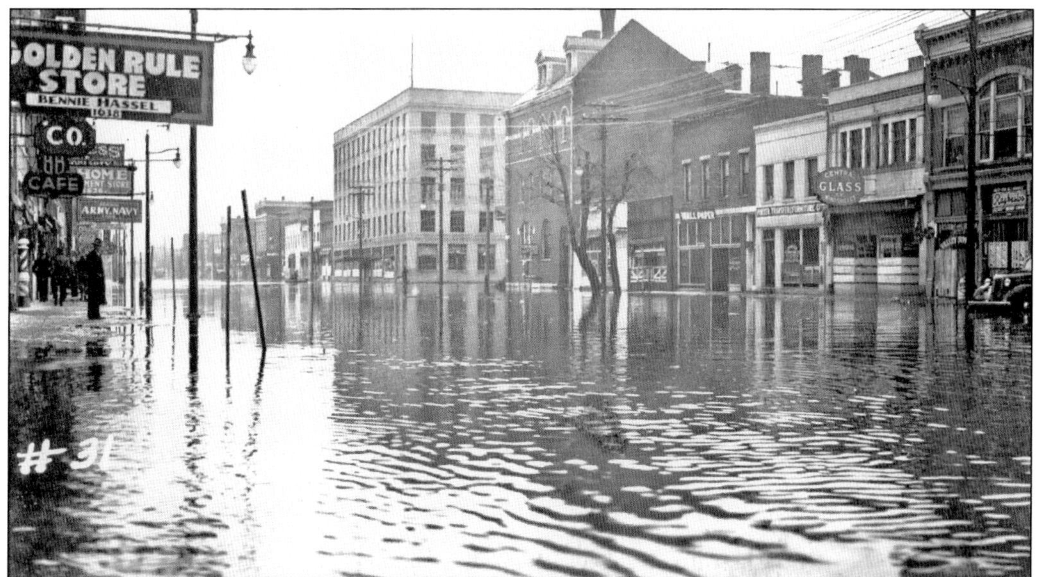

SAME SCENE, DIFFERENT FLOOD. The Coles Building can be seen in the background along Greenup Avenue and Sixteenth Street. The businesses and styles have changed since the 1913 flood, but the helplessness is the same. The water was on its way down by the time this photograph was taken. (Courtesy of the Arnold Hanners Photographic Collection, Minnie Winder Room, Boyd County Public Library.)

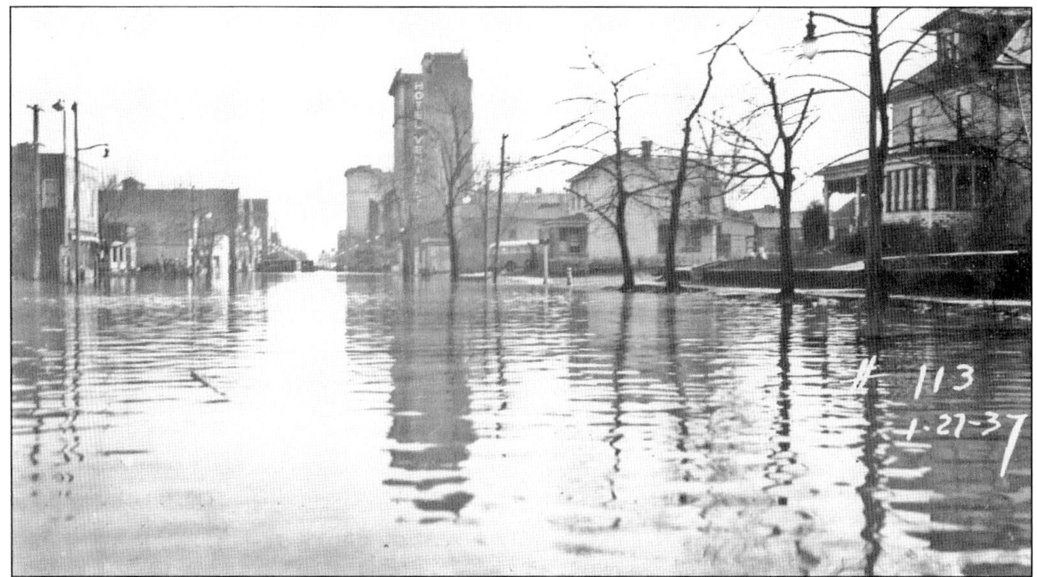

Above the Flood. Homes to the south of Winchester Avenue seem to be out of harm's way, due to being built on mound-like foundations. The business to the north, or on the right of this picture, fared much worse at their lower elevations. Flood walls erected after the 1937 flood have provided much-needed protection. (Courtesy of the James C. Powers Collection.)

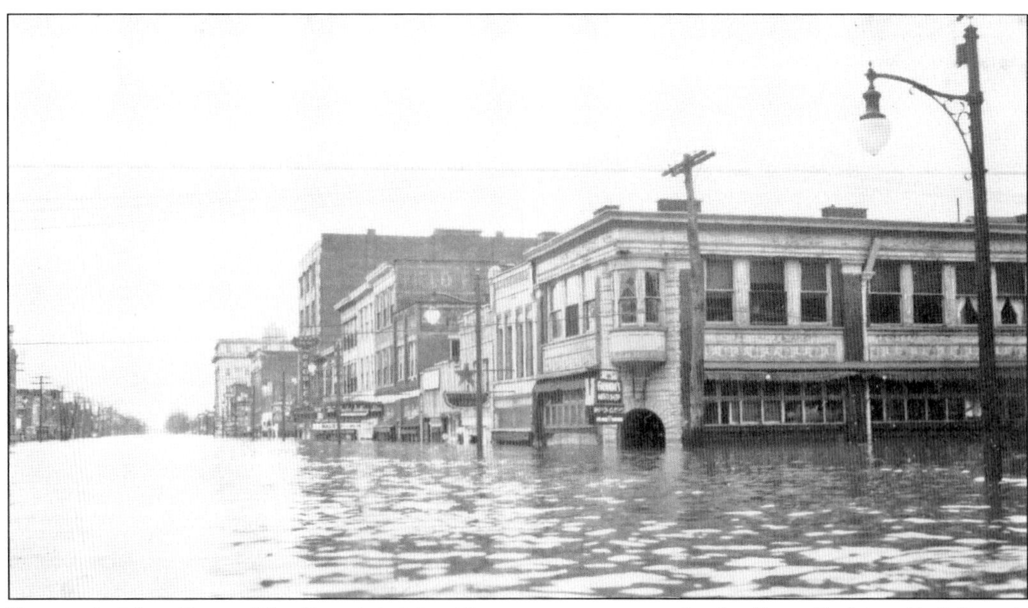

Fannin's Men Shop. The Fannin's Men Shop, or more recently the Stars Fashion Building, is on the southeast corner of Fifteenth Street and Greenup Avenue. It appears that nearly six feet of water from the Ohio River has decided to shop in this part of Ashland. (Courtesy of the Arnold Hanners Photographic Collection, Minnie Winder Room, Boyd County Public Library.)

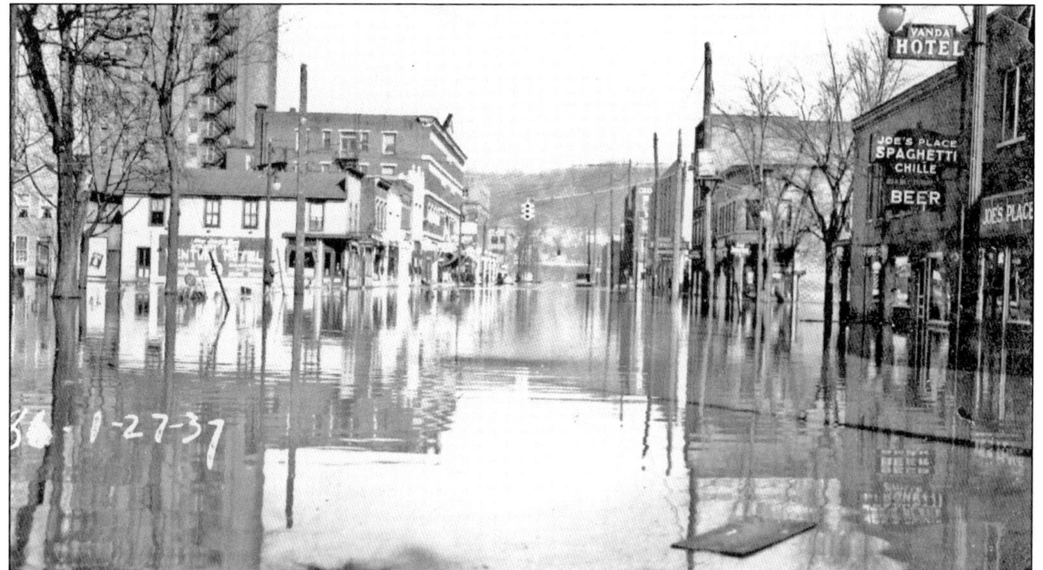

BEFORE THE BRIDGE. This photograph shows flooding reaching up to Carter Avenue and Thirteenth Street, looking north past the Paramount Theater on the right and Hotel Ventura on the left. Today a Burger King is on the right, the Paramount Arts Center is on the right, and a beautiful blue bridge leads north into Ohio. (Courtesy of the Arnold Hanners Photographic Collection, Minnie Winder Room, Boyd County Public Library.)

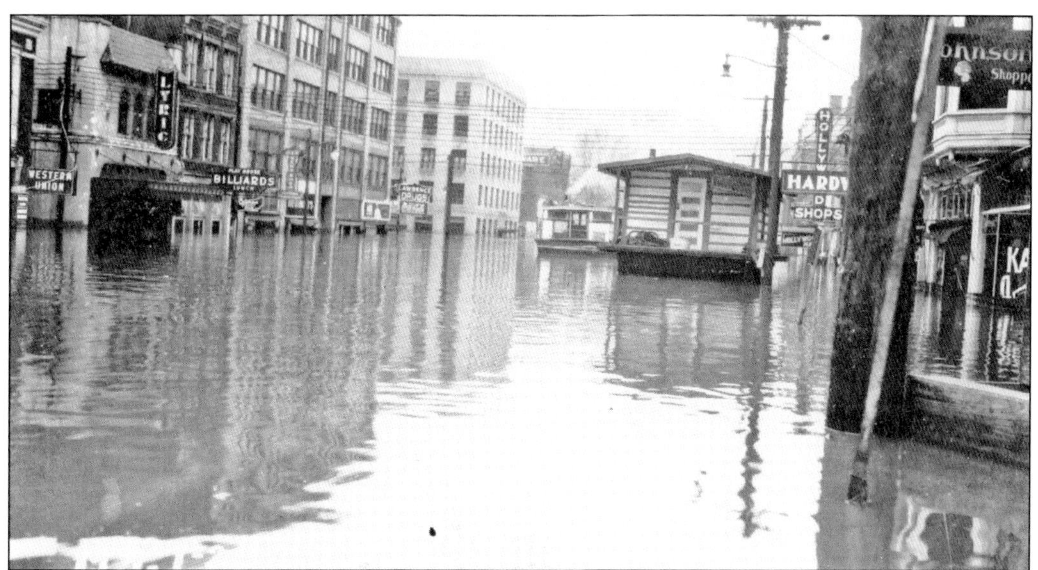

HIGH LEVEL. Water levels look to be around 6 feet or more in many of these businesses along Seventeenth Street and Greenup Avenue. A small boat makes its way in the direction of the camera, south toward Winchester Avenue. Several businesses decided to move to higher ground in South Ashland after this flood. (Courtesy of the Arnold Hanners Photographic collection, Minnie Winder Room, Boyd County Public Library.)

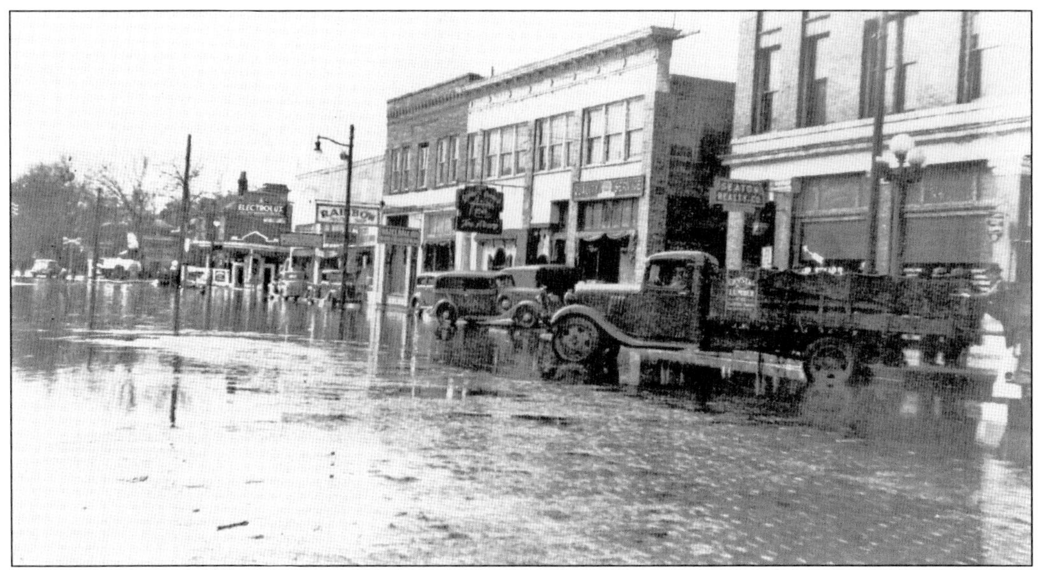

DRYING OFF. This street is drying off, which will enable the businesses to get back up and running. It is estimated that the damage done by the 1937 flood would equal almost $4 billion in today's economy. Pictured in the center is the Chimney Corner Tea Room at 333 Sixteenth Street. (Courtesy of the Arnold Hanners Photographic Collection, Minnie Winder Room, Boyd County Public Library.)

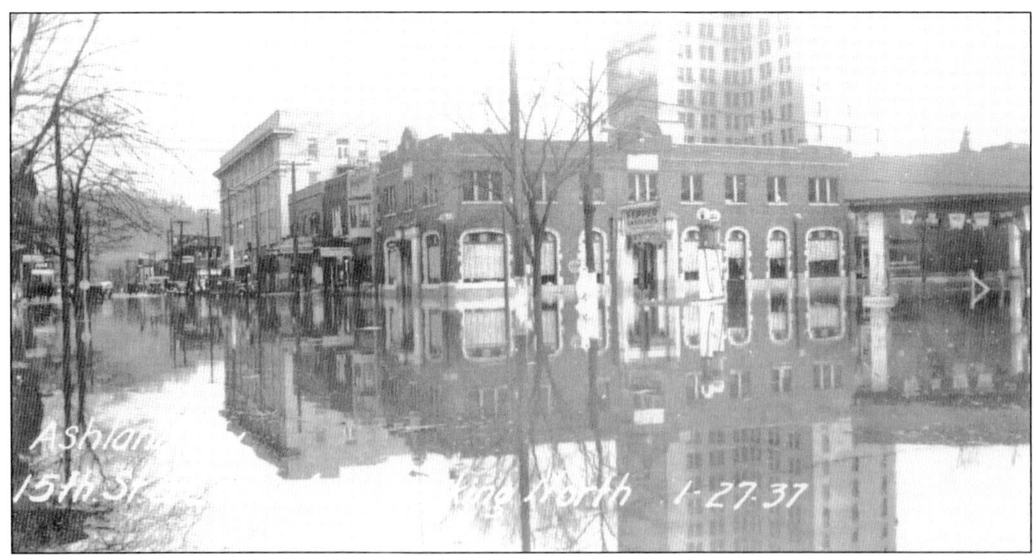

PEPPER GAS. This photograph was taken on January 27, 1937, in front of Pepper Gasolines at the intersection of Fifteenth Street and Carter Avenue. The Second National Bank Building is to the left, and the Ashland National Bank Building is climbing out of the picture to the north. (Courtesy of the Arnold Hanners Photographic Collection, Minnie Winder Room, Boyd County Public Library.)

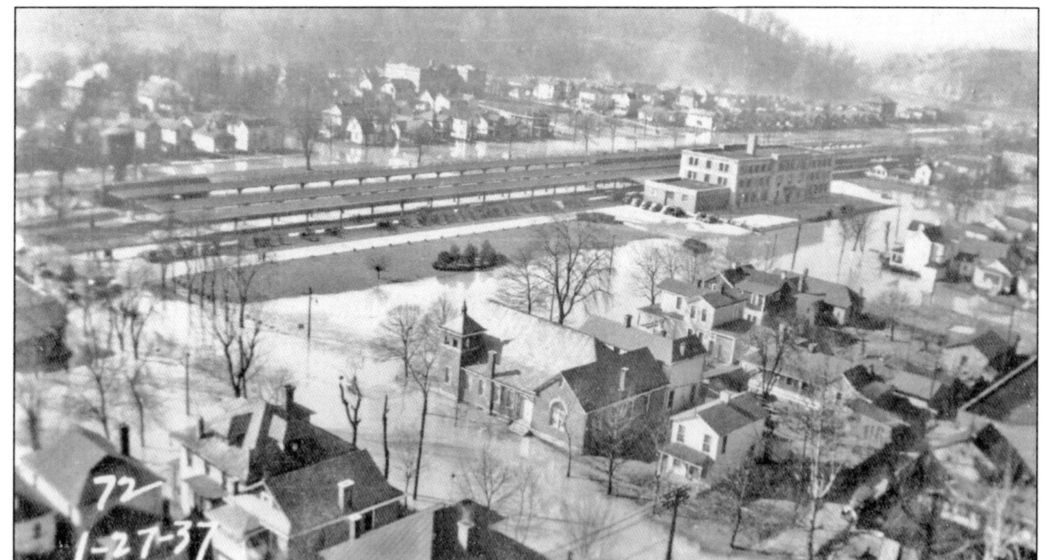

NEAR THE DEPOT. The floodwaters in 1937 were all around the C&O depot, as can be seen from this aerial view. The railroad was silent for a month after the flooding due to inspections and track replacements. Much of Carter Avenue, Central Avenue, Hagen Court, and Tenth Street resembled small creeks and rivers rather than roadways. (Courtesy of the Arnold Hanners Photographic Collection, Minnie Winder Room, Boyd County Public Library.)

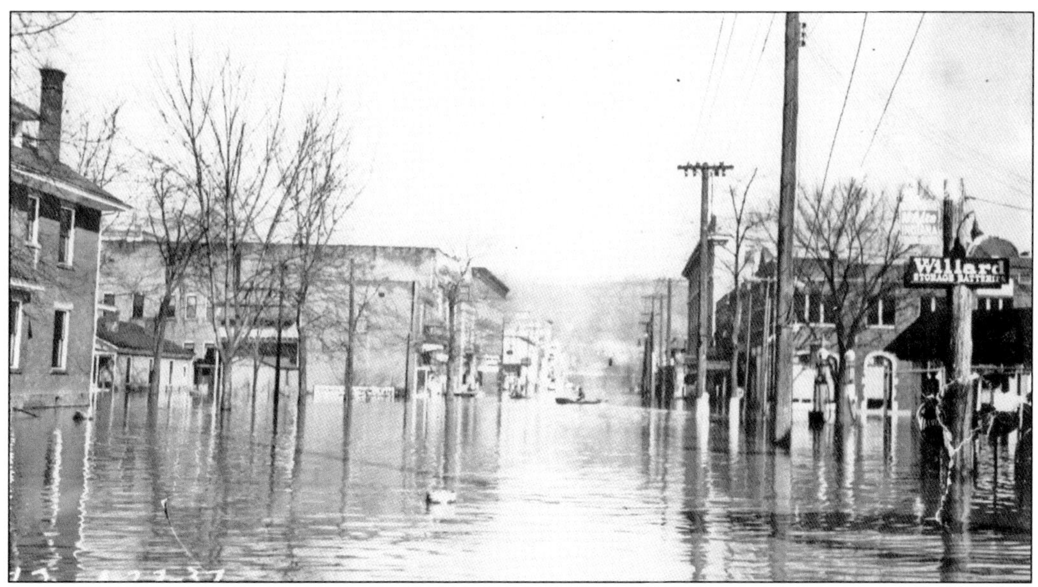

NORTH OF FIFTEENTH STREET. Water can be seen from this point on Carter Avenue north past Winchester Avenue and Greenup Avenue to dry ground in Coal Grove, Ohio. Almost 400 people lost their lives during this flood, which stretched from Pittsburgh to the Mississippi River. (Courtesy of the Arnold Hanners Photographic Collection, Minnie Winder Room, Boyd County Public Library.)

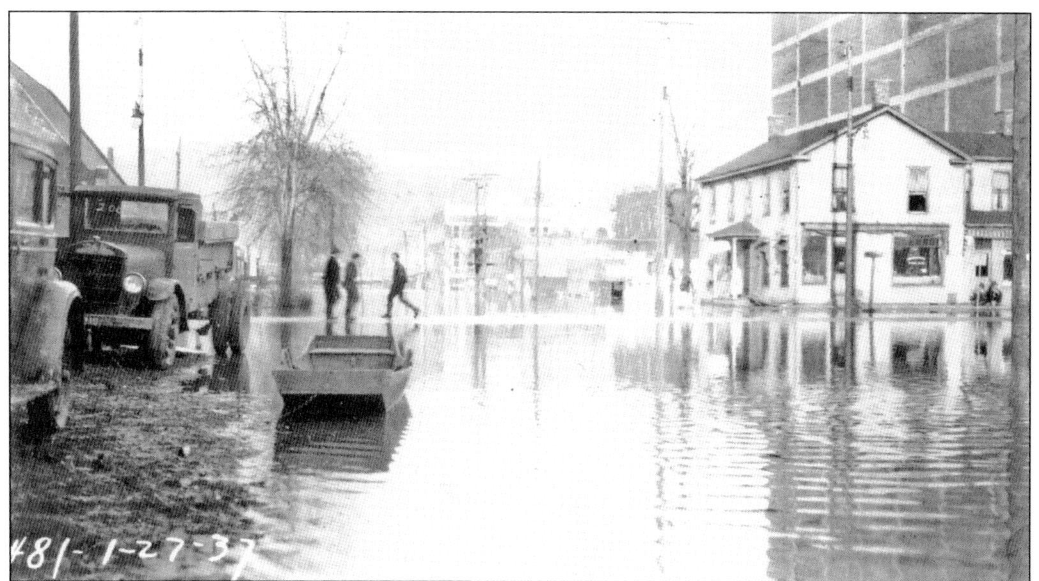

WALKWAY. Young people walk along a dry patch of brick on Winchester Avenue in front of the Joseph Burdett Home heading west. Approximately one million people lost their homes because of this great flood along the Ohio Valley. It would be 60 years after this photograph was taken before the area would see another great flood. (Courtesy of the Arnold Hanners Photographic Collection, Minnie Winder Room, Boyd County Public Library.)

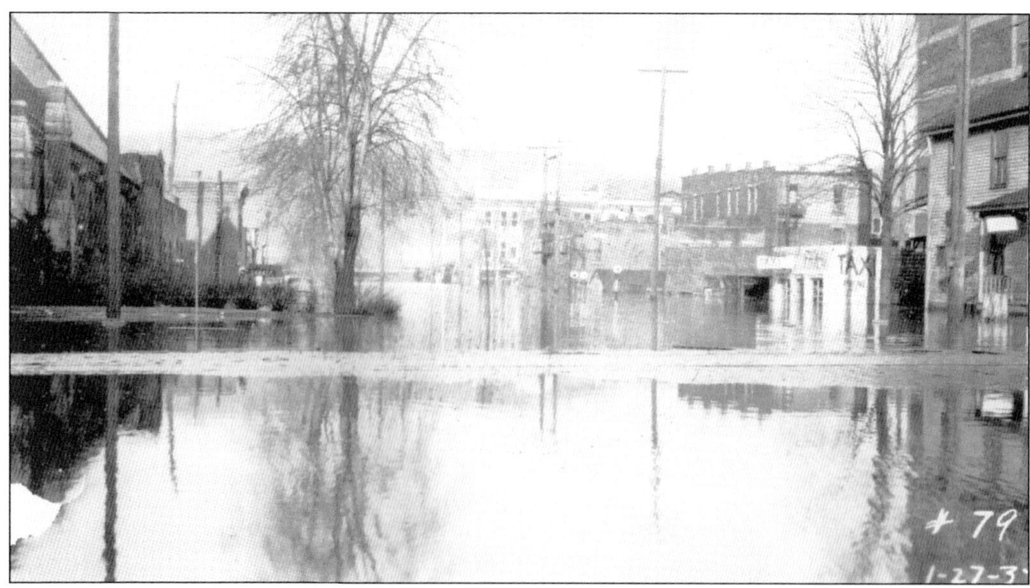

STREETCAR TRACK. Only the slightly higher elevation of the streetcar track separates the floodwaters north and south of Winchester Avenue. The Crump and Field Building in the distance can be seen dealing with floodwaters again. The building has been well kept throughout the years and still stands on Greenup Avenue today. (Courtesy of the Arnold Hanners Photographic Collection, Minnie Winder Room, Boyd County Public Library.)

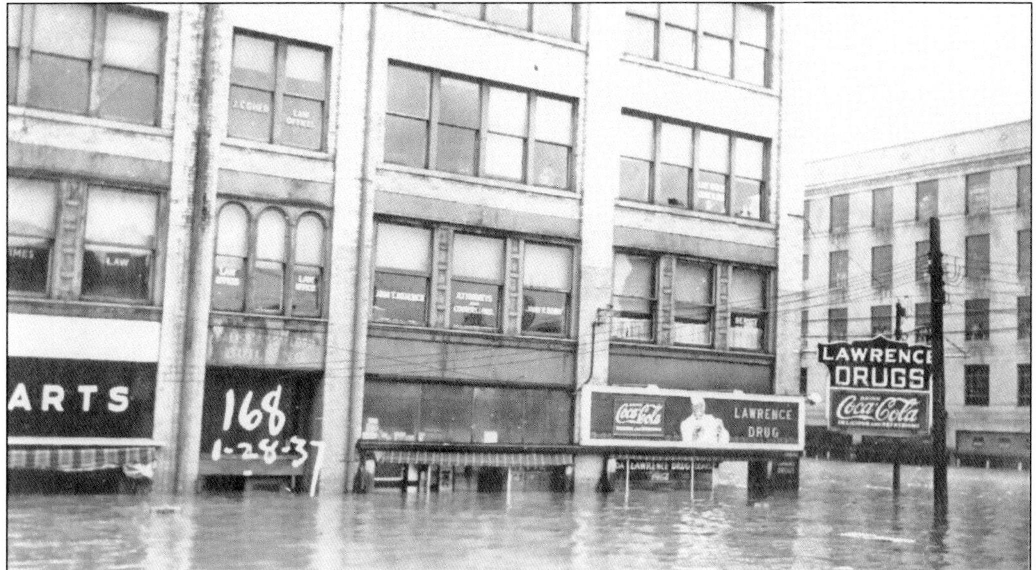

FLOATING LAW OFFICES. The Lawrence drugstore looks to have nearly 7 feet of water in and around it, and the water just across Greenup Avenue looks even deeper. In fact, the water in some areas along the north side of the avenue were up to 3 feet deeper than on the south side. (Courtesy of the Arnold Hanners Photographic collection, Minnie Winder Room, Boyd County Public Library.)

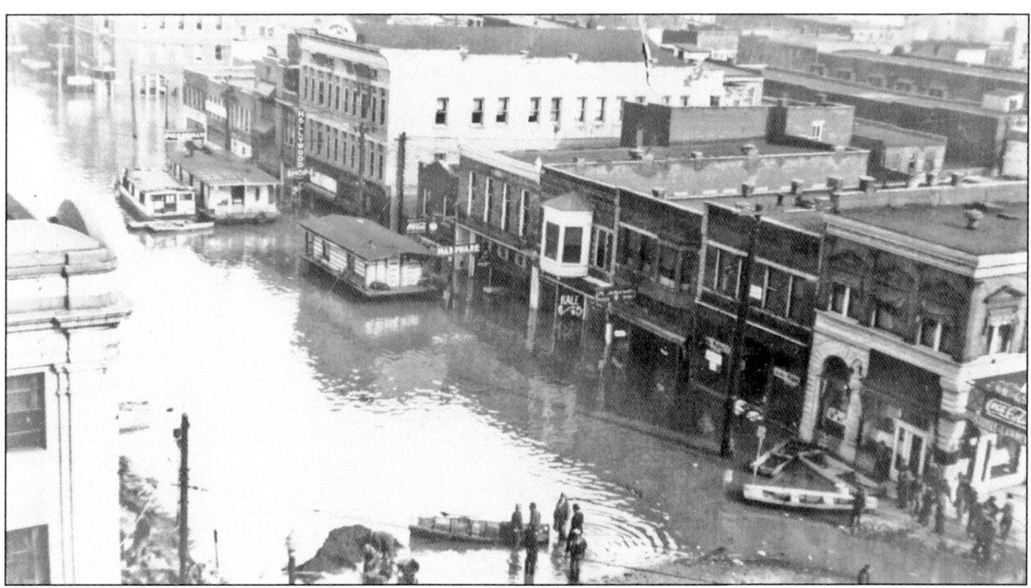

ATOP THE ASHLAND NATIONAL BANK BUILDING. Near the foot of the Ashland National Bank Building, several of the curious have come to watch waters of the Ohio River recede slowly from record flooding. Almost all of downtown Ashland was awash with the muddy river water. (Courtesy of the Arnold Hanners Photographic collection, Minnie Winder Room, Boyd County Public Library.)

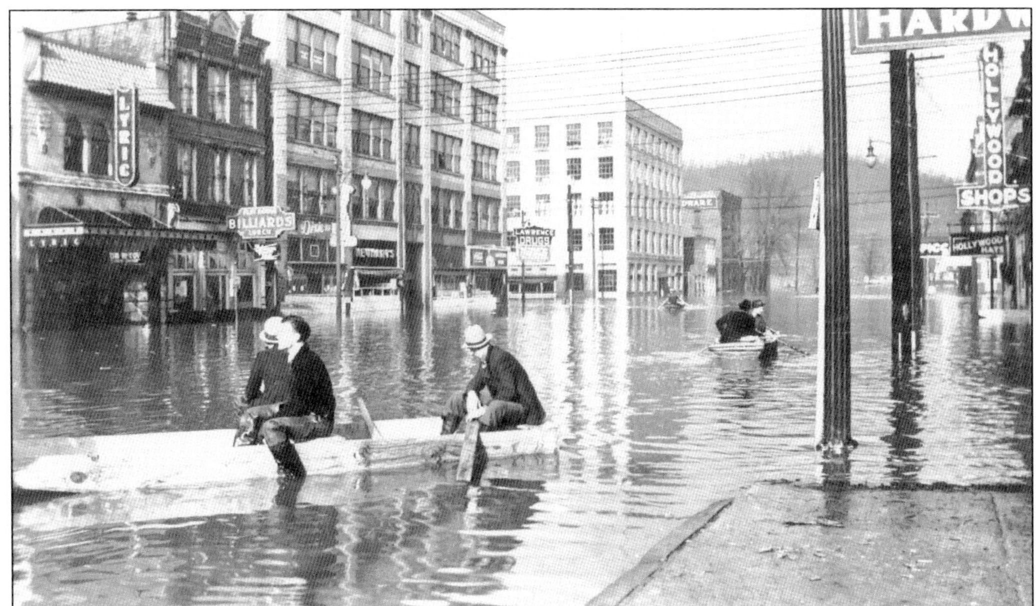

ASHLAND GONDOLAS. Sixteenth Street looks more like an Appalachian Venice than the worst flood in recorded history. Several men in a makeshift boat look as if they are waiting their turn to make it to Greenup Avenue and on to the unending Ohio River. (Courtesy of the Arnold Hanners Photographic Collection, Minnie Winder Room, Boyd County Public Library.)

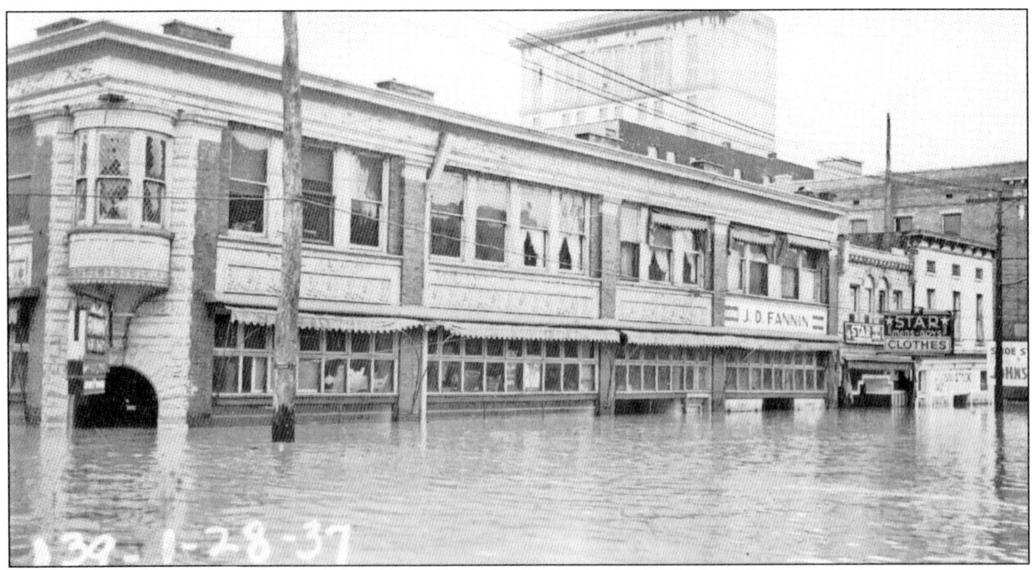

WATERFRONT DWELLINGS. The Ashland National Bank building stands tall over the deluge that has engulfed the city. The 1902 Murphy and Abrams Block Building looks as if it has just two stories, as the floodwaters completely cover the first story. This photograph was taken on January 28, 1937. (Courtesy of the Arnold Hanners Photographic Collection, Minnie Winder Room, Boyd County Public Library.)

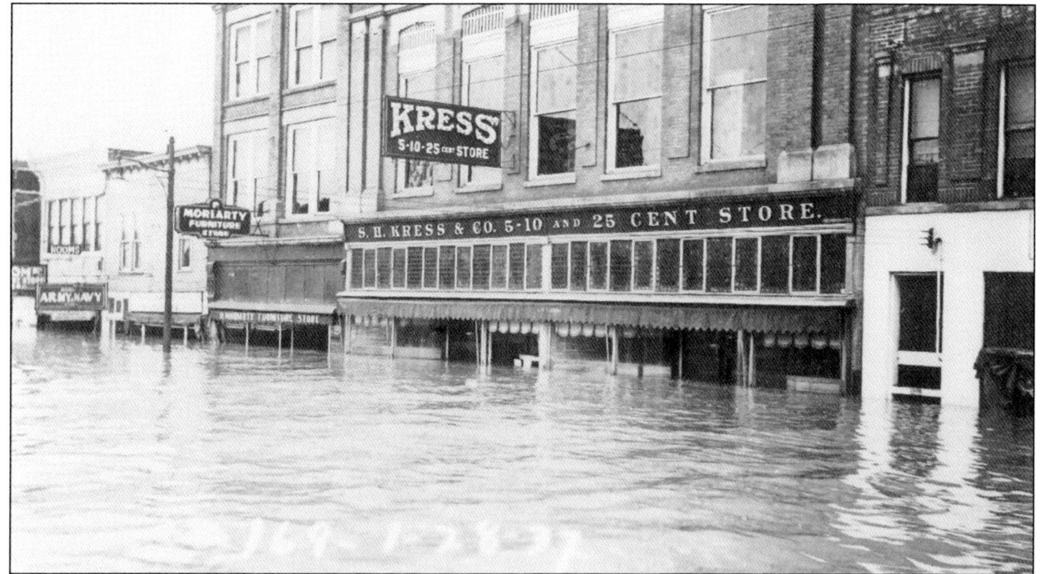

WASHOUT. Several businesses along Greenup Avenue will have unwanted time off as the Ohio River comes ashore to shop. Business in the photograph are the Army Navy Store, the Moriarty Furniture Store, and the Kress 5, 10, and 25¢ store. The old Army Navy Store structure is showing a sag in the center. (Courtesy of the Arnold Hanners Photographic Collection, Minnie Winder Room, Boyd County Public Library.)

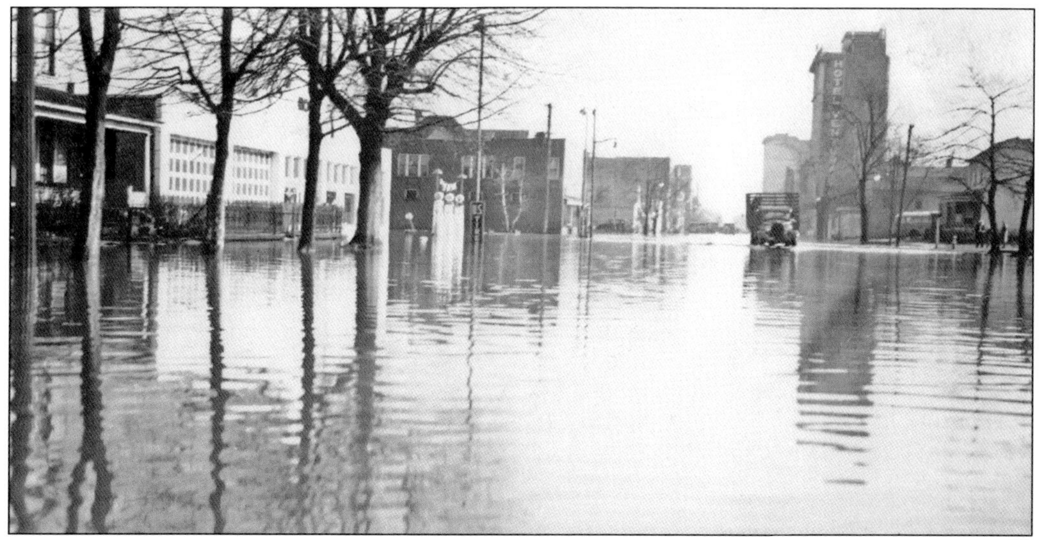

NO GAS. A truck makes its way through high water traveling west on Winchester Avenue past a flooded gas station. Most businesses and homes along Winchester fared much better during the flood, only receiving a foot or two of water damage. Huntington, Ironton, Portsmouth, Greenup, Maysville, and other river cities experienced widespread damage. (Courtesy of the Arnold Hanners Photographic Collection, Minnie Winder Room, Boyd County Public Library.)

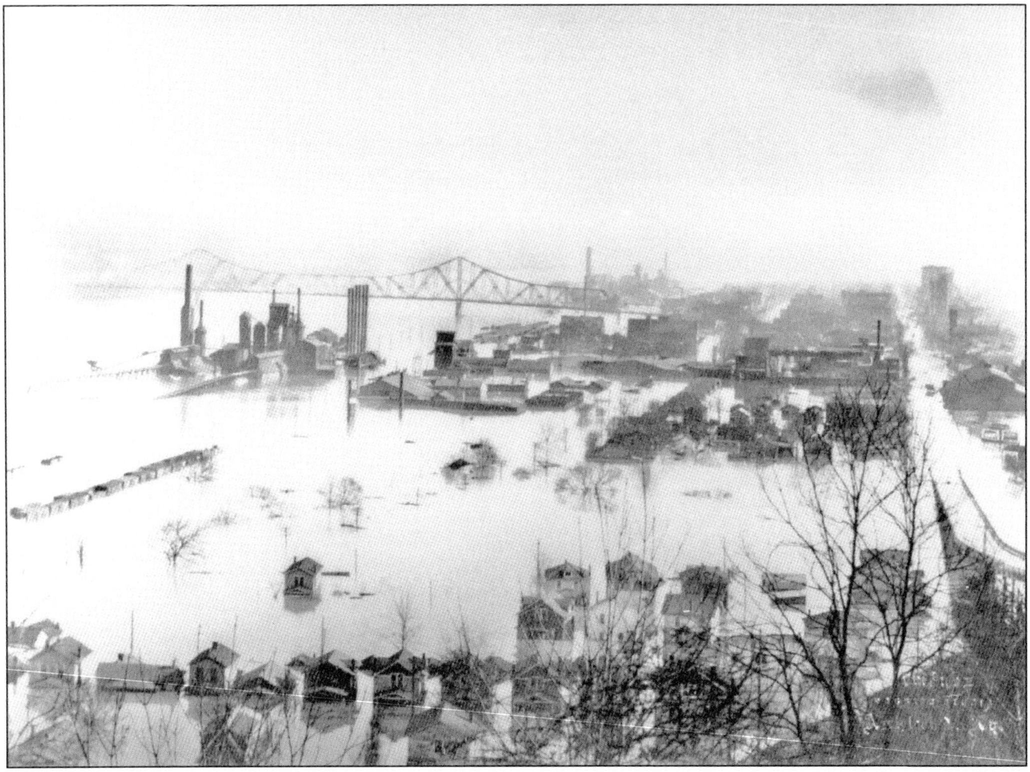

WATER AND IRON MEET. In this photograph taken from the west looking east into flooded Ashland, Winchester Avenue north has become part of the great Ohio River. The ironworks and railroad cars to the left are in the water, as are the homes in the foreground. (Courtesy of the Arnold Hanners Photographic Collection, Minnie Winder Room, Boyd County Public Library.)

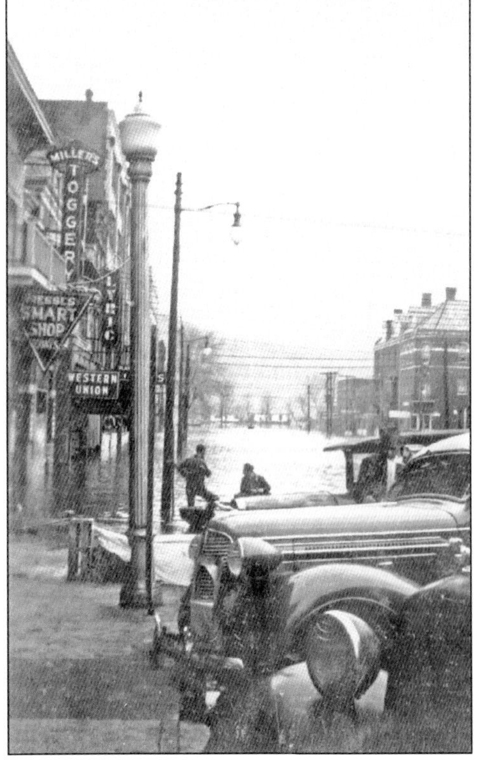

WESTERN UNION. This photograph is looking north from the west side of Sixteenth Street toward the Coles Building. The Western Union office, which is flooded in the picture, is in the same location as the cigar shop where, during the flood of 1913, two men stood outside and watched the floodwaters rise onto the street. (Courtesy of the Arnold Hanners Photographic Collection, Minnie Winder Room, Boyd County Public Library.)

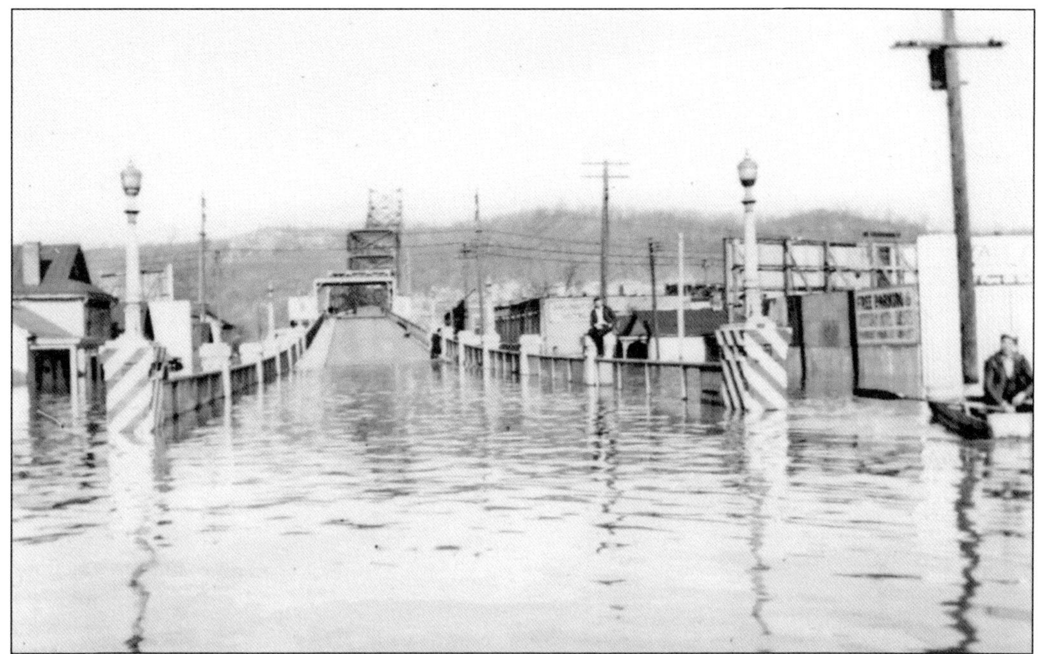

A Bridge over Water? A gentleman sits on the Ashland side of the Twelfth Street Bridge, now the Ben M. Williams Sr. Bridge. The roadbed of the bridge was dry from Coal Grove to this point, where it met the water it was designed to bridge. No other flood in Ashland's history did as much damage as the 1937 flood. (Courtesy of the Arnold Hanners Photographic Collection, Minnie Winder Room, Boyd County Public Library.)

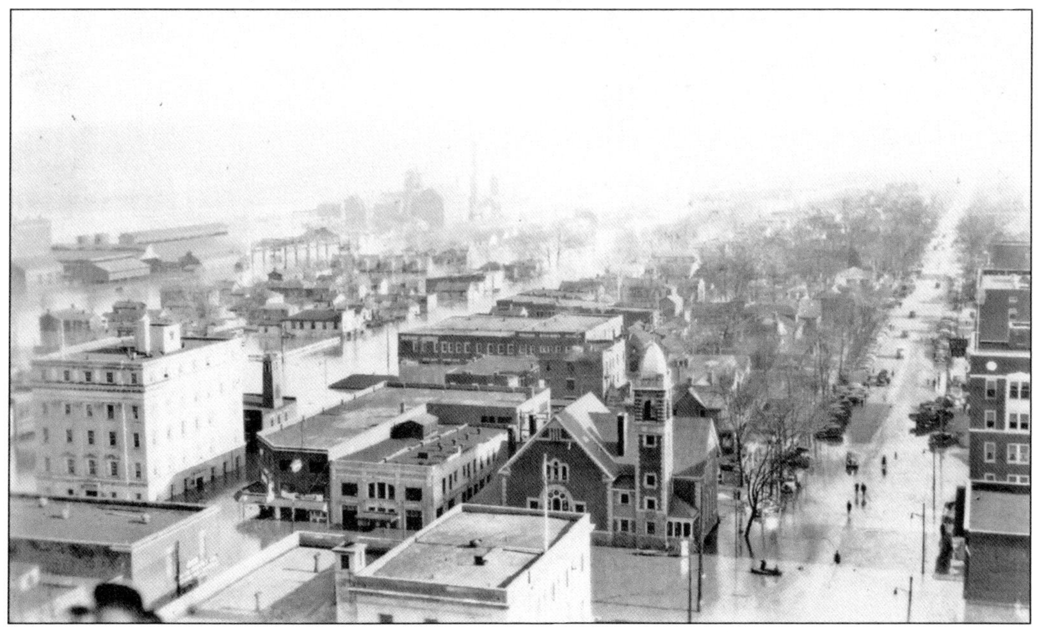

A Northeast View. The Henry Clay Hotel, as well as much of northeast Ashland, can be seen. City hall, at Greenup Avenue and Fifteenth Street, can be seen as well as the Mansbach Scrap Iron Company, founded in 1918 by Joseph Mansbach. (Courtesy of the Arnold Hanners Photographic Collection, Minnie Winder Room, Boyd County Public Library.)

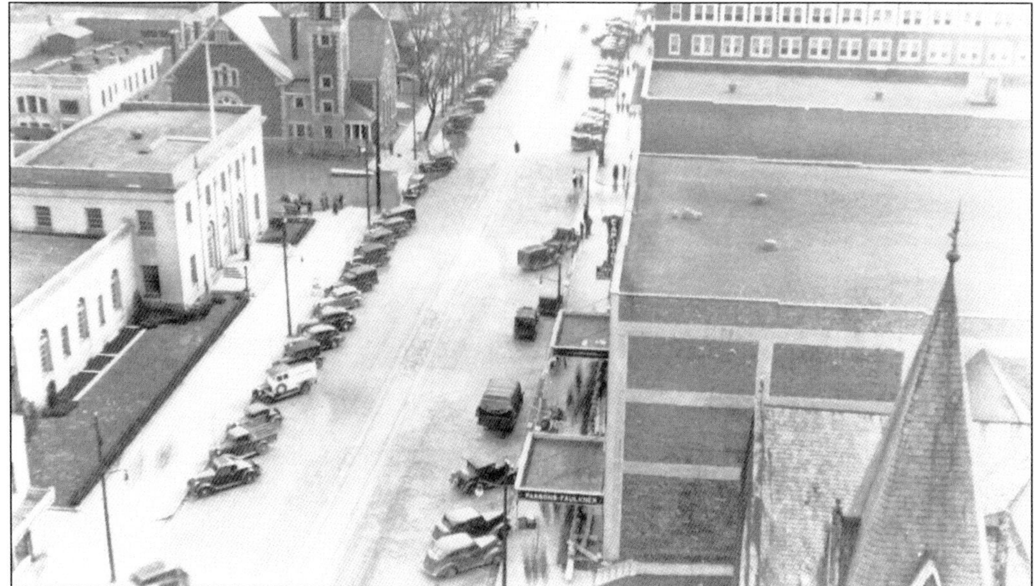

MUDDY WINCHESTER. Automobiles and drying mud line Winchester Avenue looking east from the Ashland National Bank Building. The C. H. Parsons Building and the Capital Theater sustained little or no flood damage. The post office continues to operate as the floodwaters recede toward Greenup Avenue. (Courtesy of the Arnold Hanners Photographic Collection, Minnie Winder Room, Boyd County Public Library.)

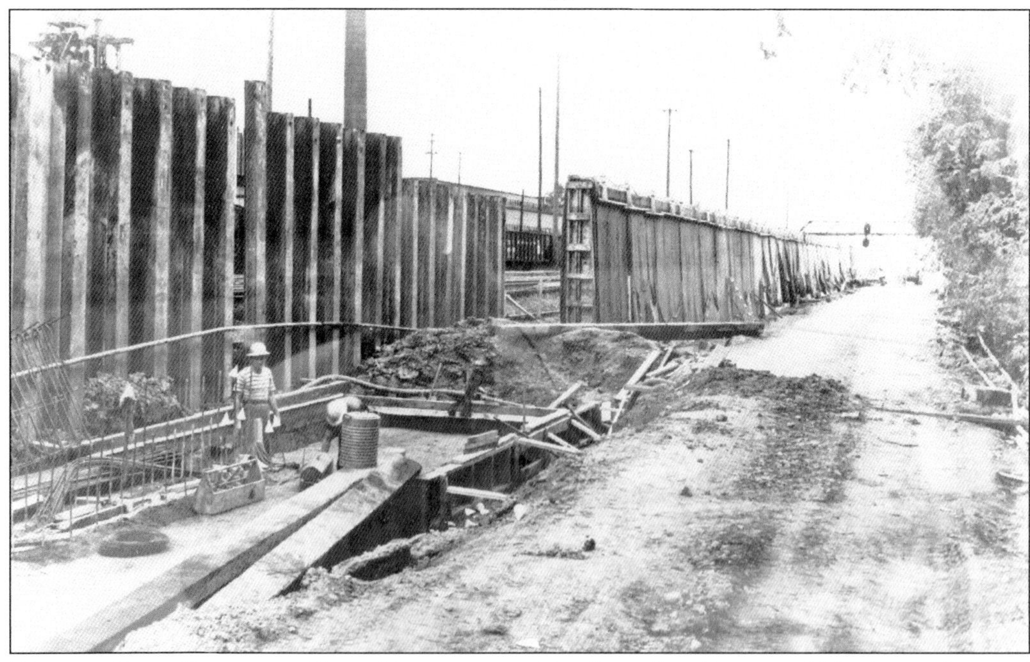

WALLED CITY. To protect Ohio River communities from flooding, the U.S. Army Corps of Engineers built dams along the river in the early 1940s. During this same time period, Ashland and Catlettsburg began constructing flood walls around their cities. In 1997, the Ashland flood wall was put to the test by the river—it passed. (Courtesy of the Arnold Hanners Photographic Collection, Minnie Winder Room, Boyd County Public Library.)

Four

OLD FASHION FUN

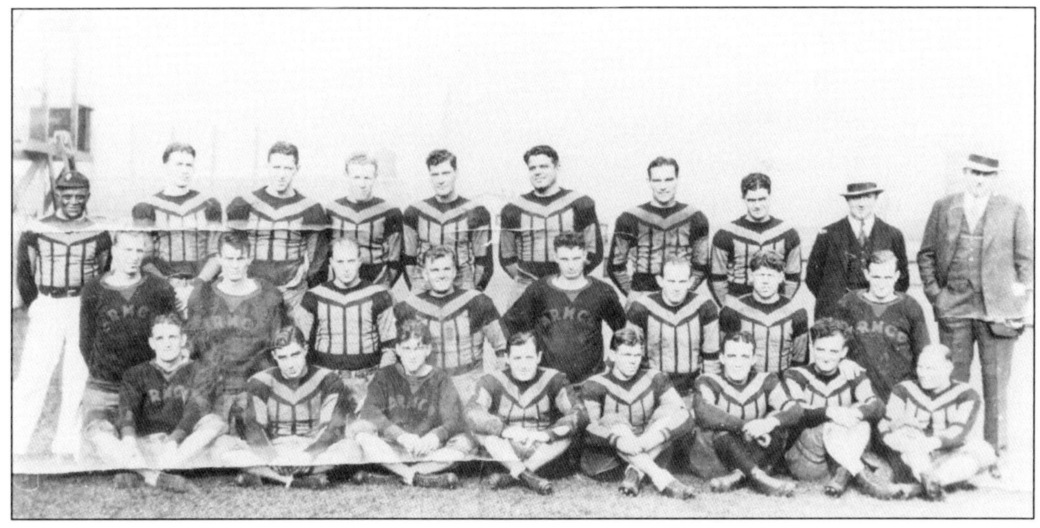

THE ASHLAND ARMCOS. This is the only professional team that Ashland has ever fielded. The Ashland Armcos played professional football on Armco Field from 1925 to 1929 against teams such as the Cleveland Panthers, Cincinnati Guards, Ironton Tanks, and Portsmouth Spartans. The 1928 team posing in front of Armco Steel won a total of eight games that year, with just four loses. By 1929, the Ashland community was not interested in supporting a professional football team, so the team dissolved, with some players finding their way to Portsmouth, Chicago, or Green Bay. Ashland, as well as many Boyd County school teams throughout the years, won Kentucky State titles in basketball, football, and baseball. Ashland once won a national high school basketball title, a claim that very few cities in the state are able to make. (Courtesy of the Arnold Hanners Photographic Collection, Minnie Winder Room, Boyd County Public Library.)

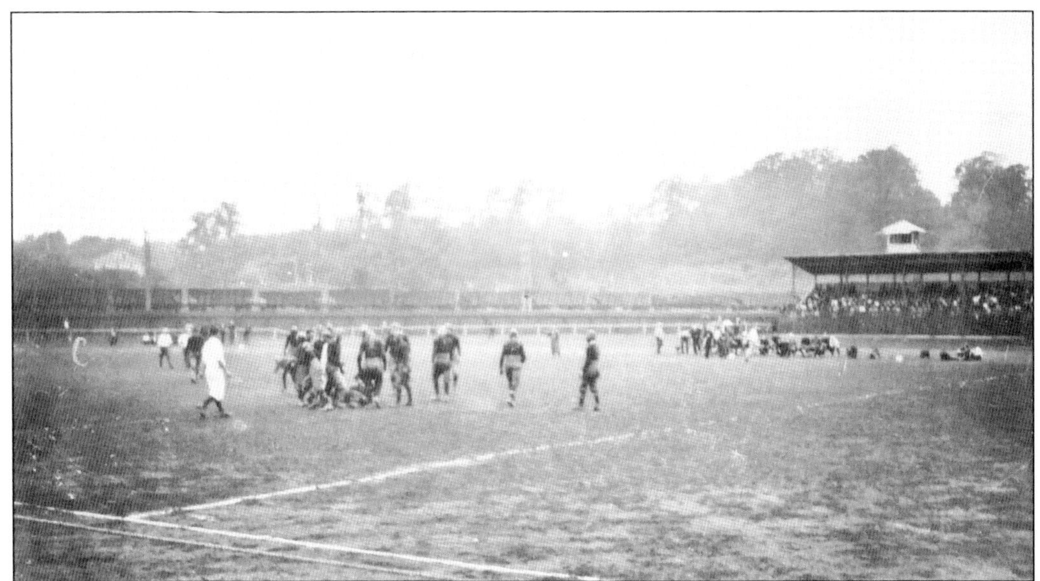

ACTIVITY ON ARMCO FIELD. The Ashland Armcos play an unidentified team at Armco Field around 1928. Ashland beat local powerhouses Ironton and Portsmouth at home that year, but the Armcos suffered away losses to Ironton at Tank Stadium and Portsmouth at Spartan Stadium later in the season. (Courtesy of the Arnold Hanners Photographic Collection, Minnie Winder Room, Boyd County Public Library.)

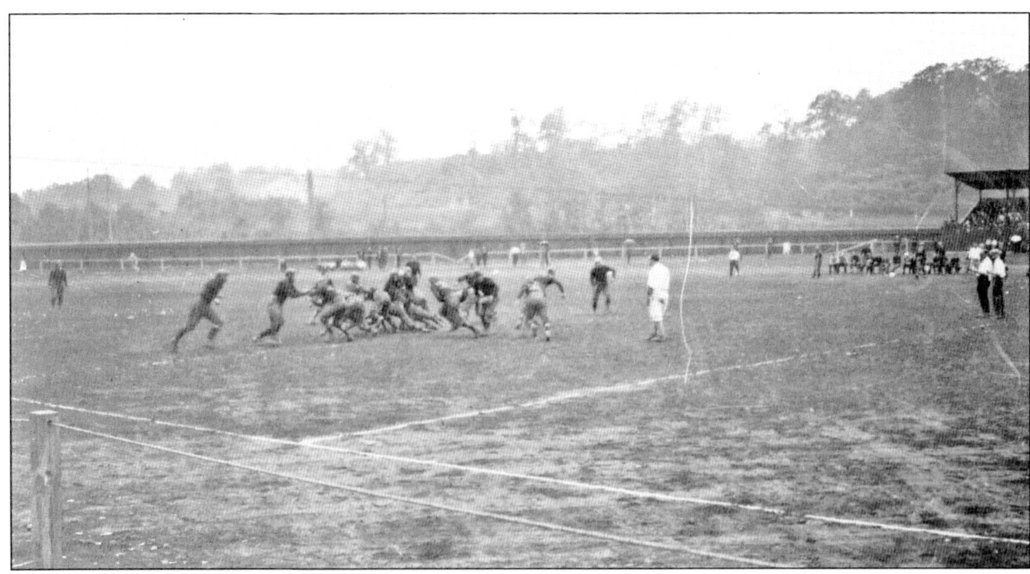

HANDOFF. The quarterback hands the football off to a running back in this rare action photograph of an Ashland Armco football game. The stands seem filled to capacity as referees look on at the action. With the exception of just one year, the Armcos enjoyed winning seasons. (Courtesy of the Arnold Hanners Photographic Collection, Minnie Winder Room, Boyd County Public Library.)

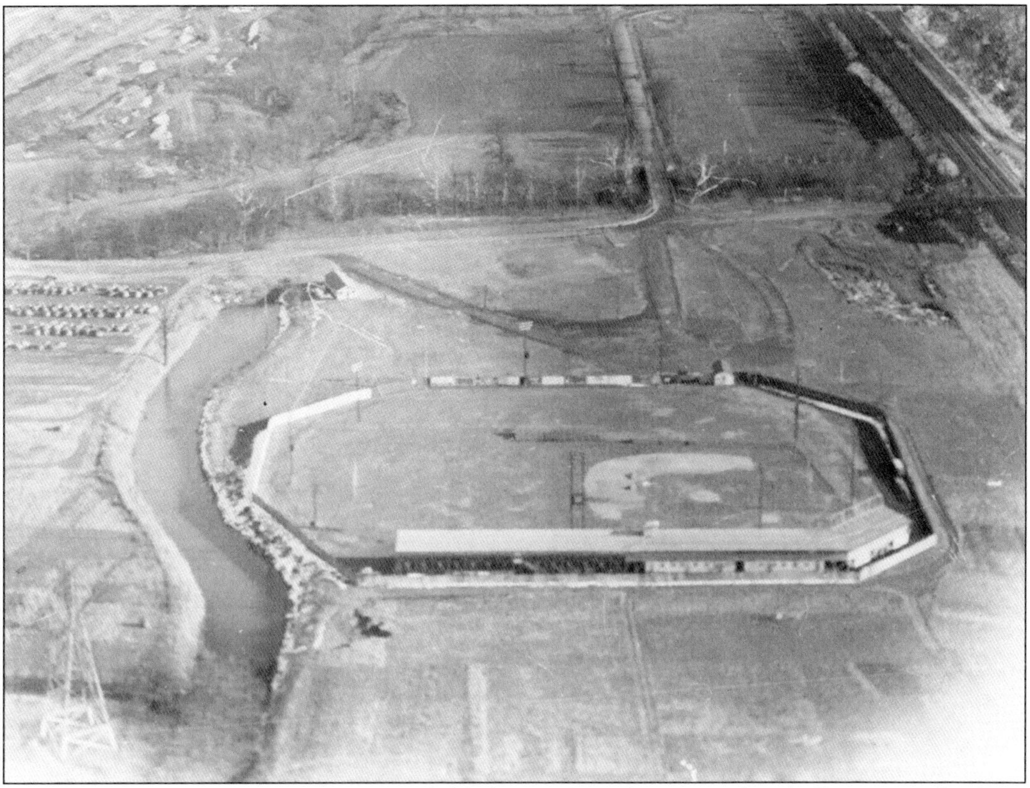

ARMCO FIELD FROM THE AIR. Armco fielded a number of company baseball teams and at least one professional football team on the field pictured. Several legendary players in both sports played at this field, including Jim Thorpe, the great professional football, baseball, and basketball player. He won two gold medals at the Olympic games in Sweden. (Courtesy of the Arnold Hanners Photographic Collection, Minnie Winder Room, Boyd County Public Library.)

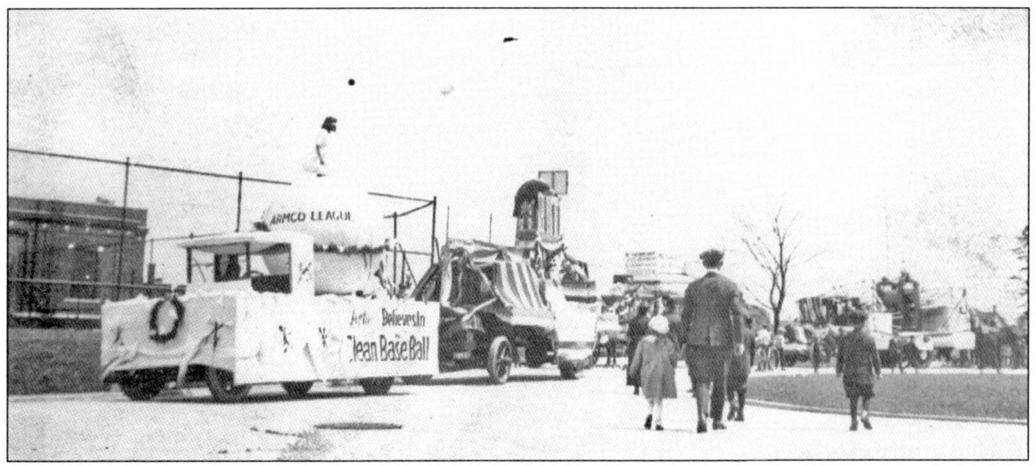

BASEBALL PARADE. A parade through Ashland is lead by a float advertising the Armco Baseball League. Baseball fans from all over the tri-state area would fill up Armco Field and watch teams from area businesses compete for trophies and bragging rights. Almost every business in Ashland, Ironton, and Huntington sponsored a baseball team. (Courtesy of the Arnold Hanners Photographic Collection, Minnie Winder Room, Boyd County Public Library.)

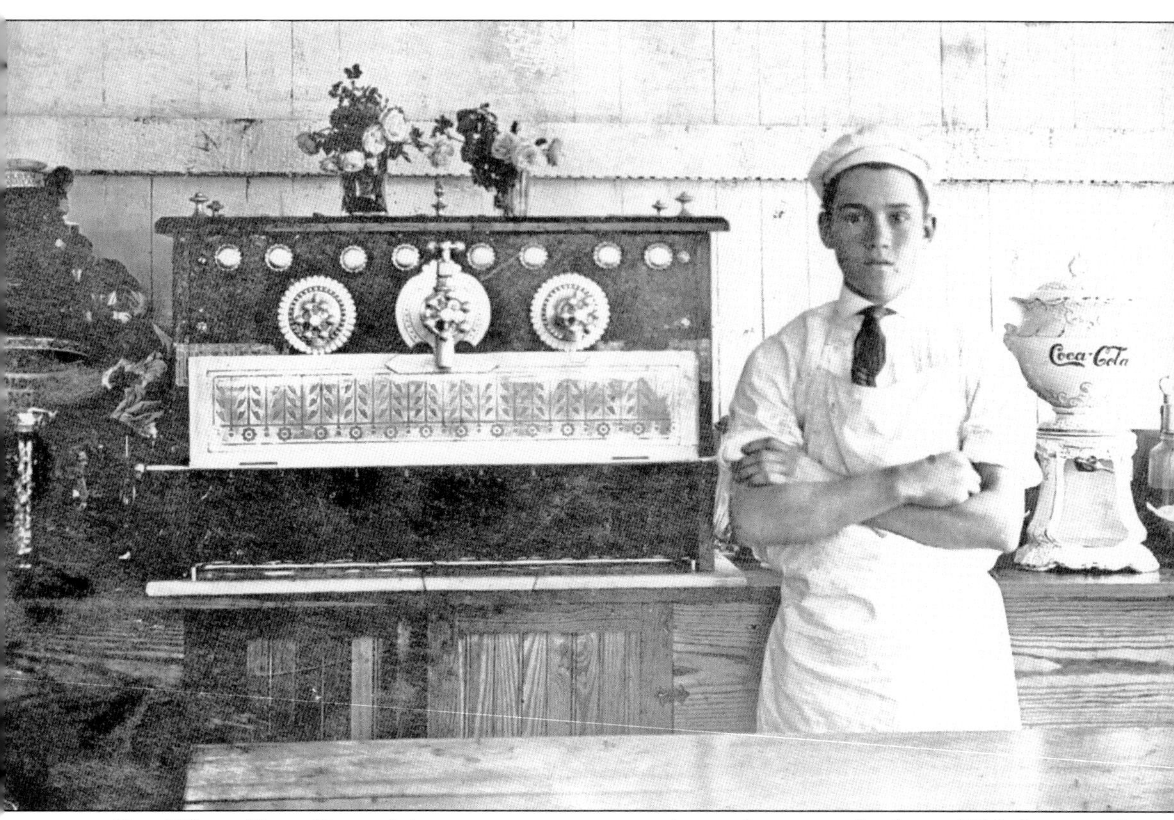

CAN I TAKE YOUR ORDER? A young concession stand attendant poses for this *c.* 1900 photograph at Clyffside Park. Also pictured behind the young man is a very early cola dispenser, as well as an Orangeade dispenser. Drinks were actually made up prior to being poured into the dispensing machines. A customer could order a drink with a small amount of ice if it had not melted away by the end of a hot summer day—a real treat during the early days of Ashland. Clyffside Park was located at Thirty-ninth Street and Fortieth Street on the east end of Ashland, across Route 23 from the coke plant. Today there are no discernable landmarks remaining of the buildings, rides, or the pond. The park closed and the lots sold in the mid-1920s. The last structure, an electric utility building, was leveled several years ago. (Courtesy of the James C. Powers Collection.)

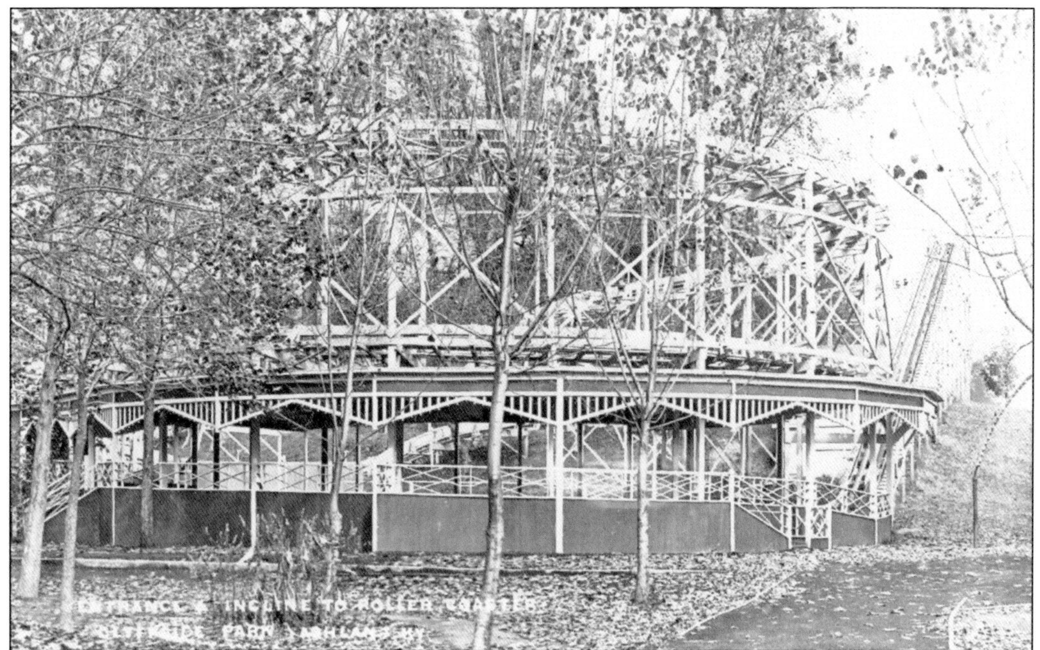

ASHLAND'S ROLLERCOASTER. This rare photograph from around 1900 shows Ashland's only rollercoaster, which was located in Clyffside Park. At one time, this rollercoaster was in Ashland, another located at Camden Park in Huntington, and a large coaster located at Millbrook Park in Portsmouth, Ohio. (Courtesy of the James C. Powers Collection.)

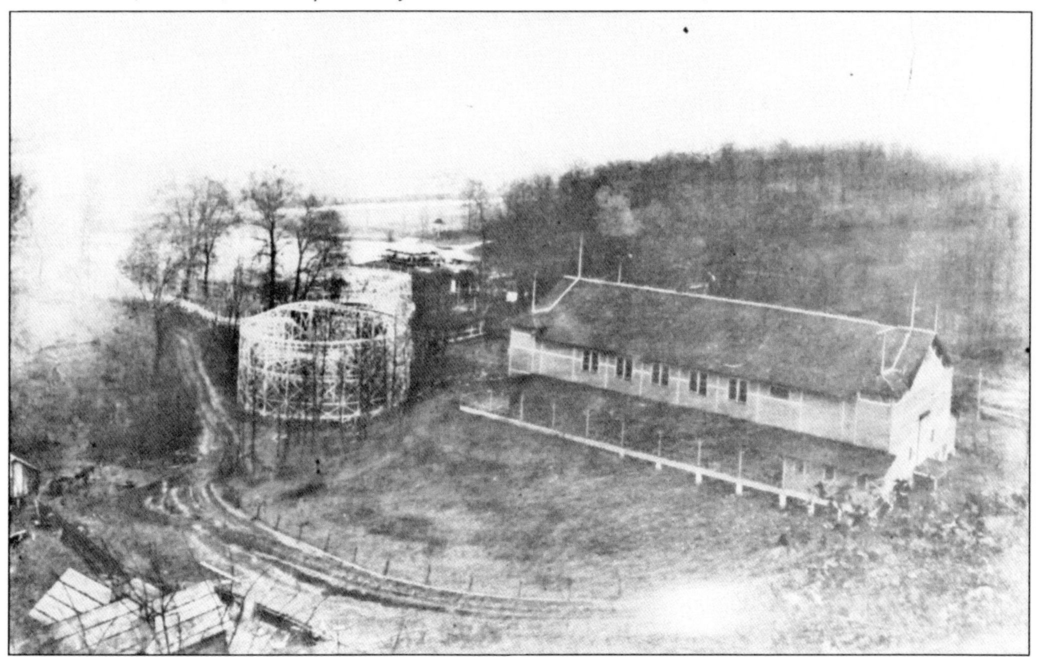

THE CASINO AND COASTER. To the right is the casino located at Clyffside Park, and to the left is the nearly complete rollercoaster. The lake is in the background, as are the dance pavilions and bandstand. In the distance, the highway and railway can be seen just behind the lake. (Courtesy of the James C. Powers Collection.)

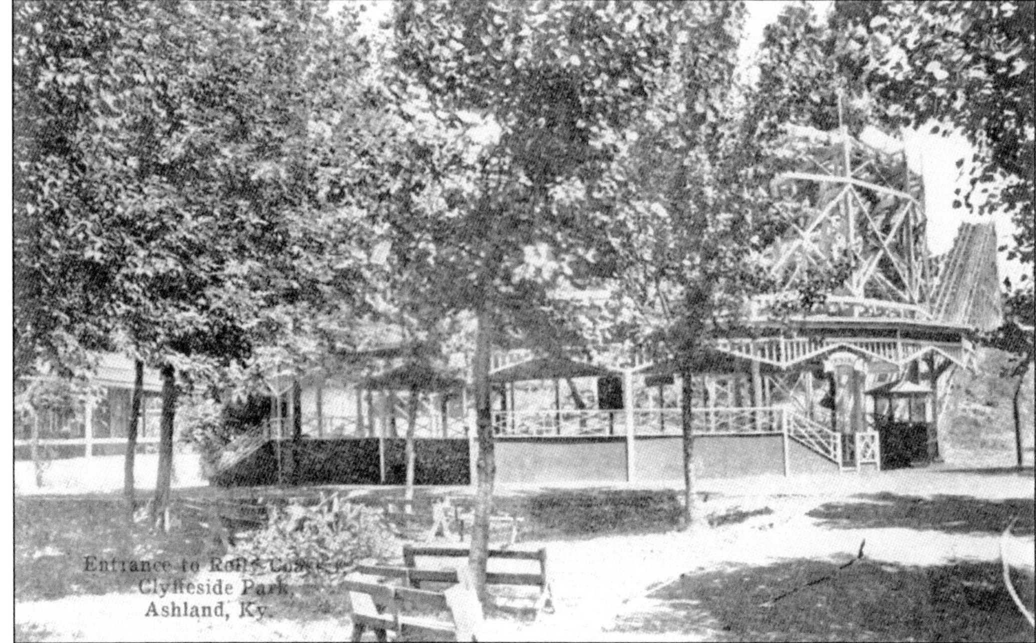

GET YOUR TICKETS! This rare postcard shows the entrance to the rollercoaster and the first large hill on the ride. The ticket booth and entrance can be seen in the image. Many people would just sit and watch the ride make its complete circuit over and over. The seats pictured provided a place to relax and enjoy. (Courtesy of the James C. Powers Collection.)

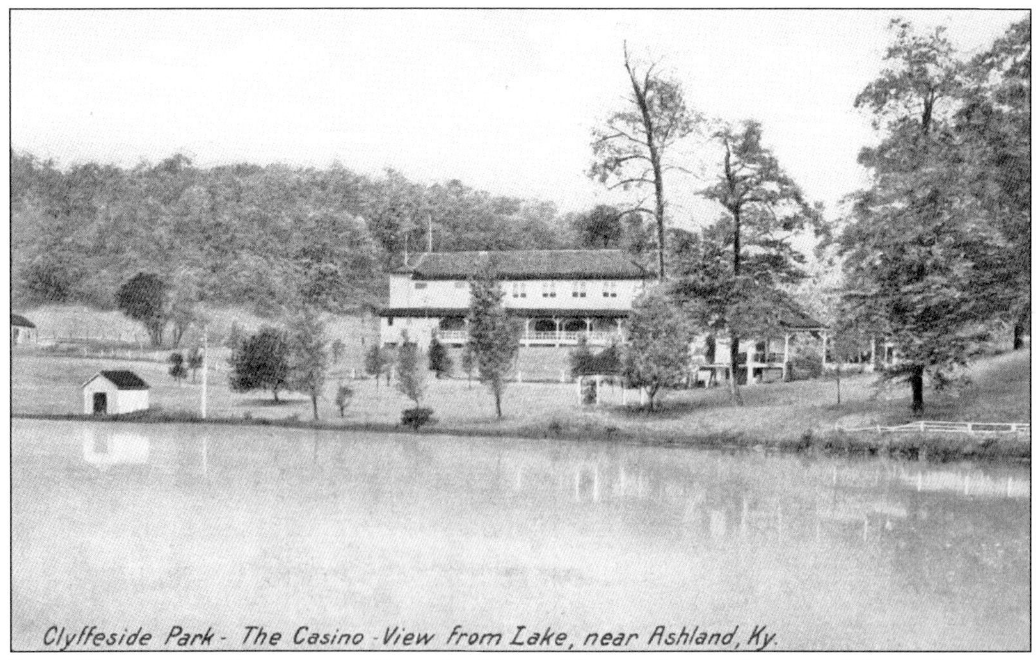

LAKE VIEW TO THE SOUTHWEST. From the lake looking southwest, the casino's lowest level can be seen in this image from around 1910. The casino provided ways to loose or win money but also hosted various popular acts, which stopped here regularly to perform for eager audiences. (Courtesy of the James C. Powers Collection.)

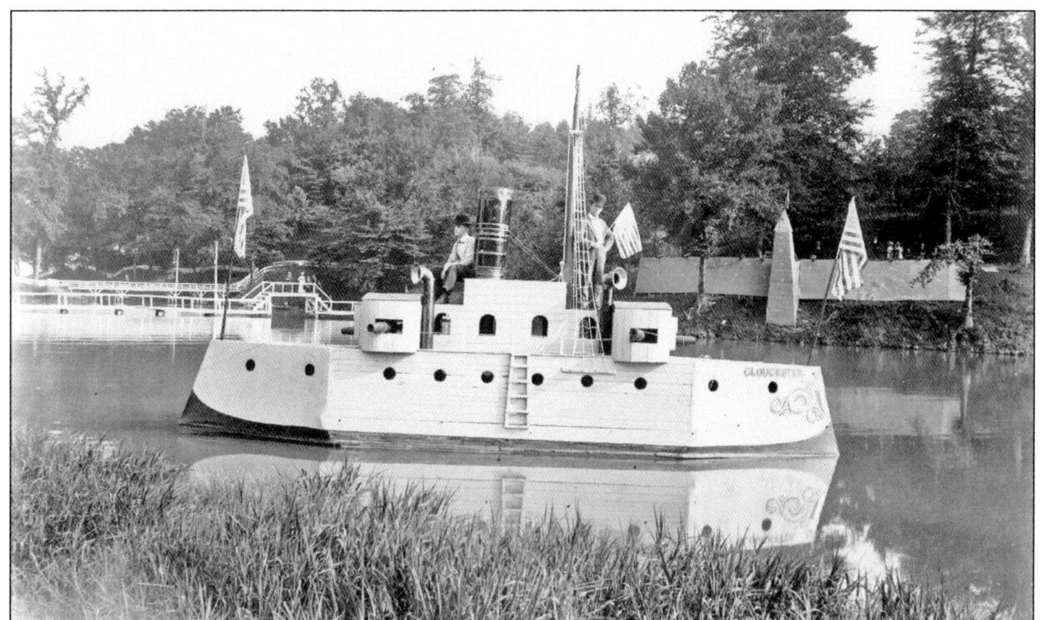

The *Gloucester*. During the summers in the early 20th century, Clyffside Park would run their battleship, the *Gloucester*, on the lake nearby. The battleship is characteristic of the ships of the time and was very popular to ride during patriotic celebrations, such as the one pictured. (Courtesy of the Arnold Hanners Photographic Collection, Minnie Winder Room, Boyd County Public Library.)

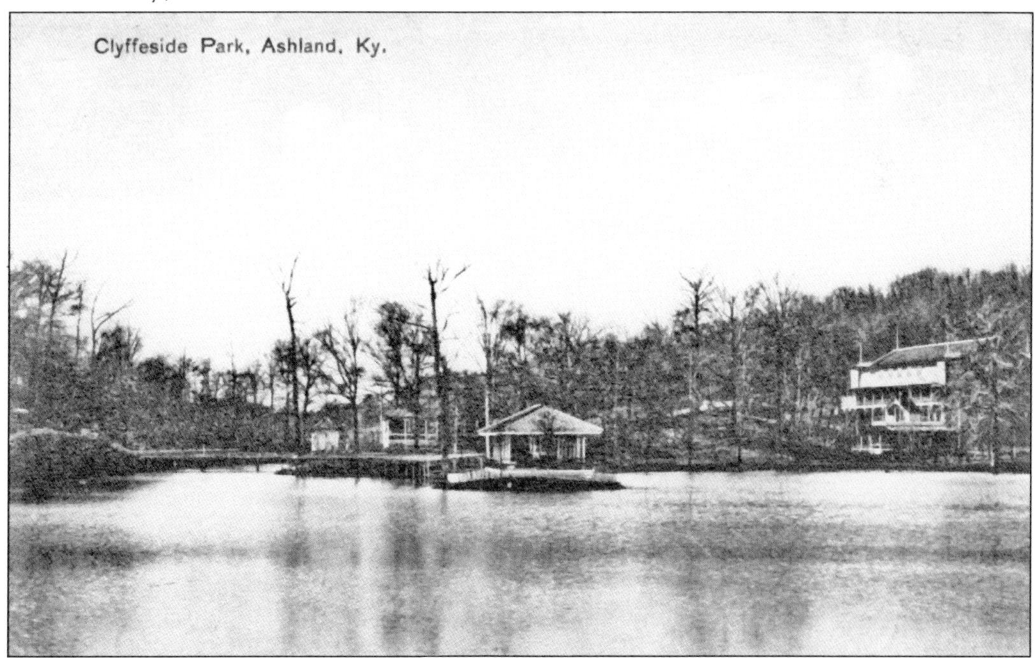

Silent Dancing. The dance pavilion sits idle in this 1905 image, with the casino to the right. The casino was open all year, as opposed to the seasonal operation of the rides and other attractions in the park. For many years after the park's closing around 1924, people held fond memories of dancing near the lake under electric lights. (Courtesy of the James C. Powers Collection.)

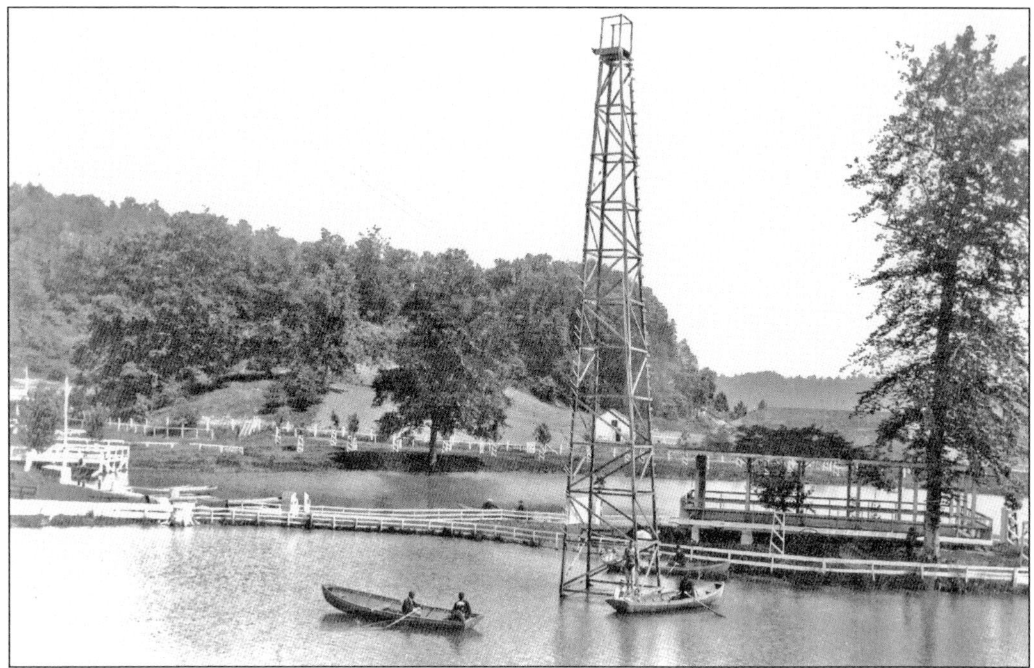

DIVING PLATFORM. A daredevil diver stands at the base of the diving platform at Clyffside Park Lake. The man would jump as a crowd gathered on the banks and in rented boats to watch the spectacle unfold. The lake was filled in and sold as lots after the mid-1920s. (Courtesy of the Arnold Hanners Photographic Collection, Minnie Winder Room, Boyd County Public Library.)

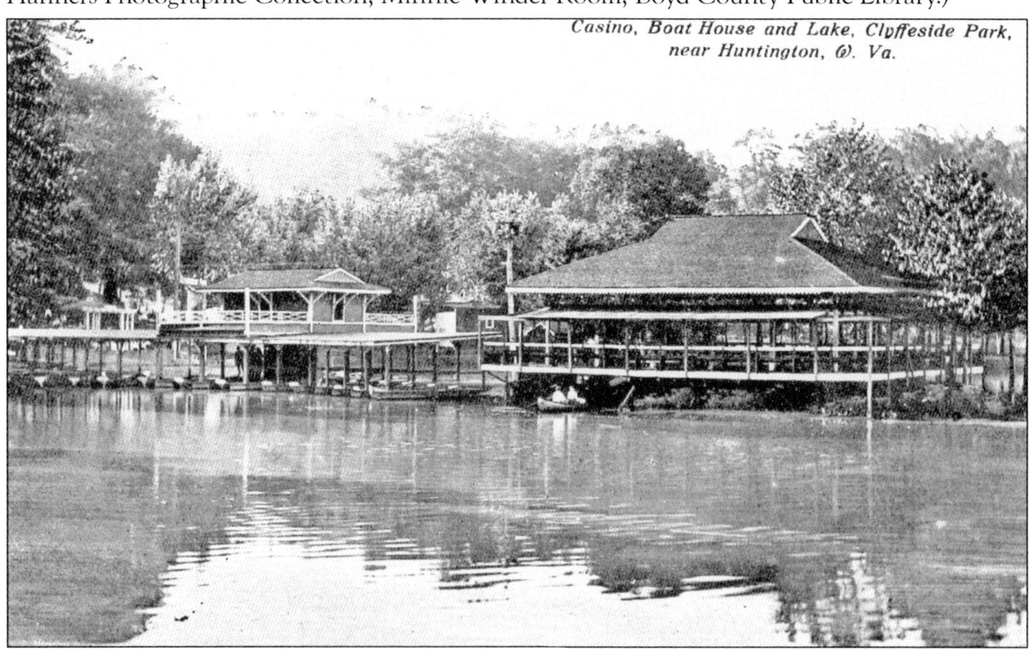

BOATHOUSE. Clyffside Park rented boats to the curious, and to young lovers rowing around the lake and eventually into each other's arms. Many couples in the early 1900s came to the park on a date or honeymooned nearby and left with a lifetime of fond memories of this long-gone park. (Courtesy of the James C. Powers Collection.)

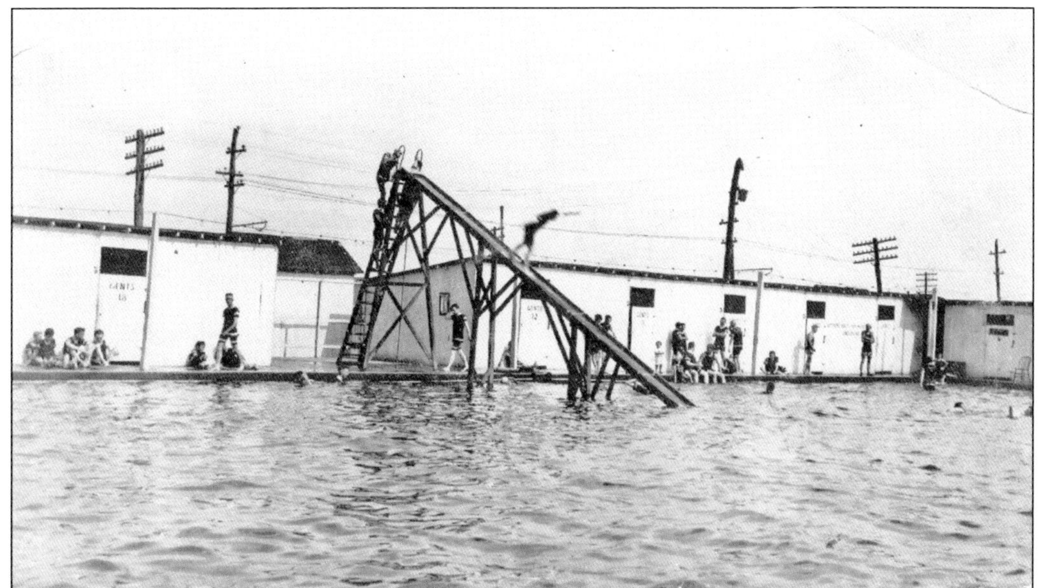

CLYFFSIDE POOL. Near the entrance of the park was one of the area's first cement pools. The pool had several gentlemen's dressing rooms, two diving boards, and a large slide as pictured. A young man is going down it as a skier would down a slope while a half dozen young men look on. (Courtesy of the James C. Powers Collection.)

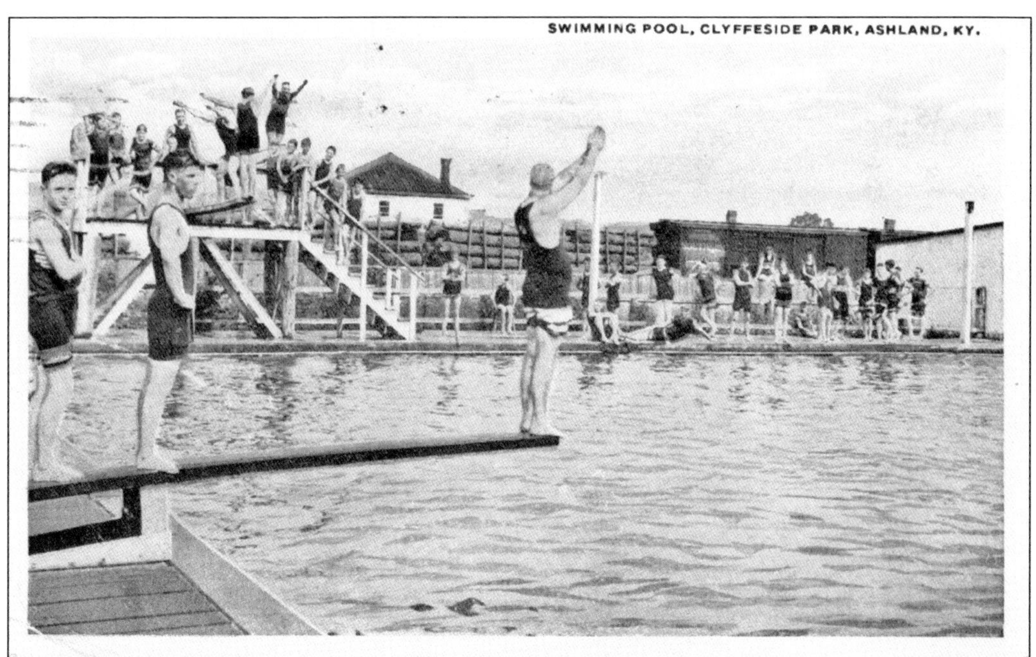

WAITING IN LINE. Quite a few young men and boys eagerly await their turn to dive into the pool at Clyffside Park as logs and freight cars line the railway north in the background. The pool was males-only for many years in the early 1900s, as were larger pools in Huntington and Portsmouth. (Courtesy of the James C. Powers Collection.)

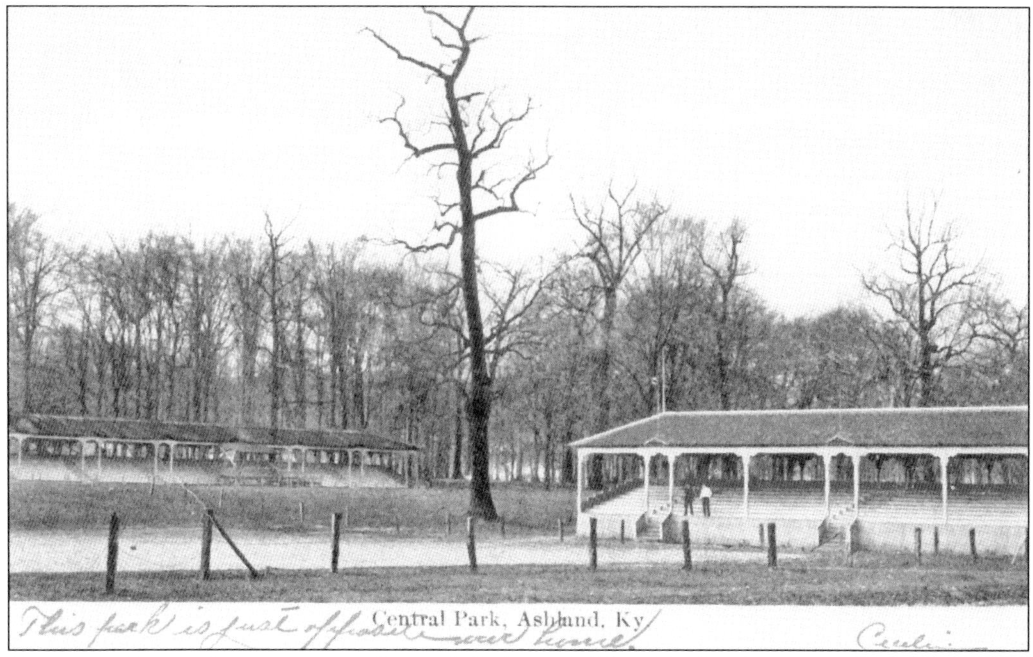

CENTRAL PARK GRANDSTAND. Central Park in Ashland had a horse track and beautiful grandstands that drew crowds from all over the area. The track was in decline at the time this image was taken. Many of the trees from this period are still standing in the park today. (Courtesy of the James C. Powers Collection.)

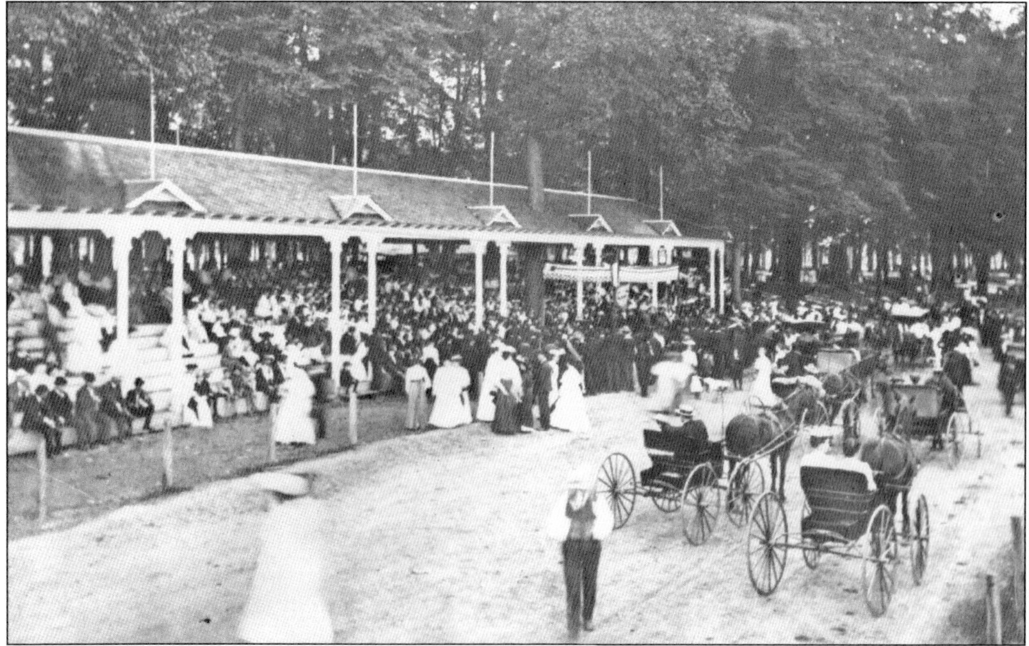

CENTRAL PARK PARADE. The grandstands are full of onlookers as horses and buggies parade around the track and park in this c. 1900 photograph. A speaker stands in the highlighted area draped with red, white, and blue, drawing the crowd's attention. (Courtesy of the Arnold Hanners Photographic Collection, Minnie Winder Room, Boyd County Public Library.)

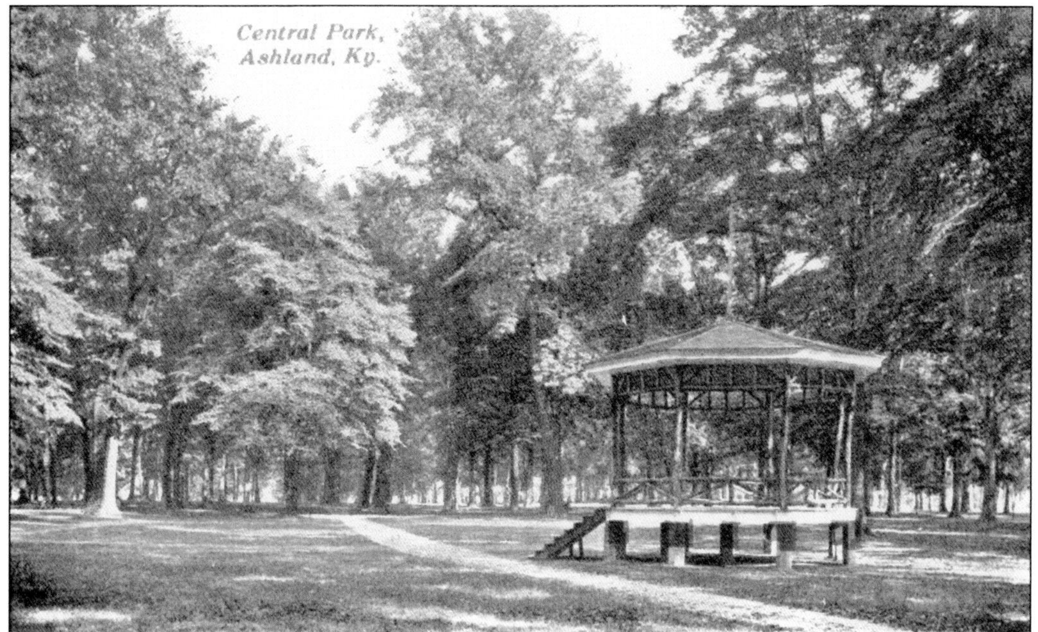

THE PARK BANDSTAND. The Central Park Bandstand is quiet on the summer day when this image was taken around 1905. Over the years, many have recalled listening to area bands play music during the day and under the stars. Eventually this old bandstand was torn down and replaced by a larger brick structure. (Courtesy of the James C. Powers Collection.)

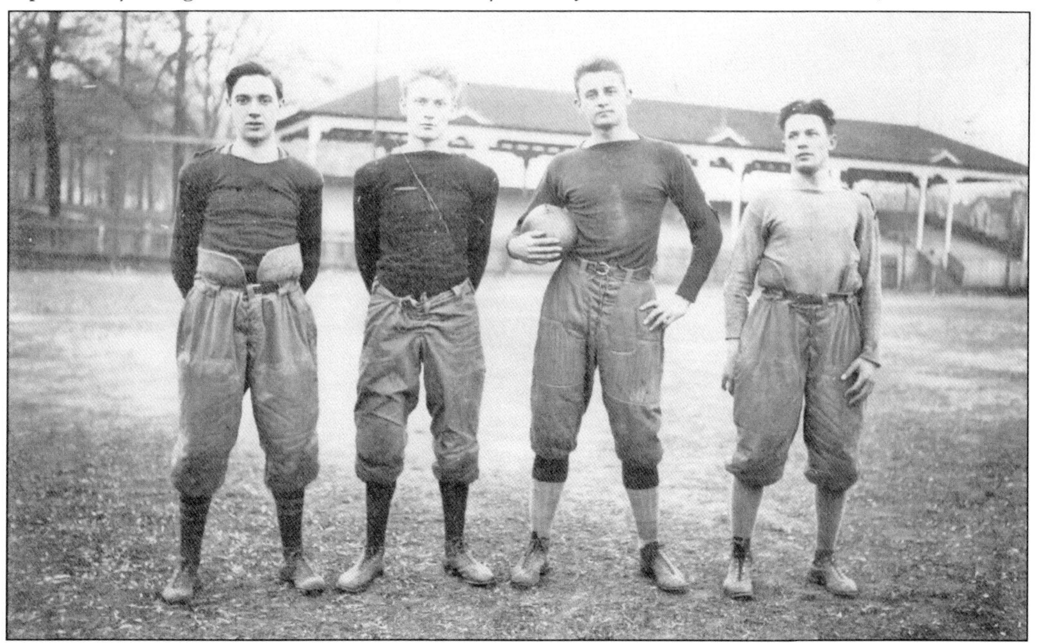

FOOTBALL AT THE PARK. Four young men from around 1918 pose for this photograph in Ashland's Central Park in front of the old grandstand. Central Park was purchased by the City of Ashland from the Kentucky Iron, Coal, and Manufactoring Company in 1900. The city paid $32,500 for this scenic piece of property. (Courtesy of the Arnold Hanners Photographic Collection, Minnie Winder Room, Boyd County Public Library.)

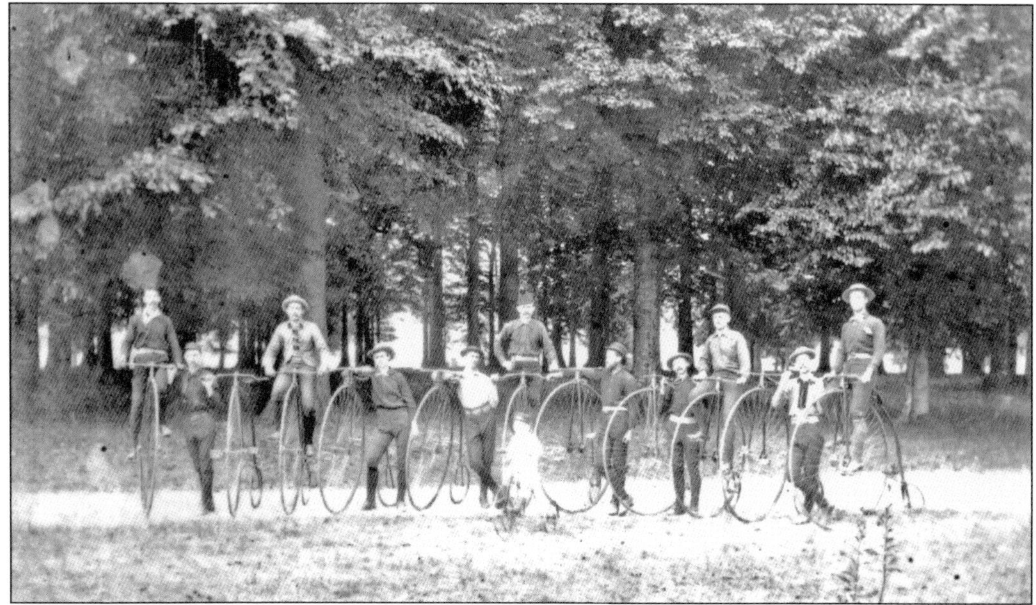

ASHLAND BICYCLE CLUB. Ashland has had many clubs and societies that have met and paraded throughout the city over the years. This photograph shows the Ashland Bicycle Club posing with their penny-farthings or high-wheel bicycles, which stood around five feet tall. Notice the boy on his smaller version in the front. (Courtesy of the Arnold Hanners Photographic Collection, Minnie Winder Room, Boyd County Public Library.)

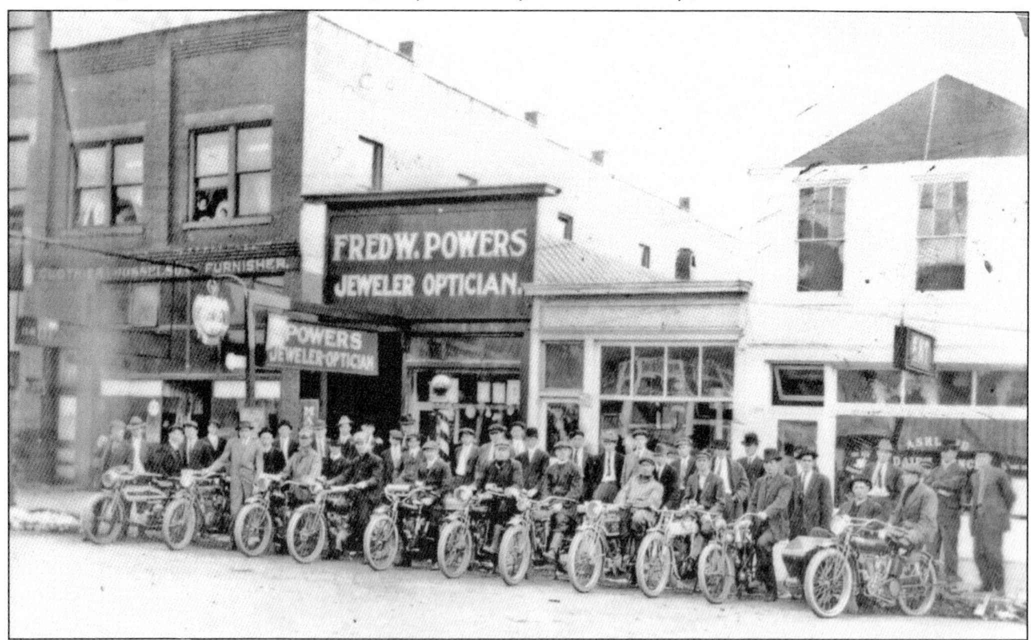

ASHLAND MOTORCYCLE CLUB. A group of young men gather on Greenup Avenue in front of Fred. W. Powers's Jewelry Store in this photograph from around 1923. The men would meet at a designated spot and ride through the city and around the countryside of Boyd, Lawrence, Carter, and Greenup Counties. (Courtesy of the Arnold Hanners Photographic Collection, Minnie Winder Room, Boyd County Public Library.)

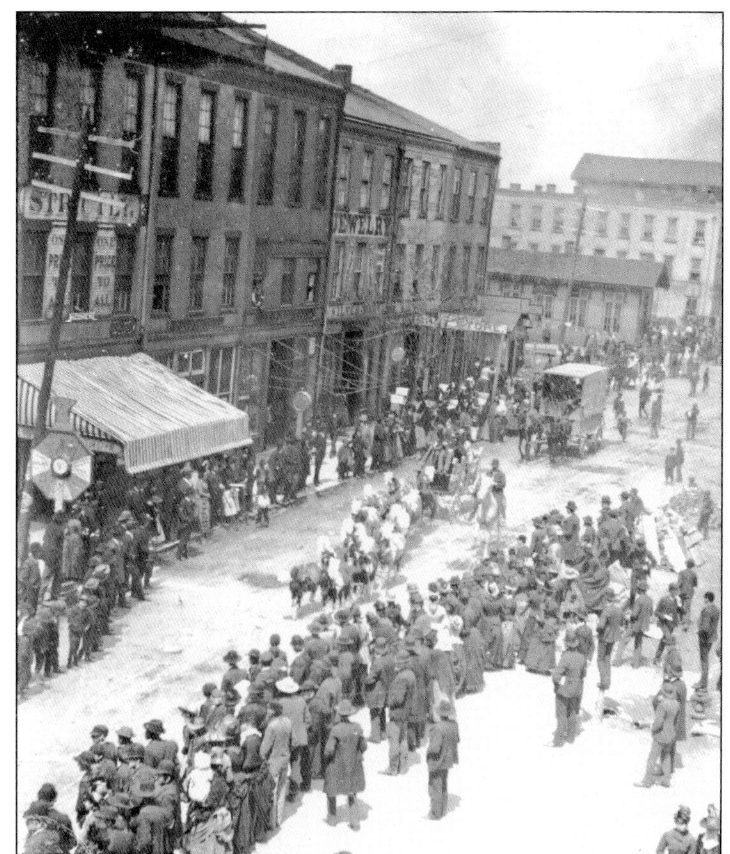

The Circus is Coming! People line both sides of Front Street in Ashland as the circus is parading east on its way to Central Park. The circus gave many folks in the area their first look at animals from various locations. The circus came via one of the four trains that ran through town. (Courtesy of the Arnold Hanners Photographic Collection, Minnie Winder Room, Boyd County Public Library.)

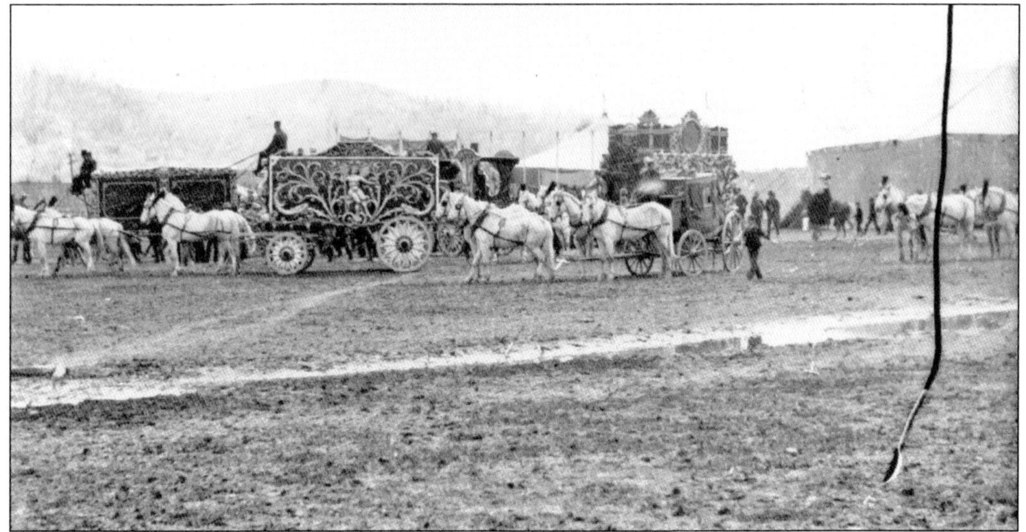

Setting up Tents. Circus wagons pull into their positions as the crew sets up the tents in this Ashland photograph from around 1890. A wintertime visit posed difficulties for the circus and public alike, as both had to deal with ice, snow, and the cold blowing off the river. (Courtesy of the Arnold Hanners Photographic Collection, Minnie Winder Room, Boyd County Public Library.)

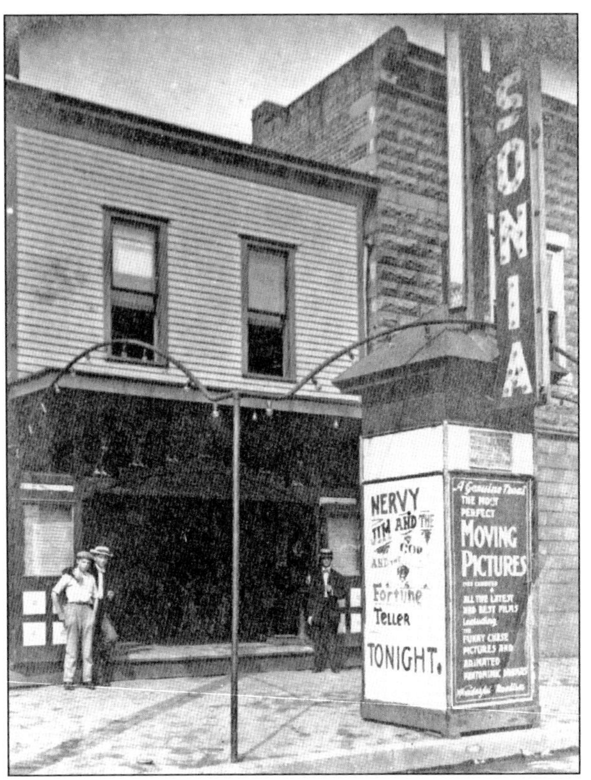

THE EDISONIA THEATER. On the north side of Greenup Avenue between Fourteenth Street and Fifteenth Street was a thin wooden structure theater called the Edisonia. Many in the area saw their first moving picture here. In 1915, the first major moving picture with synchronized sound and moving film, *The Photo-Drama of Creation*, had a showing here. (Courtesy of the Arnold Hanners Photographic Collection, Minnie Winder Room, Boyd County Public Library.)

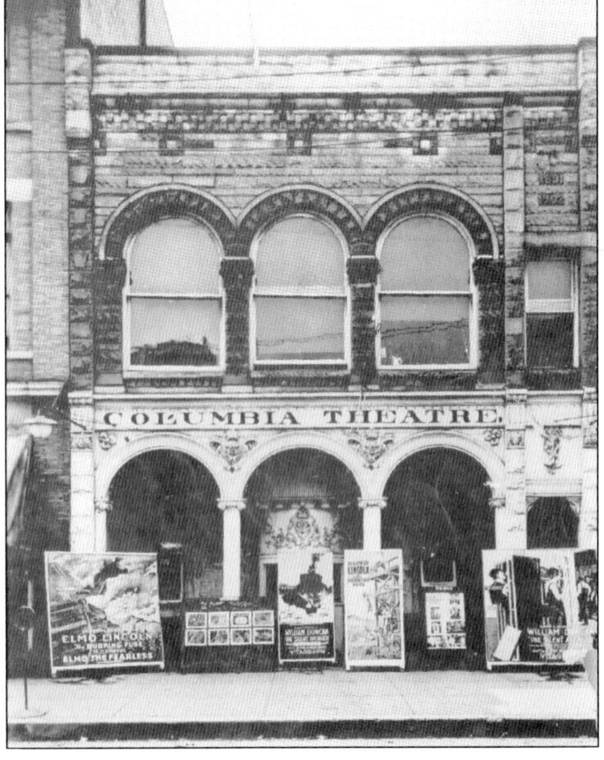

COLUMBIA THEATER. On the opposite side of Greenup Avenue was the Columbia Theater. Like many theaters, Columbia had a ticket booth in the front. Columbia did not have a marquee; instead the theater would hand out flyers and advertise their billings using posters. (Courtesy of the Arnold Hanners Photographic Collection, Minnie Winder Room, Boyd County Public Library.)

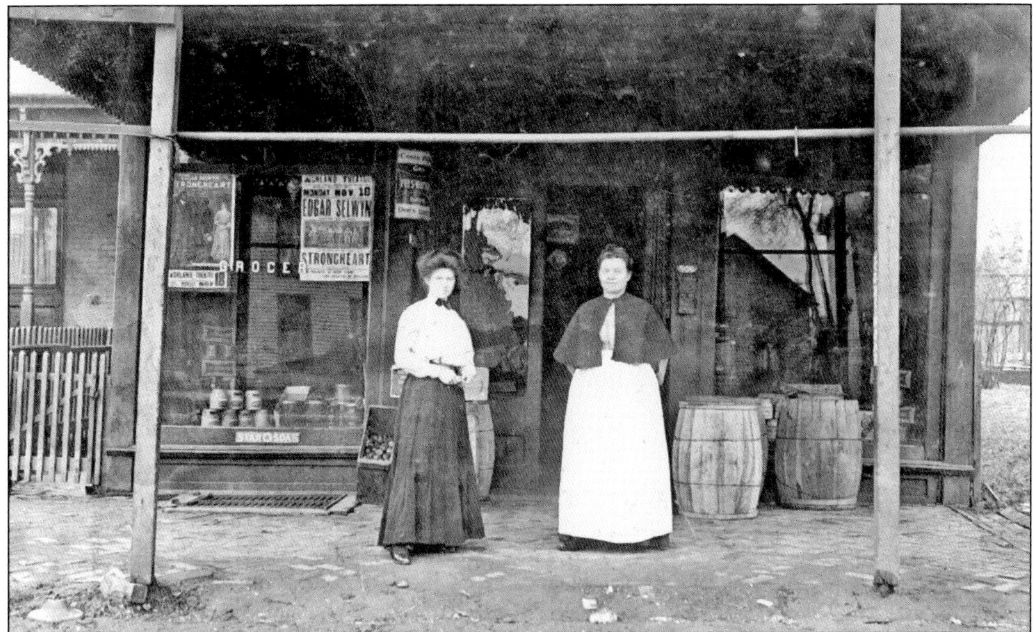

STRONGHEART! Two women pose for a photographer in front of an Ashland store around 1919. The poster advertisements in the window is advertising Edgar Selwyn's play *Strongheart* at the Ashland Theater on November 18. The theater was located on the west side of Seventeenth Street between Greenup Avenue and Winchester Avenue. (Courtesy of the James C. Powers Collection.)

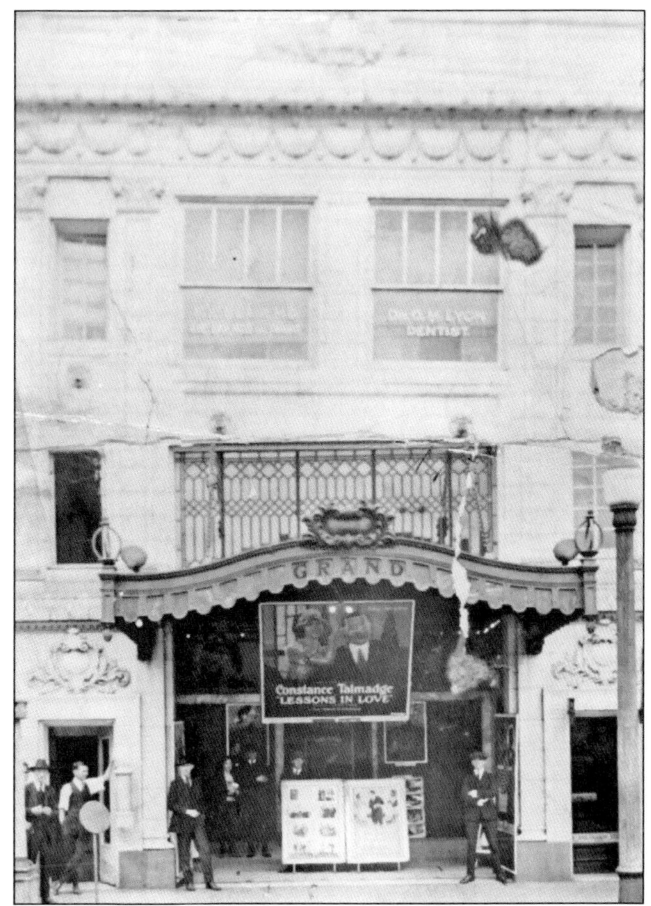

GRAND THEATER. The Grand Theater was located in the 1600 block of Winchester Avenue and changed hands several times since it opened in 1914. After the 1937 flood, the Grand was sold, and the new owner remodeled and changed the name to Alfon. The Alfon Theater remained open for nearly 20 years before closing. (Courtesy of the Arnold Hanners Photographic Collection, Minnie Winder Room, Boyd County Public Library.)

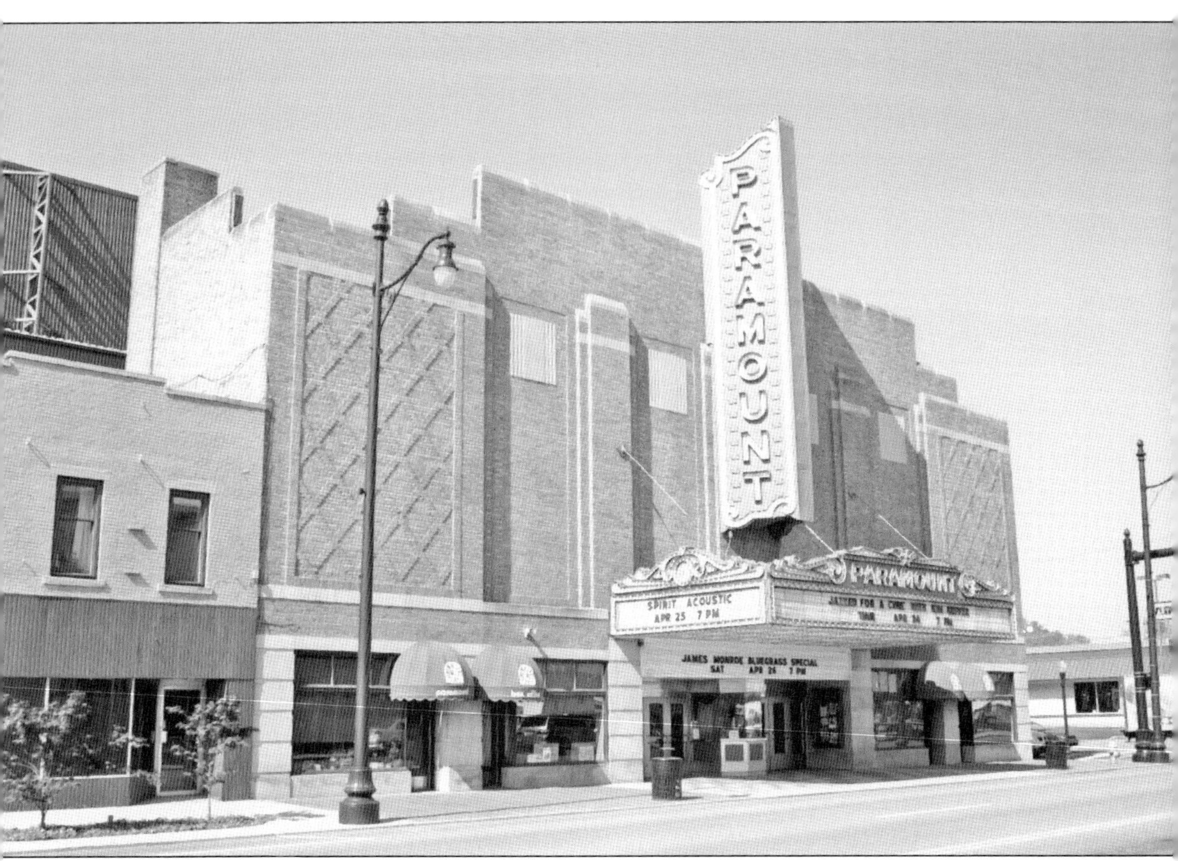

THE PARAMOUNT ARTS CENTER. The Paramount Theater was built in the art deco style in 1931 to show motion pictures instead of silent films, which were beginning to loose their appeal at this time. The first movie to premier at the Paramount was *Silent*. The Paramount Theater closed its doors in 1971, and the building was made a historic landmark around 1975. Today, as the Paramount Arts Center, the building maintains its art deco charm and elegance. The marquee demands attention when lit up during a performance at night. Many national and international talents perform yearly here, one of Kentucky's pristine arts centers. Ashland has had more than a dozen theaters during its history. Many remember the Alfon, Capitol, Lyric, Rand, and Midtown Cinemas from the 1950s to the late 1980s. Today there are the Cinemark Movies 10 across from the Ashland Town Center on the cities west side and the Phoenix Theaters at the Kyova Mall in Cannonsburg. (Photograph by Terry L. Baldridge.)

Five

A Last Look

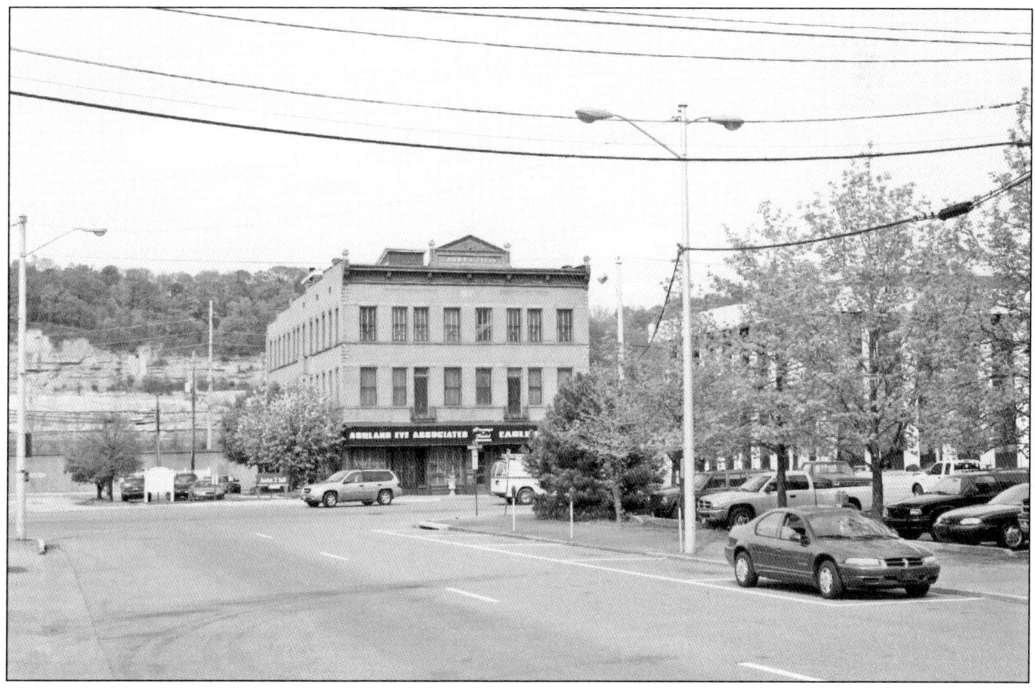

The Crump and Field Building. The Crump and Field Building at Greenup Avenue and Fourteenth Street is a wonderful example of classical architecture from the 1890s. The building has changed very little over the years despite major flooding, threats of fire, and businesses coming in and moving on. Like Ashland, many area communities have retained that small-town atmosphere despite the quickly changing pace of today's world. Portsmouth, Ohio, was founded very early in the 1800s and contains many structures that have survived the river and fire. Ironton, Ohio, was founded about 10 years before Ashland in 1849. Ironton has seen many businesses come and go over the years, but it retains its small-town charm. Catlettsburg, Westwood, South Ashland, Cannonsburg, Belefonte, Russell, Flatwoods, Raceland, Worthington, Wurtland, Greenup, Lloyd, and South Shore add elegant flavors to the Ohio River Valley on the Kentucky side. The hometown feel can also be experience today in communities such as Kenova, Ceredo, and Huntington in "wild and wonderful" West Virginia. (Photograph by Terry L. Baldridge.)

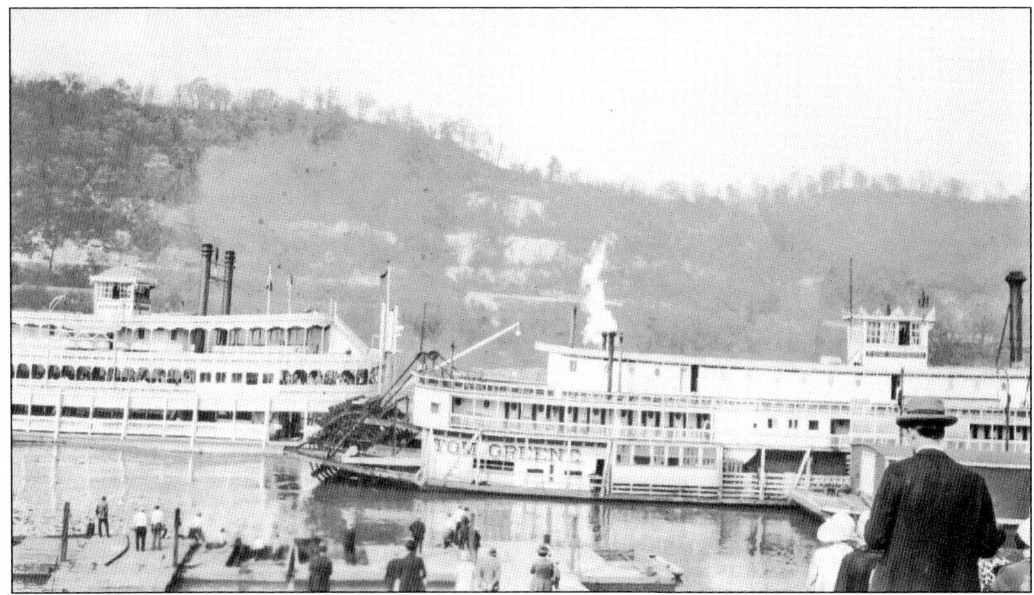

RIVERBOAT CITY. Like many towns along the Ohio River, Ashland was a regular stop for passenger travel up and down the river. Wood and coal were loaded along with waiting passengers on the Ohio River as these giant steamers docked on the riverbank. (Courtesy of the Arnold Hanners Photographic Collection, Minnie Winder Room, Boyd County Public Library.)

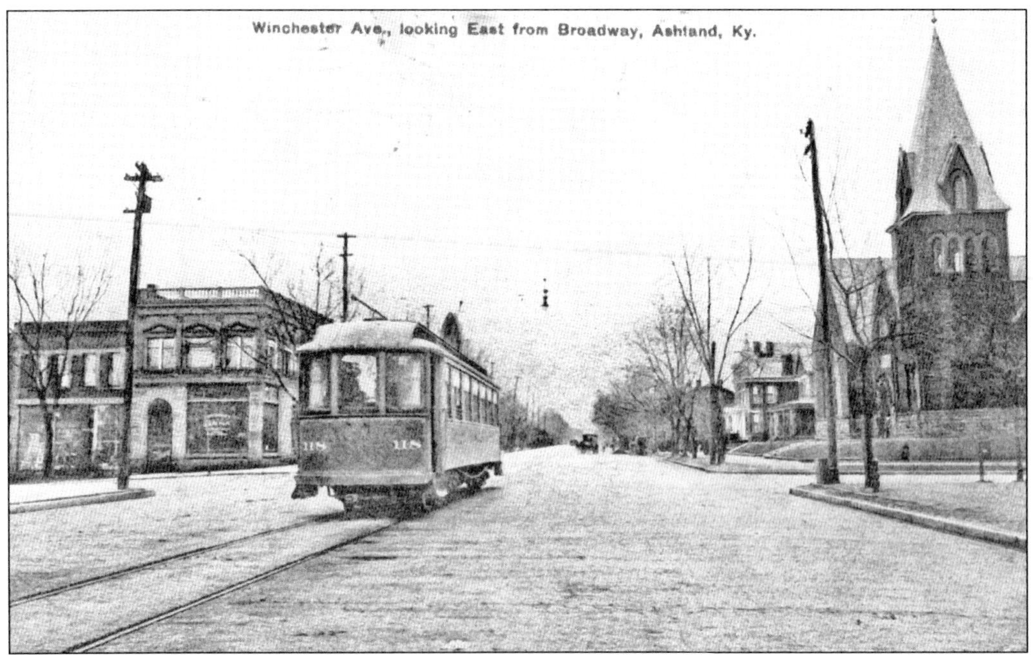

BROADWAY AND WINCHESTER. Life is quiet as a lone streetcar makes its way down Winchester Avenue moving west toward the business district of downtown Ashland. This picture shows the future Steele and Lawrence drugstore and was taken near where the 1937 cover picture. (Courtesy of the James C. Powers Collection.)

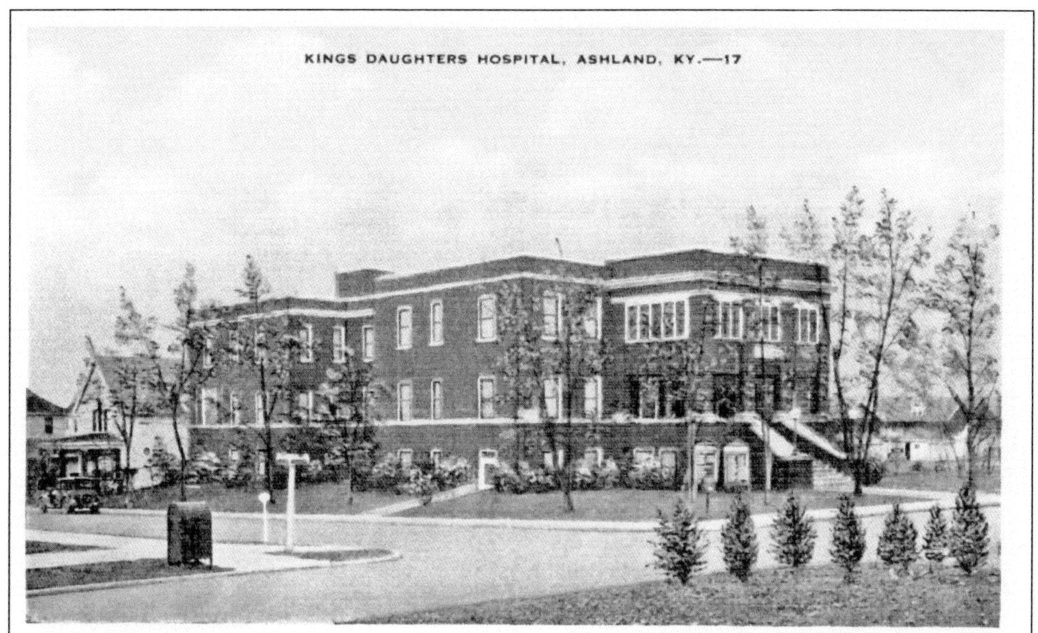

KINGS DAUGHTERS HOSPITAL. Eastern Kentucky's largest and most advanced hospital had its beginning on Winchester Avenue in the late 1890s. The hospital purchased the property at the corner of Twenty-second Street and Lexington Avenue. This image shows what the hospital's current location looked like back in 1928. (Courtesy of the James C. Powers Collection.)

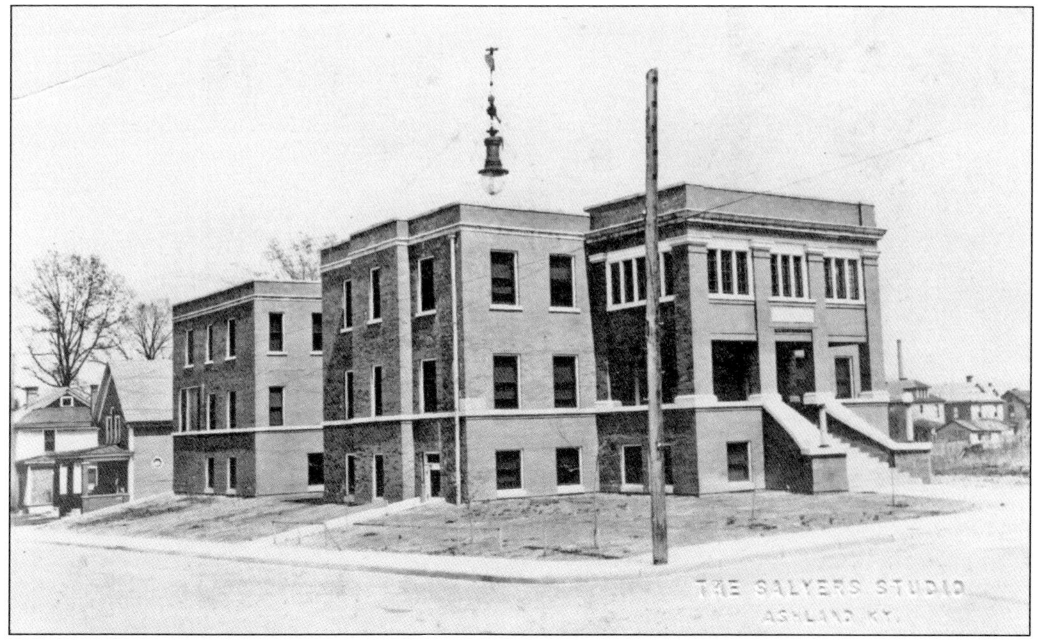

CORNER OF TWENTY-SECOND AND LEXINGTON. This photograph taken around the mid-1920s shows a streetlamp sitting above the intersection of Twenty-second Street and Lexington Avenue. The hospital has experienced tremendous growth over the years; viewing the building from this vantage point, it is unrecognizable today. (Courtesy of the James C. Powers Collection.)

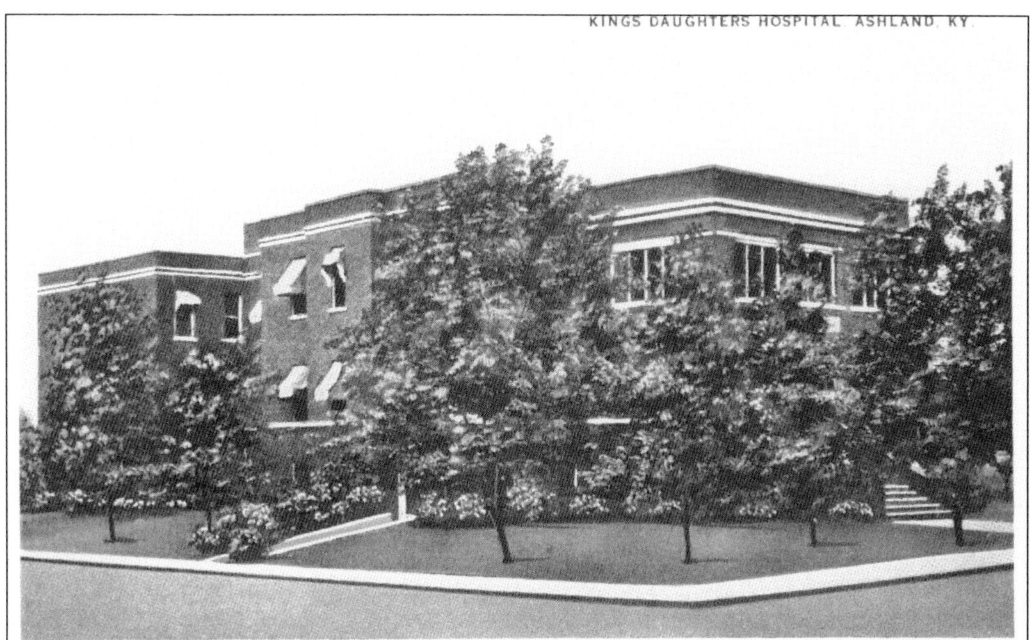

THE HOSPITAL DURING SUMMER. Kings Daughters Hospital is shown in an early-1930s postcard from Lexington Avenue and Twenty-second Street. Thousands from the Ashland, Grayson, Greenup, and Louisa areas visit the outpatient and inpatient areas of this medical center on a weekly basis. (Courtesy of the James C. Powers Collection.)

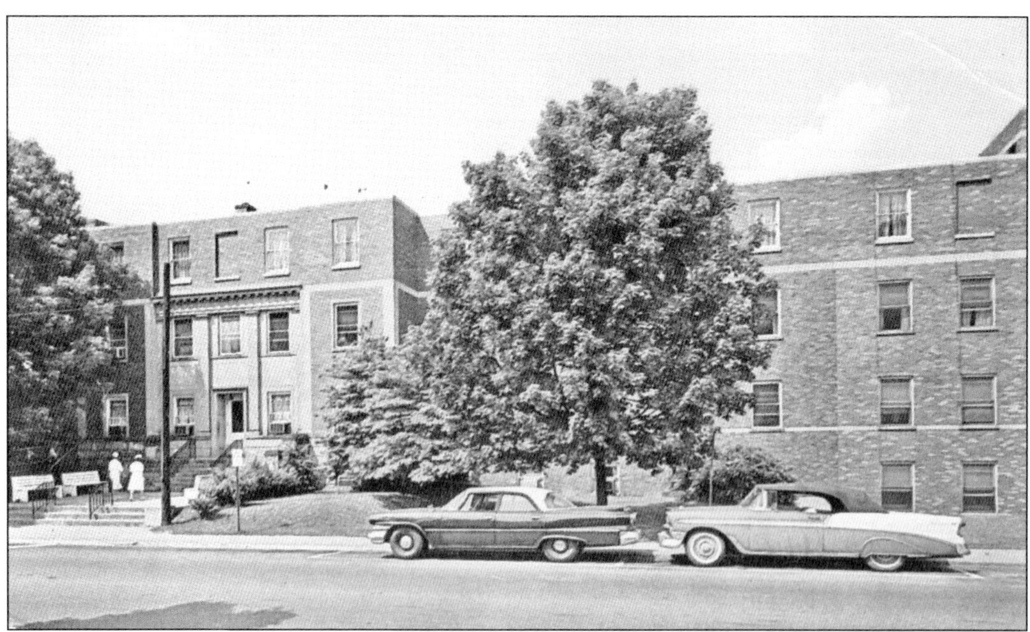

A 1950S LOOK. This photograph gives a familiar 1950s view of Kings Daughters Hospital from along Lexington Avenue. The hospital purchased the south side of Lexington Avenue across the street and constructed administration buildings. Today Kings Daughters Medical Center continues to expand to meet the healthcare needs of the area. (Courtesy of the Arnold Hanners Photographic Collection, Minnie Winder Room, Boyd County Public Library.)

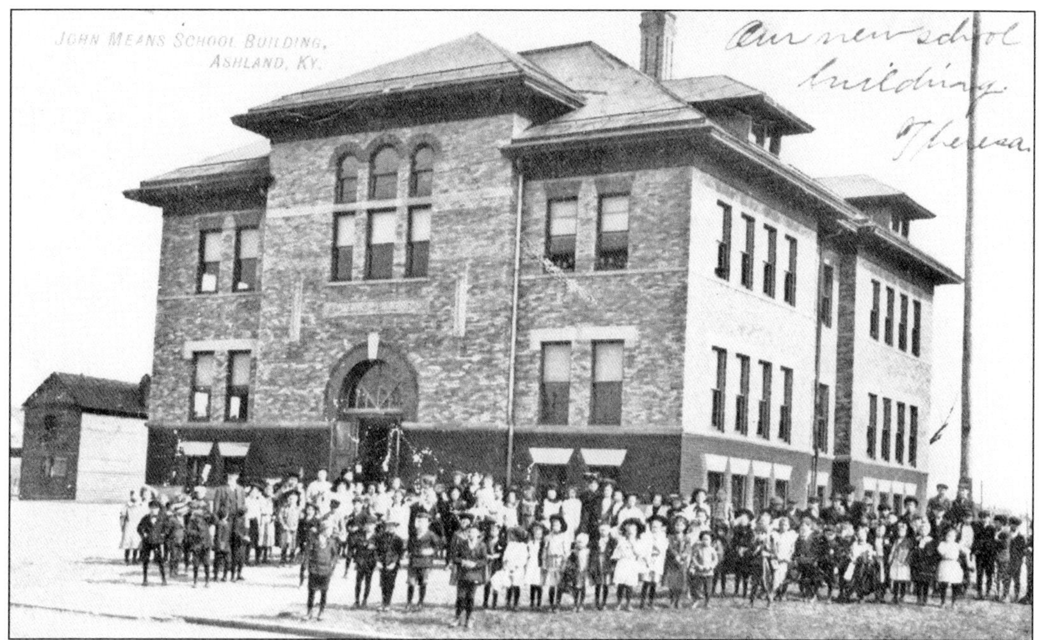

MEANS SCHOOL. Students gather outside the three-story Means School in this rare 1912 image. Means School was built in 1905 on the corner of Twenty-fifth Street and Carter Avenue. The school closed in 1960 and the structure was leveled in 1969. (Courtesy of the James C. Powers Collection.)

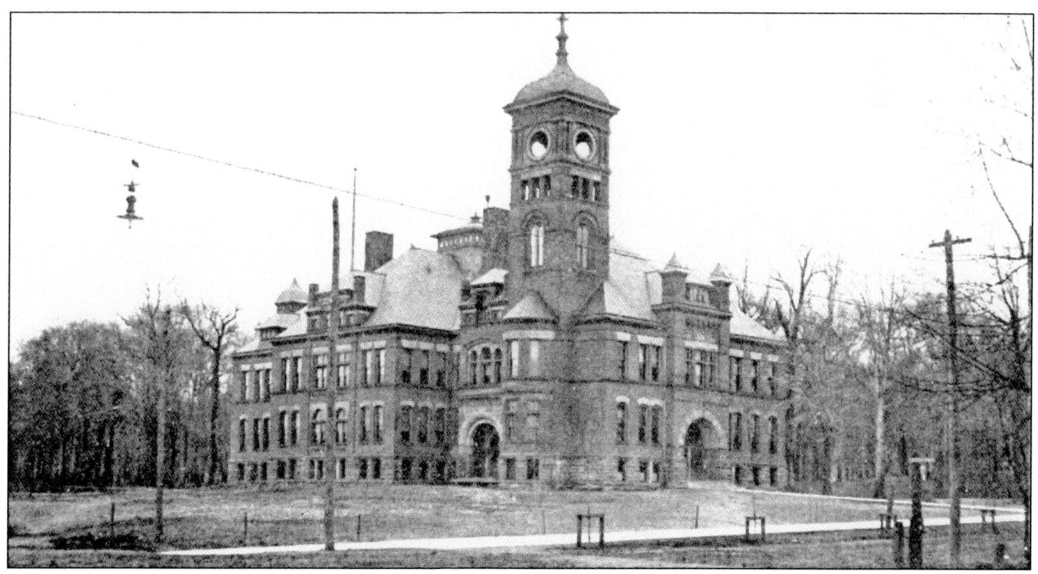

ASHLAND CENTRAL HIGH SCHOOL. Today Ashland has several area high schools: Paul G. Blazer High School, Holy Family School, Rose Hill Christian High School, Fairview High School, and Boyd County High. Pictured is the magnificent Victorian Crabbe School or Central High School, built in 1897. (Courtesy of the James C. Powers Collection.)

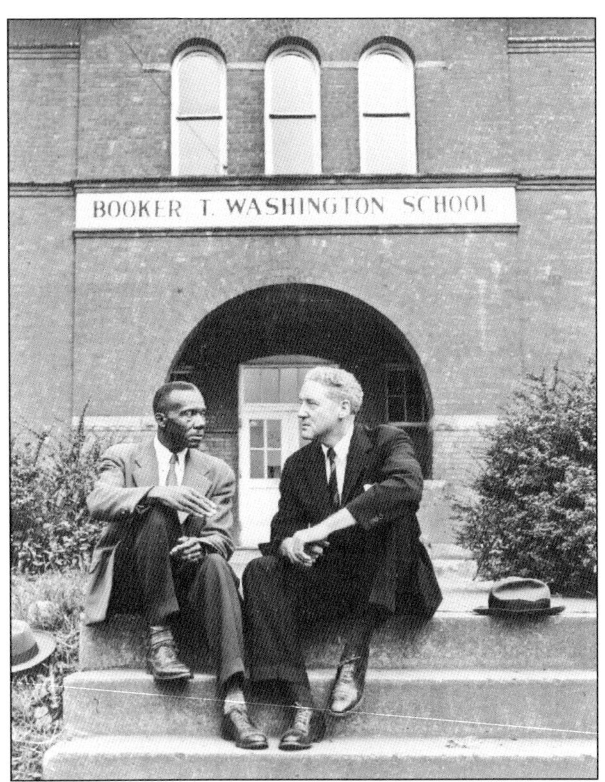

BOOKER T. WASHINGTON SCHOOL. In 1904, graves were moved from a cemetery on Central Avenue and reinterred in Ashland Cemetery. The land was used to build one of the area's first African American schools. Because of segregation, African American children in Ashland met in private homes, church rooms, and finally the Booker T. Washington School. Segregation ended in Ashland in the mid-1960s. Shown are Prof. R. W. Ross (left) and John Sherman Cooper. (Courtesy of the Arnold Hanners Photographic Collection, Minnie Winder Room, Boyd County Public Library.)

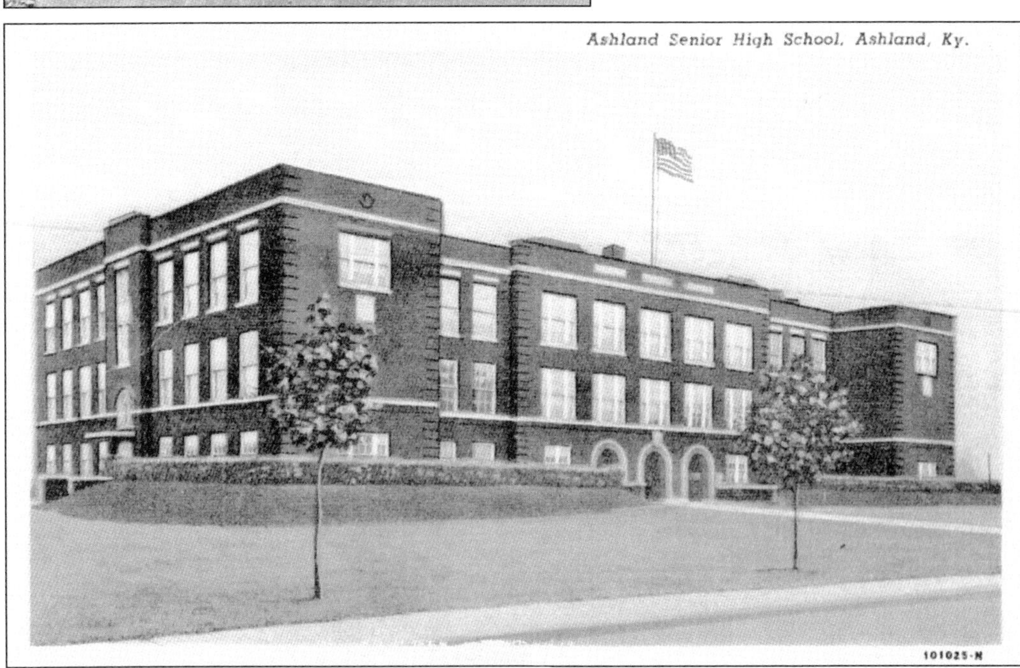

ASHLAND SENIOR HIGH SCHOOL. Ashland Senior High School is depicted in this postcard scene in the 1930s. Many people today recall going to school here and how successful the sports teams were. Today there are several high schools in the area that keep that tradition alive. (Courtesy of the James C. Powers Collection.)

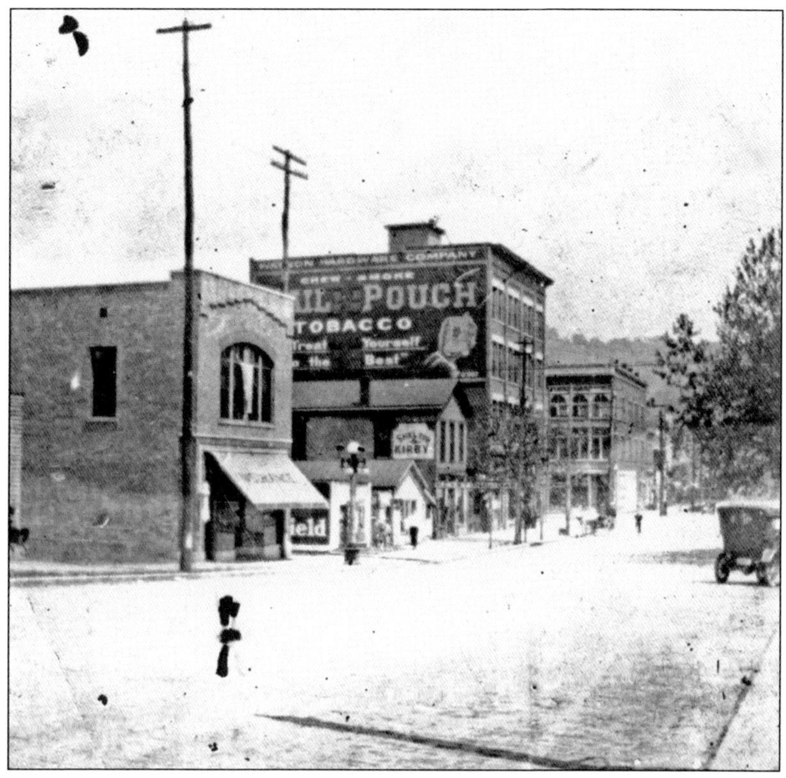

TALL LINES. In this rare 1910s photograph of Greenup Avenue near Sixteenth Street looking southwest, the poles used to hold electric lines running across Ashland are almost twice the height of poles today. The four-story building with "Mail Pouch" on it is standing today. (Courtesy of the Arnold Hanners Photographic Collection, Minnie Winder Room, Boyd County Public Library.)

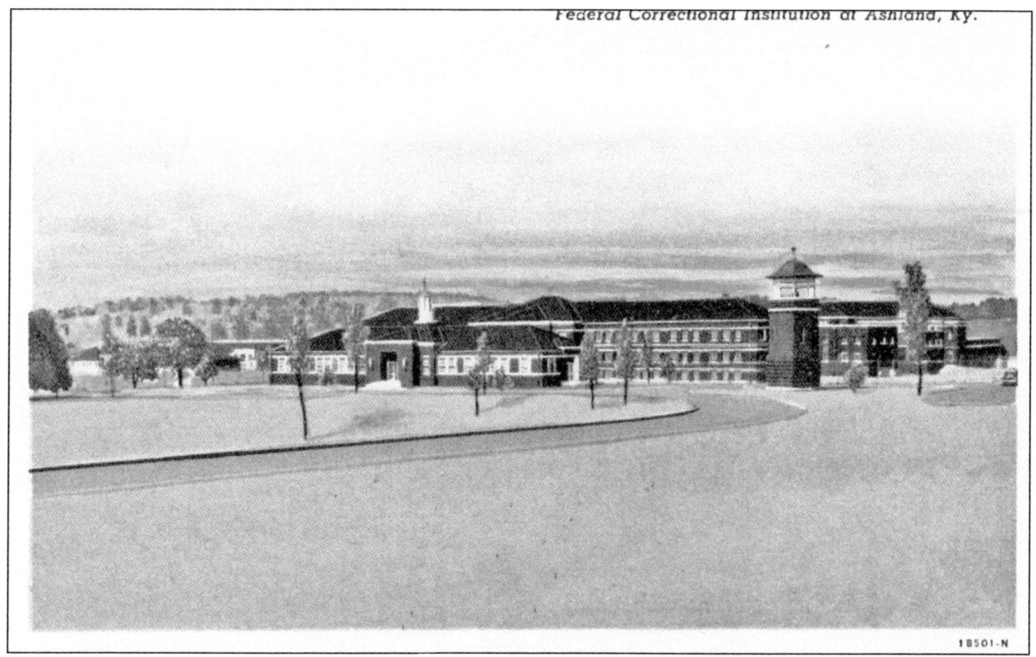

FCI AT ASHLAND. This image shows the Federal Correctional Institution located about five miles south of Ashland in Cannonsburg. The buildings that make up this institution have changed very little since the early 1940s. The institution is a minimum-security prison and houses only male inmates. (Courtesy of the James C. Powers Collection.)

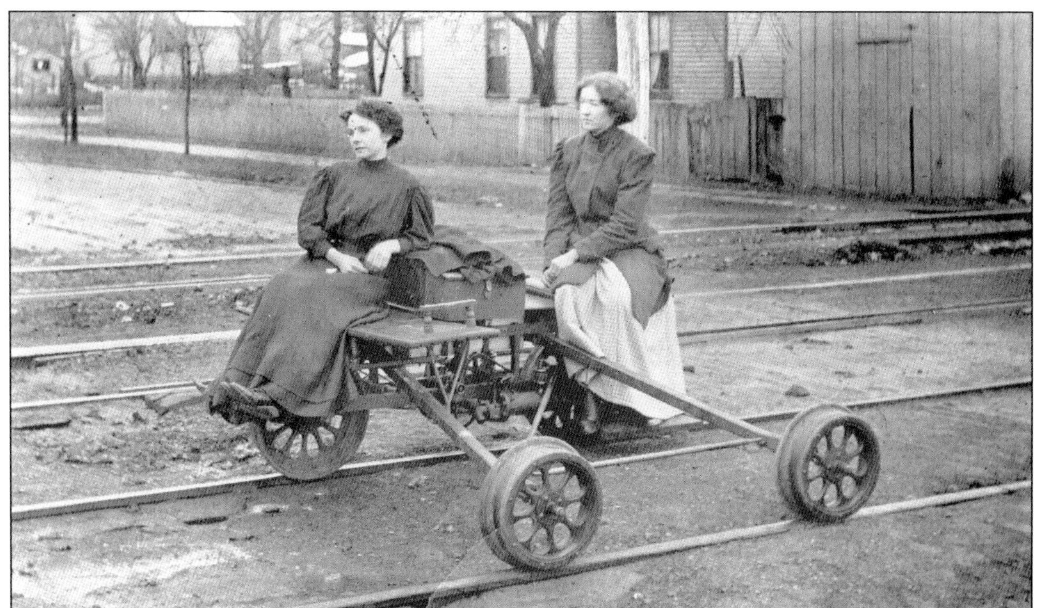

WOMEN ON A VELOCIPEDE. Near Front Street are two women from around 1920. This four-wheeled velocipede worked by pushing the feet in a rowing motion back and forth. This particular vehicle could carry up to three people at a time. The velocipede was rarely used for pleasure riding. (Courtesy of the Arnold Hanners Photographic Collection, Minnie Winder Room, Boyd County Public Library.)

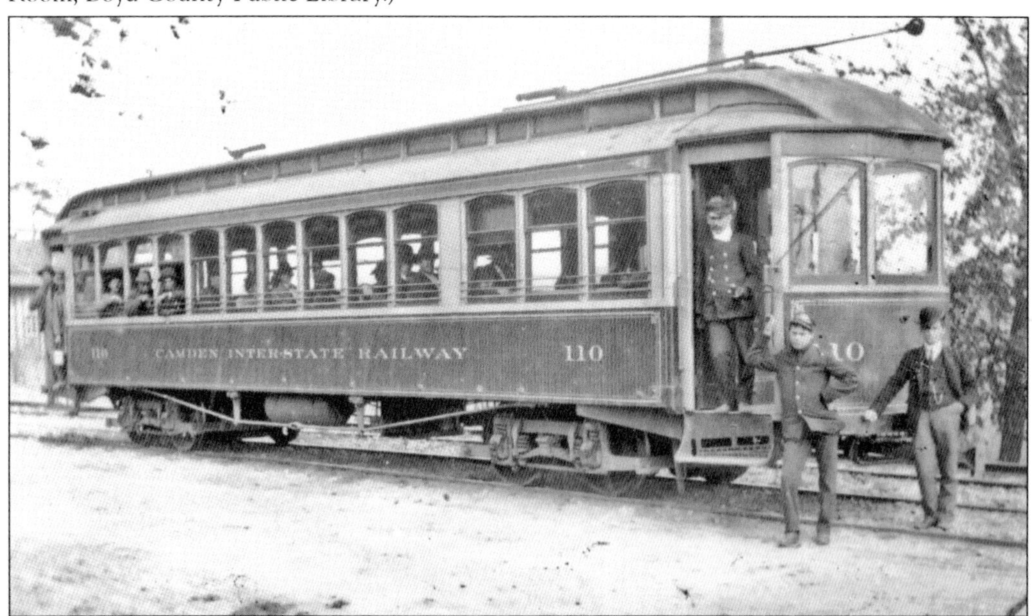

STREETCAR NO. 110. Passengers and crewmen pose for this 1910s photograph with Camden Interstate Railway Streetcar No. 110. The cars ran through Ashland on a regular basis from west end of Winchester Avenue to Catlettsburg's eastern border with West Virginia. The electric rods on the roof of the car came in contact with the electrified cable running centered above the track. (Courtesy of the Arnold Hanners Photographic Collection, Minnie Winder Room, Boyd County Public Library.)

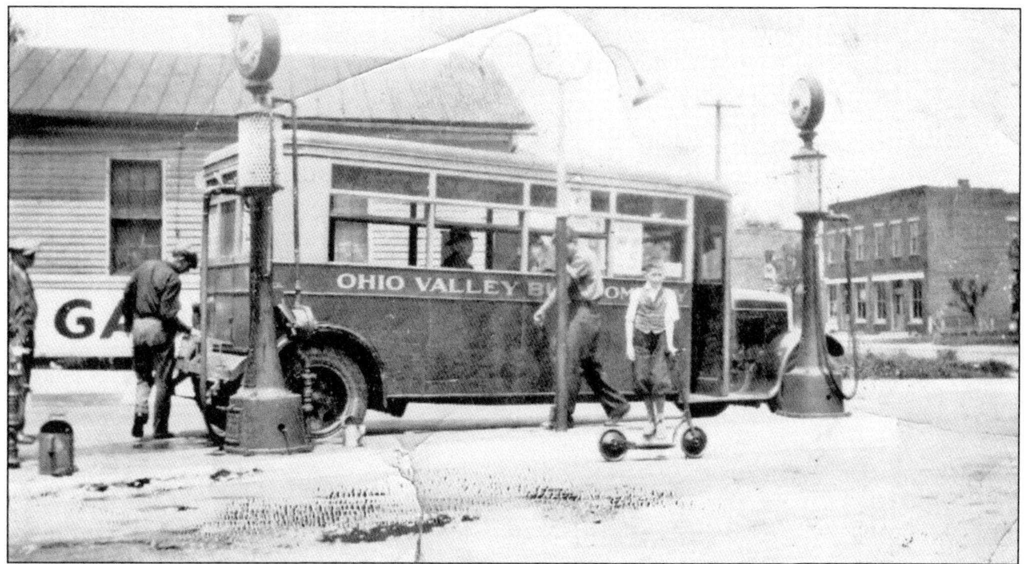

GASSING UP THE BUS. An Ohio Valley Bus Company bus stops for fuel at a filling station near Carter Avenue in the early 1930s. Ashland Bus System today offers customers a variety of routes from west Ashland to Kenova, West Virginia, six days a week. (Courtesy of the Arnold Hanners Photographic Collection, Minnie Winder Room, Boyd County Public Library.)

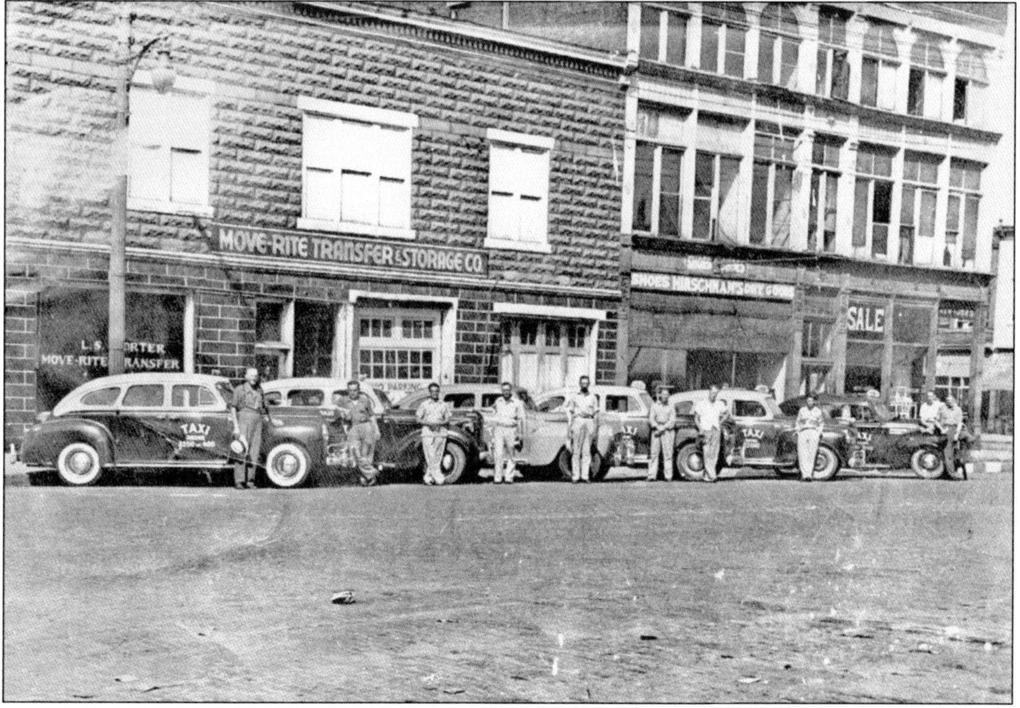

ASHLAND TAXI. Six taxis are parked and ready for use on Greenup Avenue in this late-1940s photograph. Taxis have always been more expensive than public transportation, but a driver can take customers wherever they wish to go. In the background is the Move-Rite Transfer and Storage Company Building. (Courtesy of the Arnold Hanners Photographic Collection, Minnie Winder Room, Boyd County Public Library.)

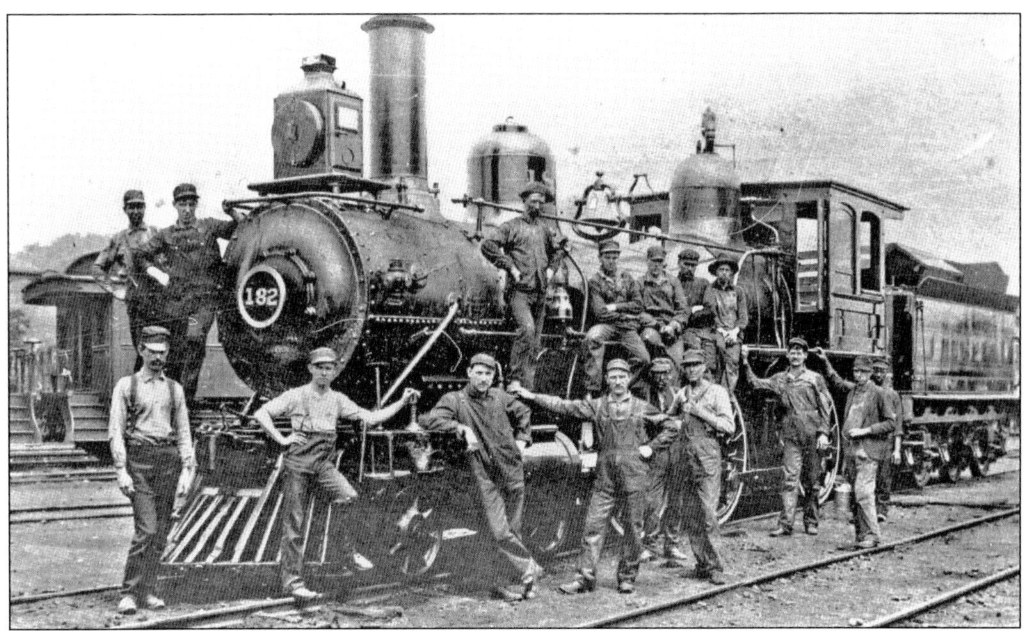

C&O's First Crew. This undated photograph shows the Chesapeake and Ohio Railway's first local crew. The engine appears to be a shiny new train just delivered to Ashland via a barge down the Ohio River from Pittsburg. CSX railroads continues to have a large presence from Ashland to Raceland. (Courtesy of the Arnold Hanners Photographic Collection, Minnie Winder Room, Boyd County Public Library.)

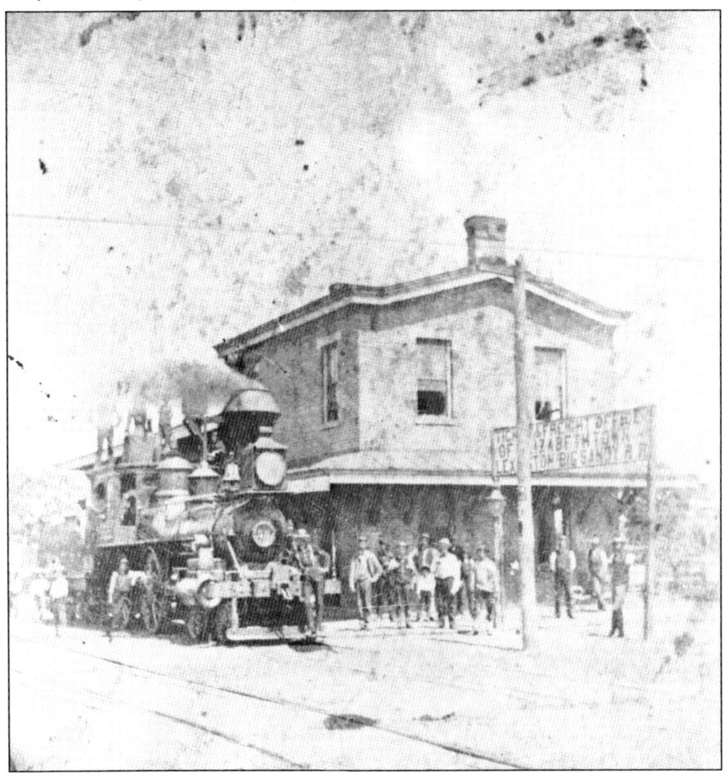

Elizabethtown, Lexington, and Big Sandy Railroad. This photograph of the Elizabethtown, Lexington, and Big Sandy Railroad Depot was taken around 1885. The wood-burning engine and people are posing in front of the two-story depot that stood on Thirteenth Street between Central and Carter Avenues. (Courtesy of the Arnold Hanners Photographic Collection, Minnie Winder Room, Boyd County Public Library.)

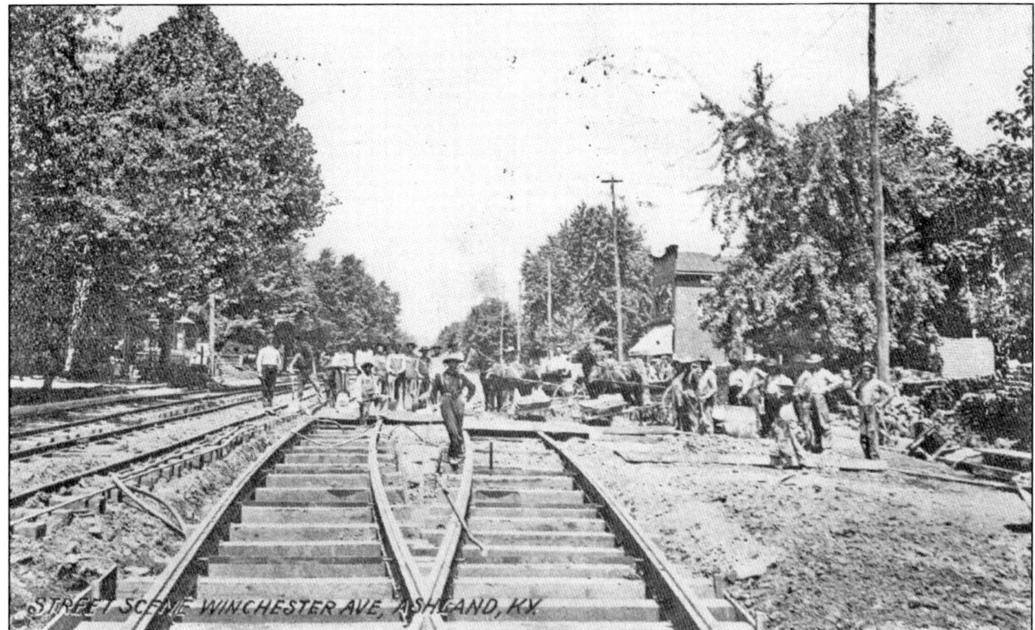

WORKING ON THE RAILROAD. This postcard from the 1890s says that it is of a street scene on Winchester Avenue, most likely near the eastern end of Ashland. Ashland had several railroad depots, such as Union Station; the Elizabethtown, Lexington, and Big Sandy Depot; the C&O Depot; and the Ashland Coal and Iron (AC&I) Depot. (Courtesy of the James C. Powers Collection.)

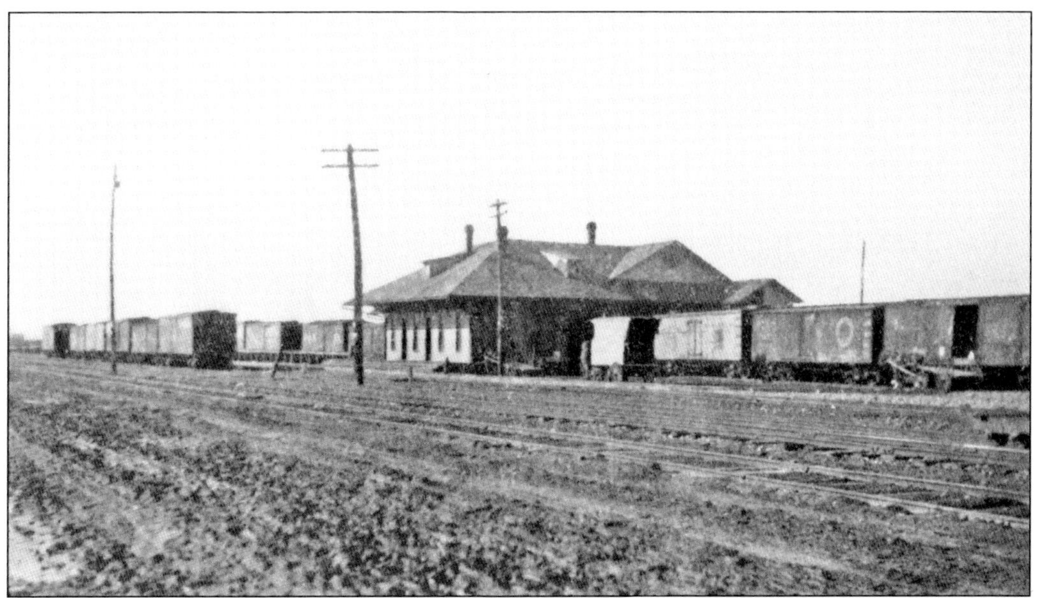

AC&I DEPOT. This rare photograph shows the classical depot structure of the Ashland Coal and Iron Railway Company in the 1930s. This depot replaced the grand Union Depot, which that was destroyed by fire in 1897. The AC&I owned shares in iron manufacturing, coal mining, and river transportation. (Courtesy of the Arnold Hanners Photographic Collection, Minnie Winder Room, Boyd County Public Library.)

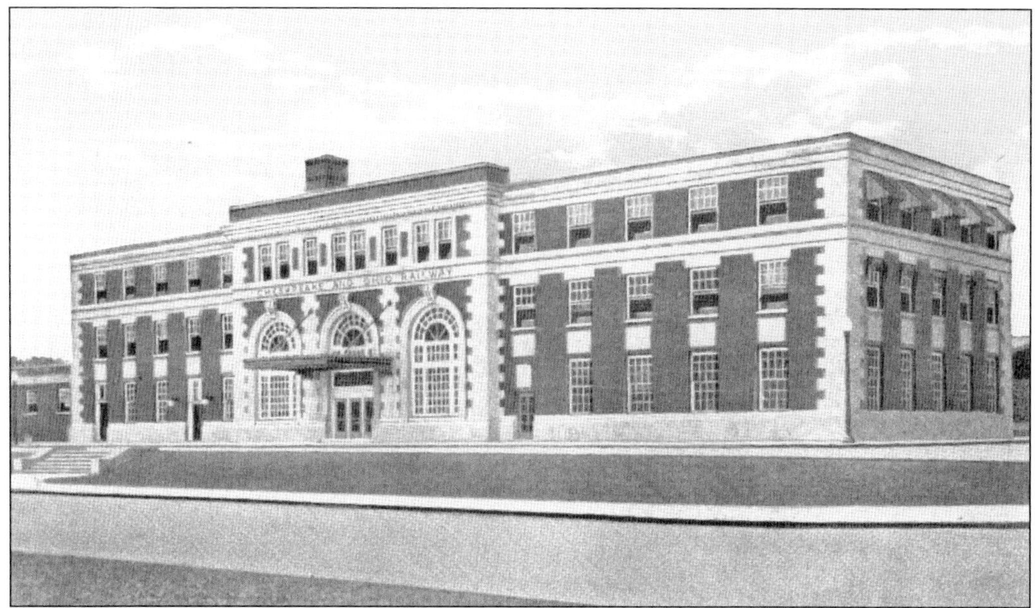

C&O Depot. The C&O Depot was built on Carter Avenue in the 1920s. The red-brick structure was one of the more modern depots in the area when constructed. This was one of the busiest depots that belonged to the C&O in this part of the country. (Courtesy of the Terry L. Baldridge Collection.)

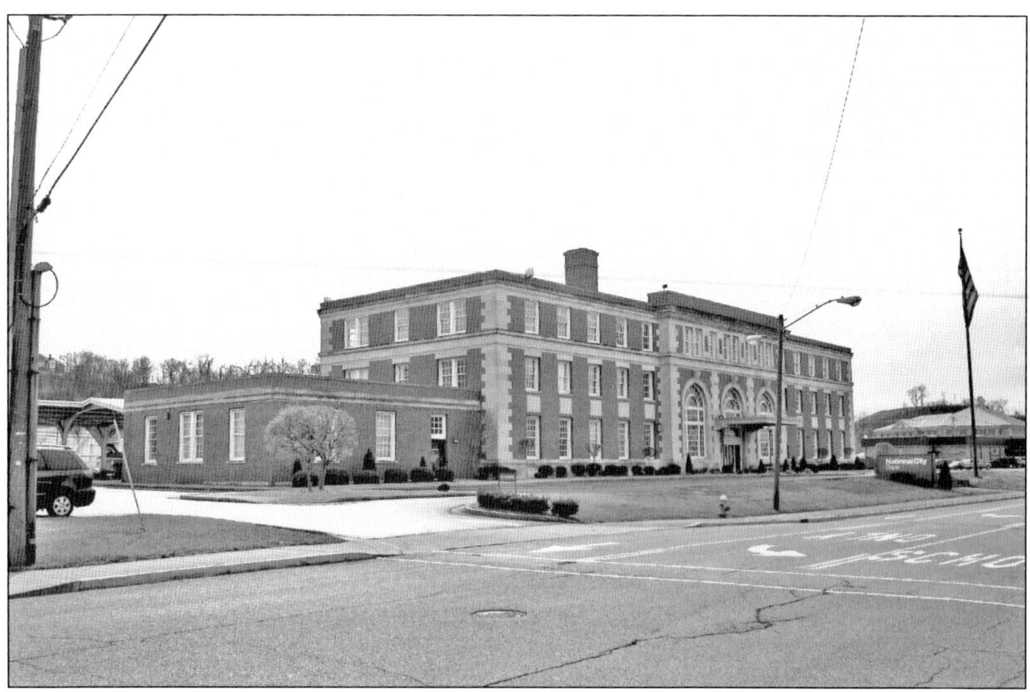

The C&O Depot Today. The C&O Depot still retains the splendor it had when it was first built. The building was turned into a bank in the early 1980s and today is owned by National City Bank. A passenger car is parked and ready on the small portion of remaining track in the back of the bank. (Photograph by Terry L. Baldridge.)

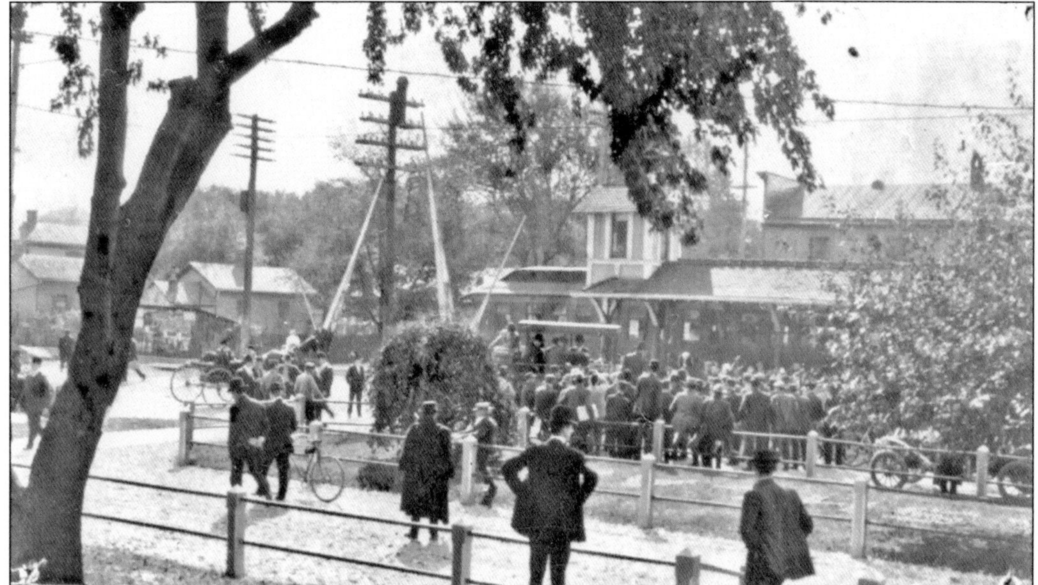

A Teddy Roosevelt Visit? This picture was taken of a crowd gathering near a parked passenger train outside the old C&O depot around 1912. Teddy Roosevelt came through the area during his 1912 presidential bid. This depot replaced the Elizabethtown, Lexington, and Big Sandy Depot that stood this spot. (Courtesy of the Arnold Hanners Photographic Collection, Minnie Winder Room, Boyd County Public Library.)

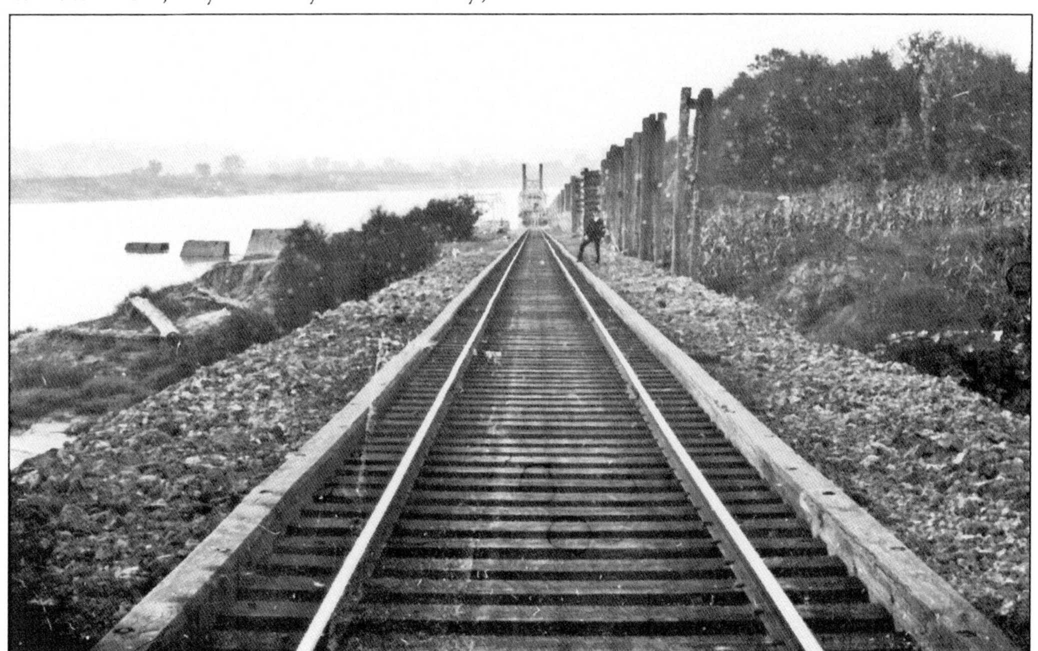

Railroad River Transfer. This photograph from the early 1900s shows the Coal Grove, Ohio, river-to-rail transfer across the Ohio River from Ashland. Ashland Coal and Iron transferred products across the river via railcars here. The operation began around 1883 and discontinued with the construction of the Kenova Bridge around 1915. (Courtesy of the Arnold Hanners Photographic Collection, Minnie Winder Room, Boyd County Public Library.)

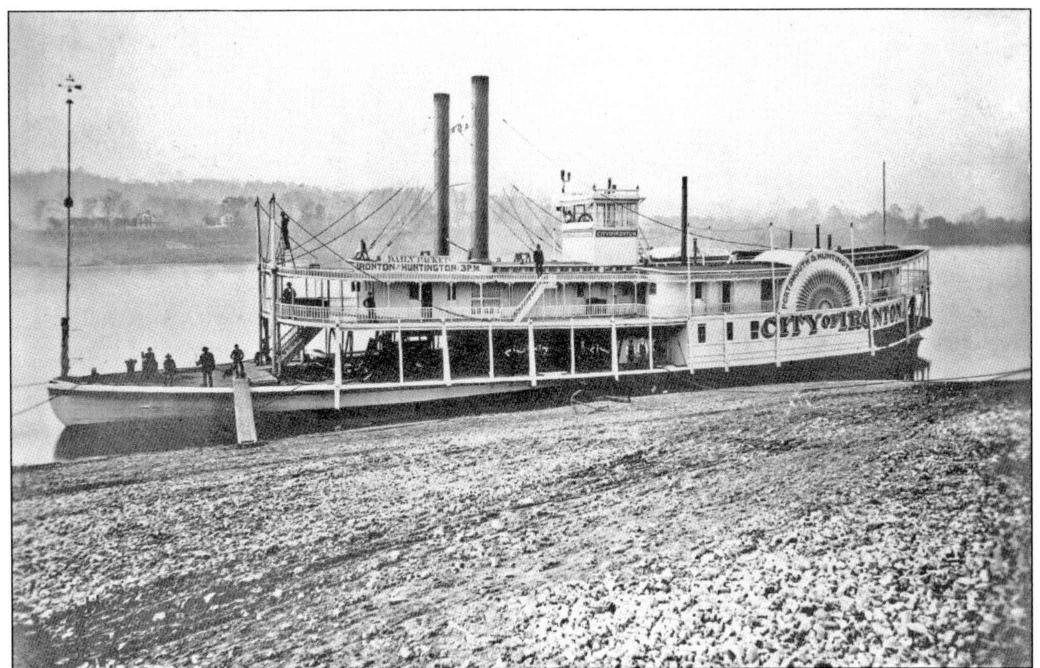

IRONTON TO HUNTINGTON. The *City of Ironton* riverboat traveled daily from Portsmouth, Ohio, to Huntington, West Virginia, during the late 1800s. The boat carried passengers on a regular schedule that coincided with city train schedules. The boat was also used to carry dry goods, livestock, and the U.S. mail. (Courtesy of the James C. Powers Collection.)

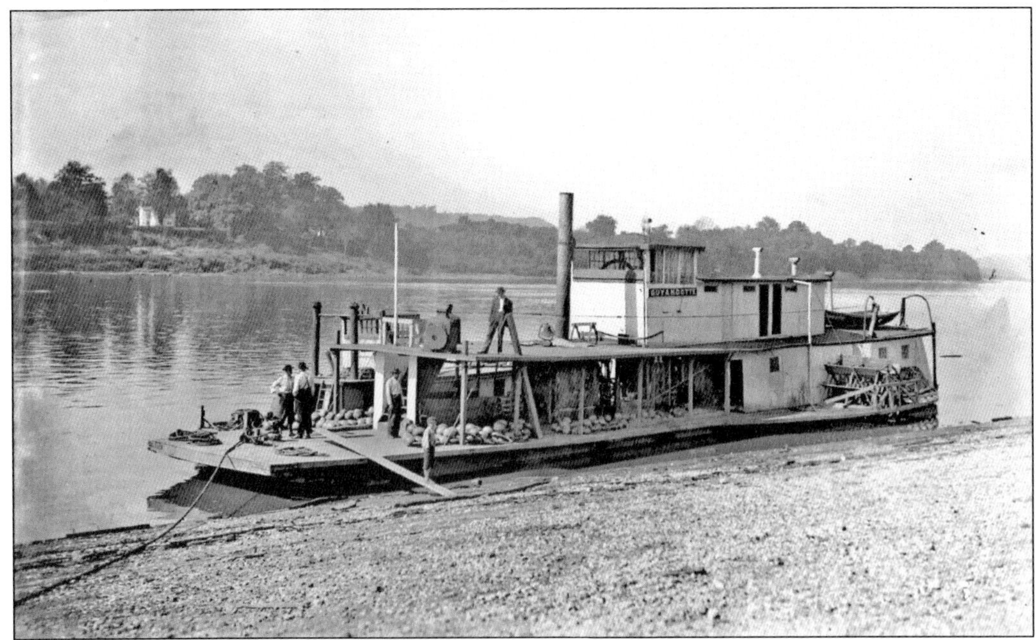

THE *GUYANDOTTE*. Small riverboats such as the *Guyandotte* pushed barges filled with raw materials or finished products between Huntington, Ashland, and Cincinnati. The crew could earn extra money for the boat through services such as being a river steamboat mechanic or selling fish caught on a slow day. (Courtesy of the James C. Powers Collection.)

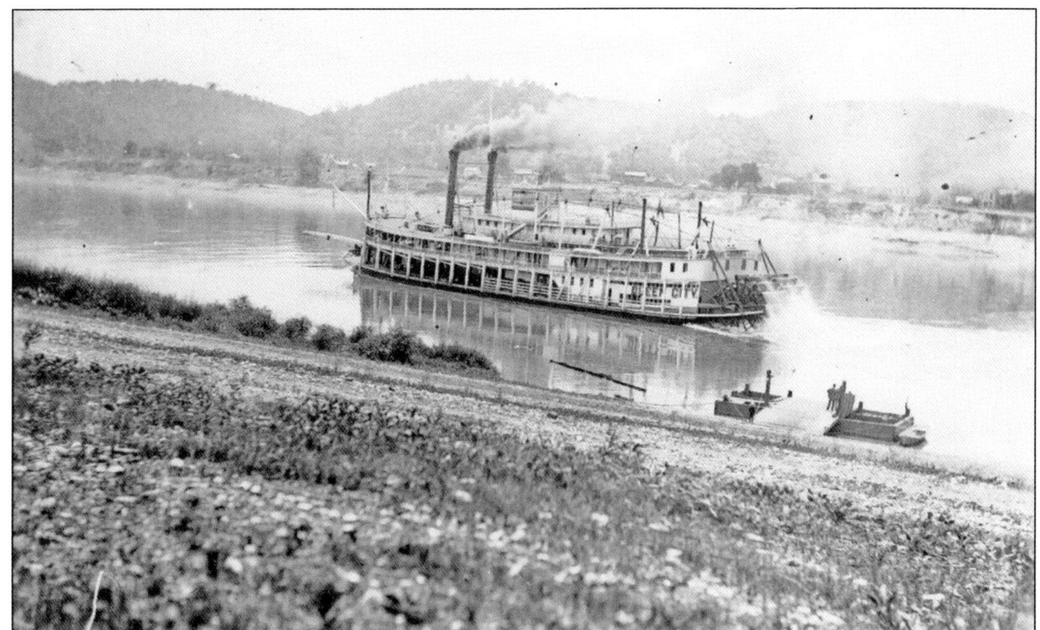

QUEEN CITY. Many Ohio River passengers made their trips back and forth from Pennsylvania to the Mississippi via the *Queen City* riverboat. The riverboat was built in the late 1890s and ran thousands of trips along the Ohio River until 1933. The riverboat had several dozen furnished rooms and served three hot meals a day. (Courtesy of the Arnold Hanners Photographic Collection, Minnie Winder Room, Boyd County Public Library.)

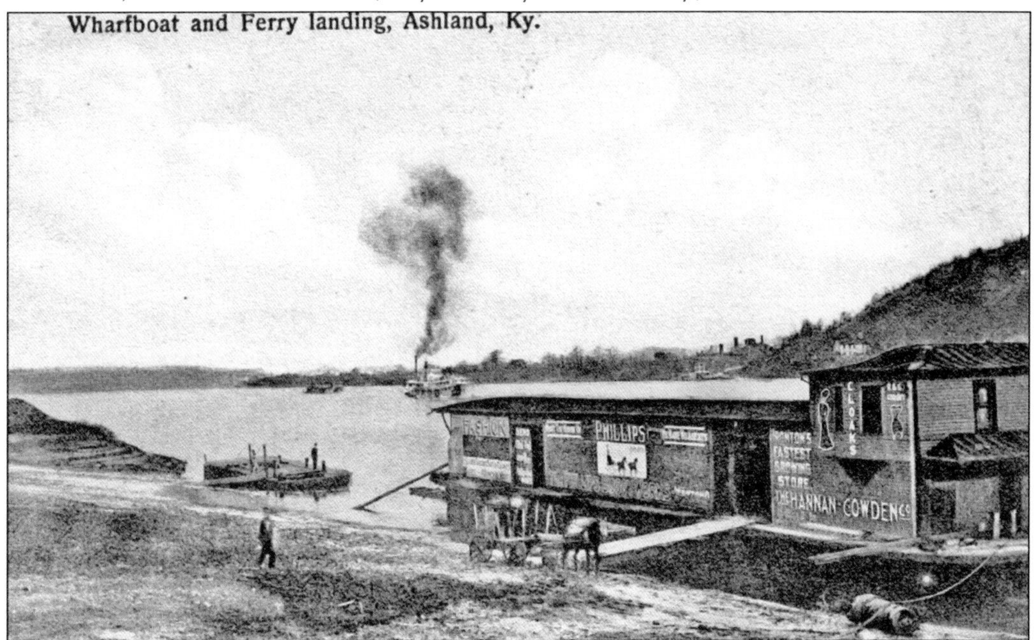

TRAVELING STORES. Several stores are built on one barge in this early-20th-century postcard. These barges would dock at a landing of a city and sell their products, then move on to the next Ohio River town. This image is of a barge from Ironton at the Ashland Ferry Landing. (Courtesy of the James C. Powers Collection.)

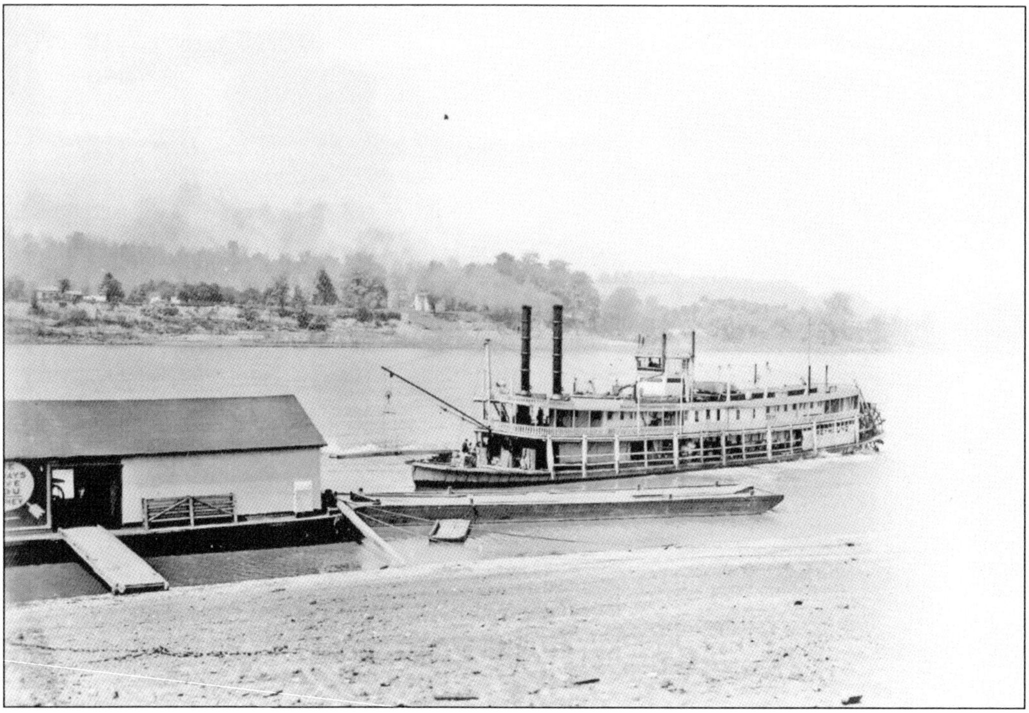

THE *GREYHOUND*. The stern-wheeler *Greyhound* backs away from a dock near Ashland. The boat pilots had to know the river like the backs of their hands. Potential danger was a constant thought that kept these men on the lookout. Sandbars, dead wood, and debris were threats not to be taken lightly. (Courtesy of the James C. Powers Collection.)

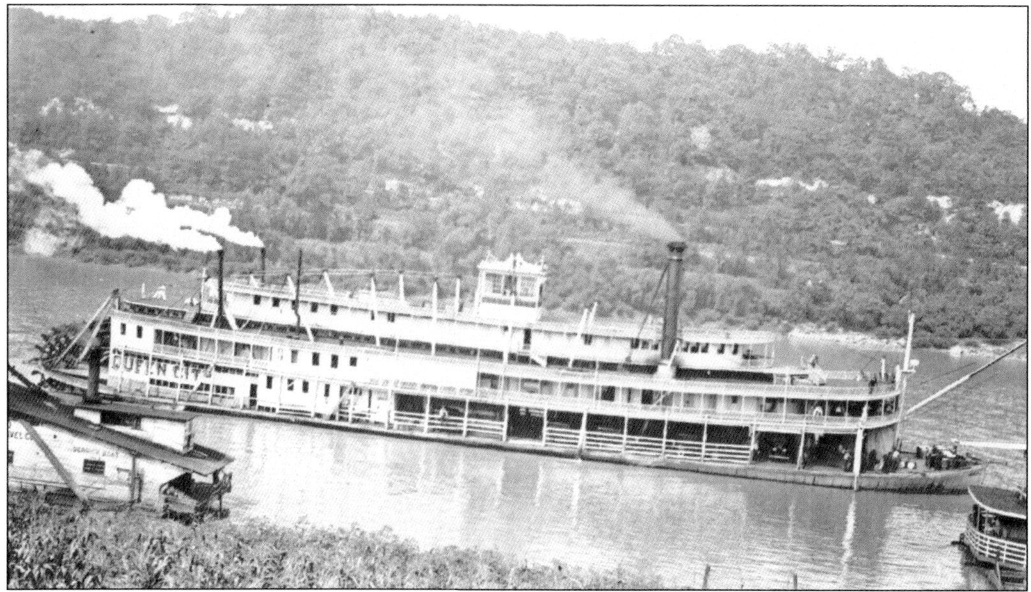

DOCKING ON THE GRAND OHIO. The *Queen City* slows as she readies herself to drop off cargo, including passengers, store goods, and automobiles. This photograph was taken near the Ashland Ferry Landing in the mid-1920s. This is near the spot where the Ben Williamson Bridge is located today. (Courtesy of the James C. Powers Collection.)

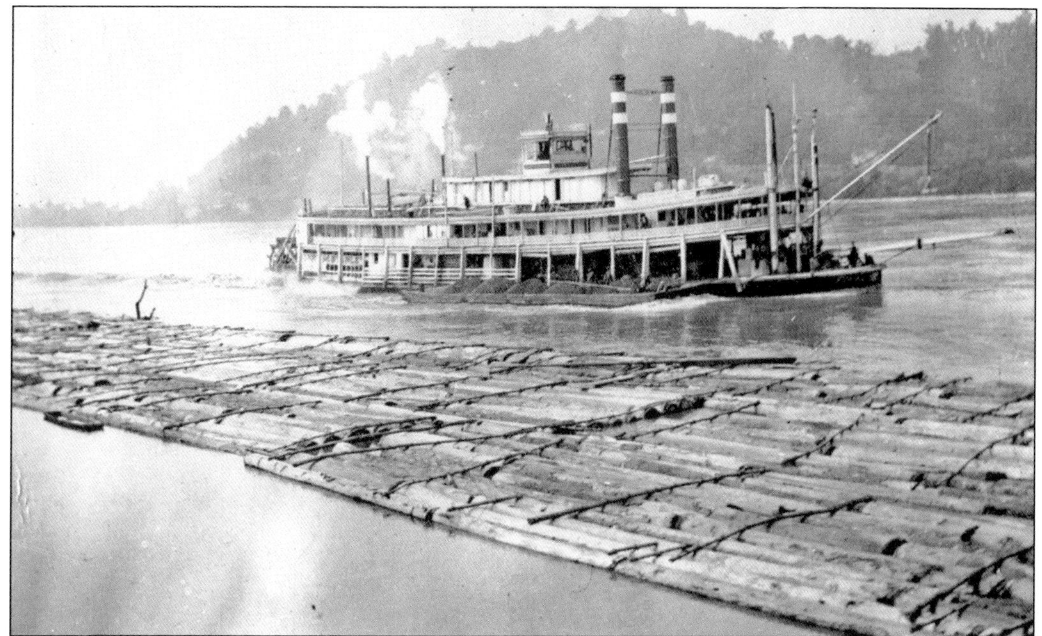

LOGS AND COAL. The riverboat M. *Stanley* ferries coal up the Ohio River in this photograph from around 1910. The coal is in a barge on this side of the boat. Logs have been nailed together to prevent single logs from drifting away and for easy passage to their destinations. (Courtesy of the James C. Powers Collection.)

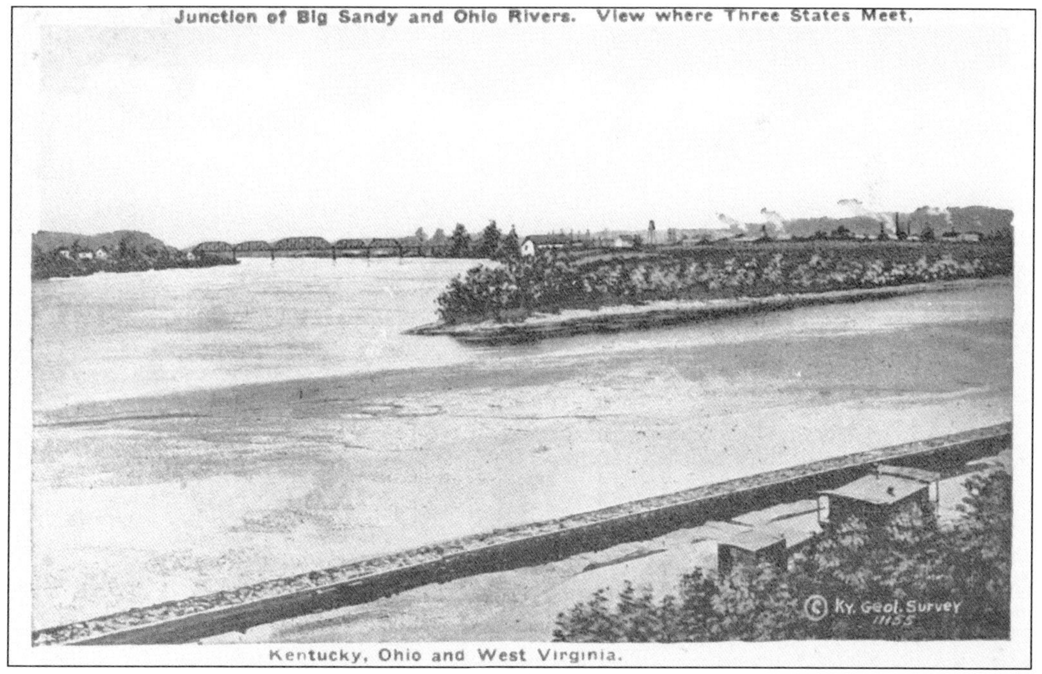

THREE STATES. This postcard from around 1915 shows the mouth of the Big Sandy River and its junction with the Ohio River. Kenova, West Virginia is in the center just across the Big Sandy; South Point, Ohio, is to the left; and Catlettsburg, Kentucky, is in the right-hand corner. (Courtesy of the James C. Powers Collection.)

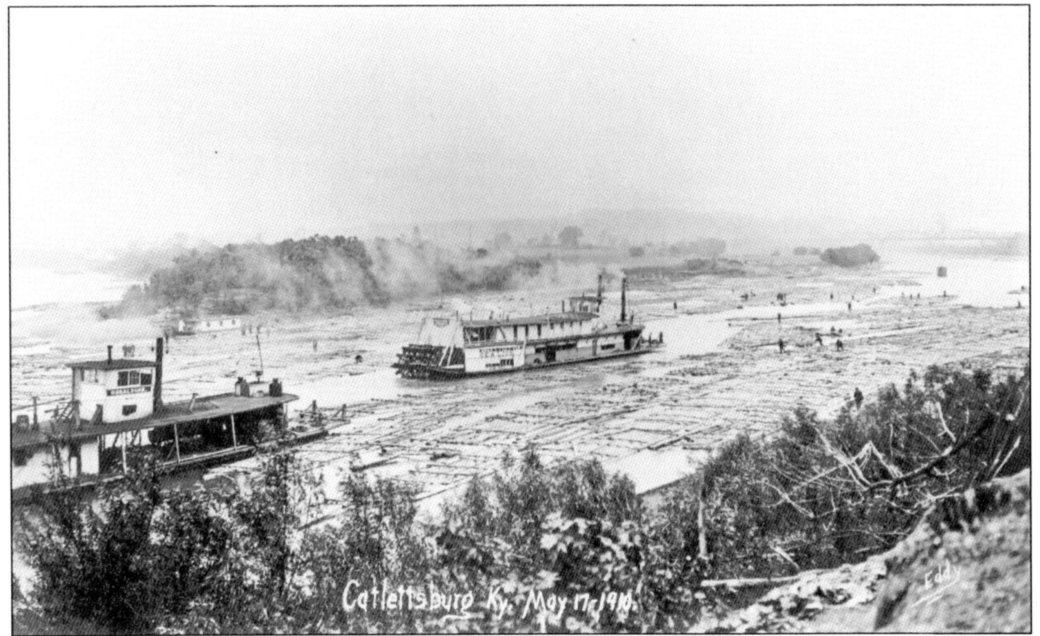

LOGGING ON THE BIG SANDY. Laborers and sawmill managers inspect barges of logs in preparation for transport to mills throughout the Ohio Valley. Much of this lumber came from Louisa and beyond. The riverboats *Sea Lion* and *Geraldine* maneuver themselves into position in this photograph from 1910. (Courtesy of the James C. Powers Collection.)

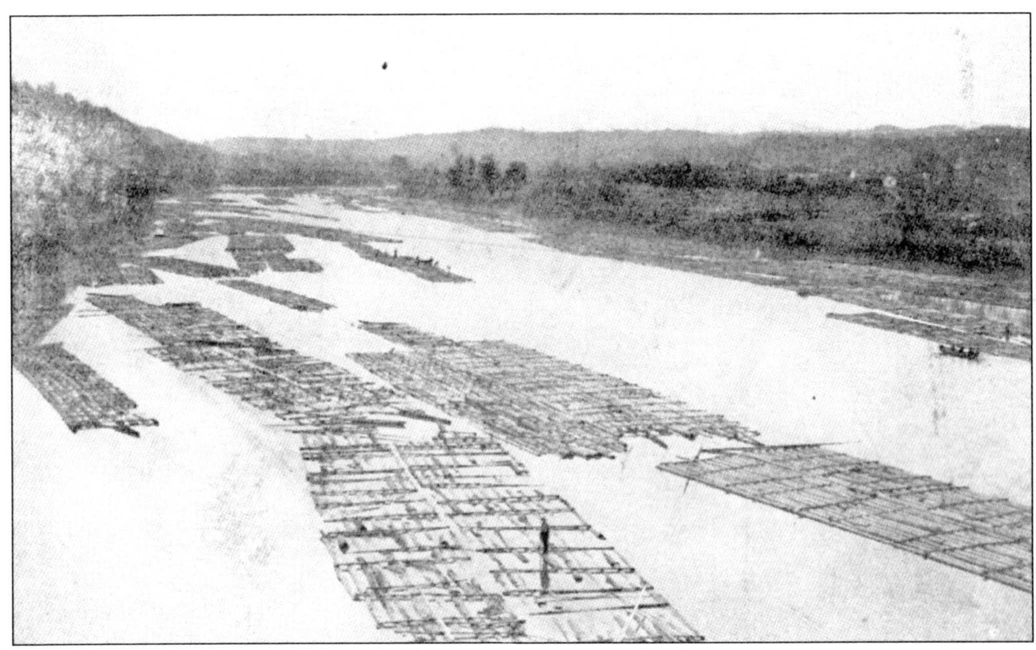

WATER TRANSPORT. Brave men walk from log barge to log barge readying their product for transport. This job posed many dangers that claimed lives and limbs throughout the years. The logging trade began to dry up in the area around 1915, causing families to migrate to more forested areas west. (Courtesy of the James C. Powers Collection.)

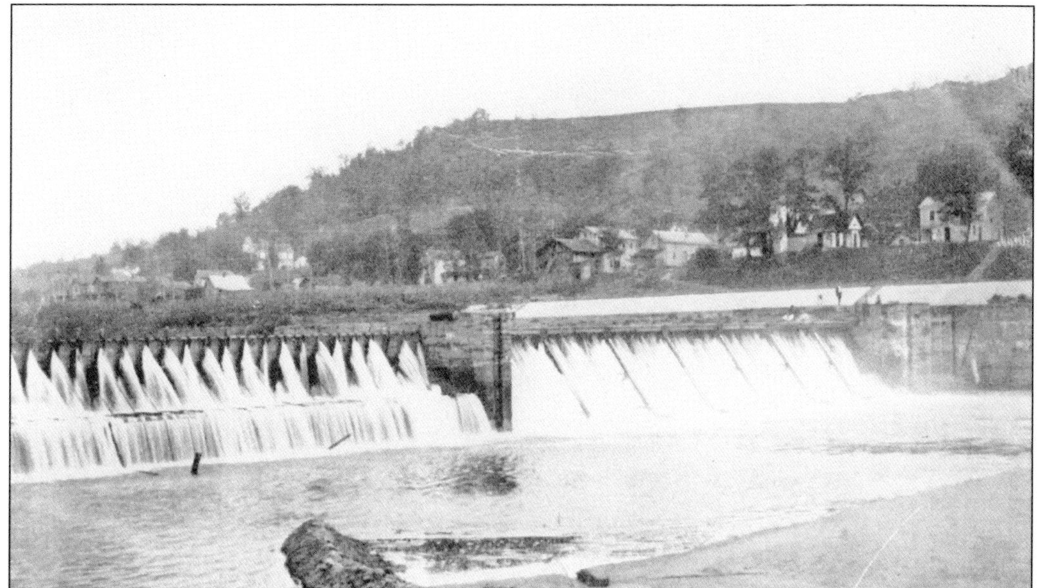

Big Sandy Lock and Dam No. 1. This photograph shows the Big Sandy Dam, located between Catlettsburg and Kenova just above Thirty-first Street in Catlettsburg. The lock portion was constructed by contractors Floz and Jonte. The dam was constructed by contractors Sheridan and Kirk. (Courtesy of the James C. Powers Collection.)

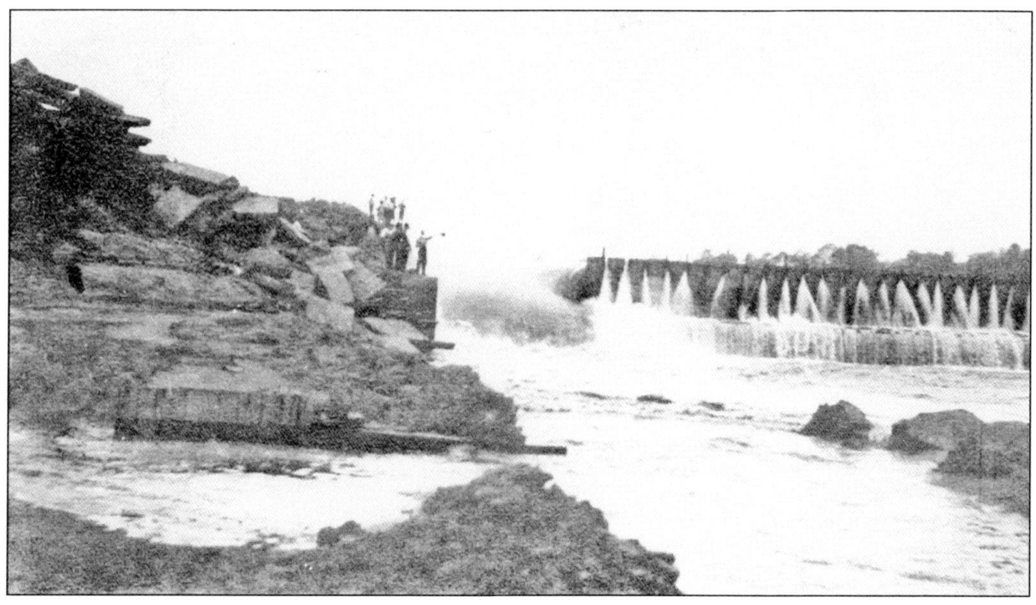

Highest in the World. At a height of 18.2 feet, the Big Sandy Dam was the highest needle dam in the world. The 14-foot needle dam in France was the world's second highest during this time. Several people are standing on the West Virginia side of the dam, which was built in 1902. (Courtesy of the James C. Powers Collection.)

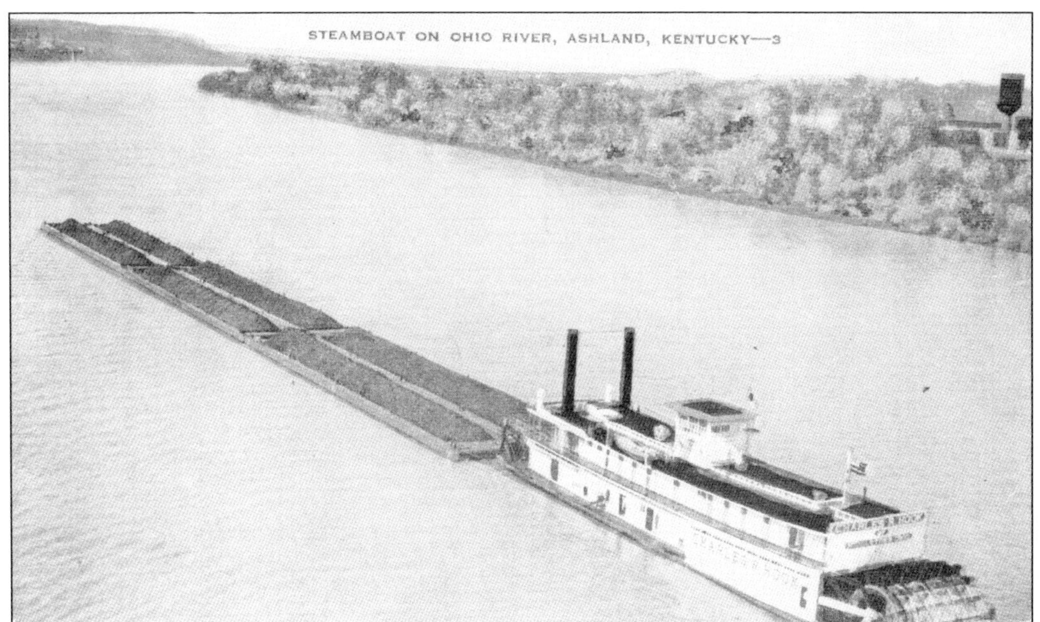

WHERE COAL MEETS IRON. Boyd County came about because of hard-working, industrious people. Several generations later, the people are just as hard working and proud of their heritage, which is centered on iron and coal. Many in the area worked in the coal mines and steel mills that made Boyd County and Ashland the wonderful area it is today. (Courtesy of the James C. Powers Collection.)

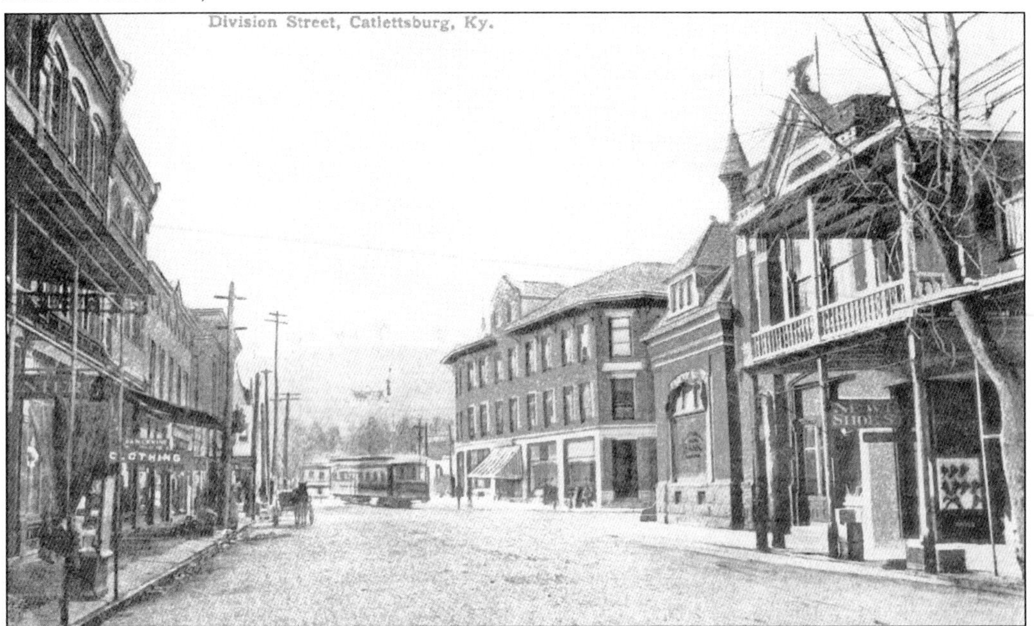

A CATLETTSBURG STREET. This image from around 1908 shows Division Street in downtown Catlettsburg. Several of the buildings shown stand today in this beautiful Ohio River town. Note the Camden Interstate Railway streetcar running in the background. The railway operated streetcars from Ashland to Huntington during this time. (Courtesy of the James C. Powers Collection.)

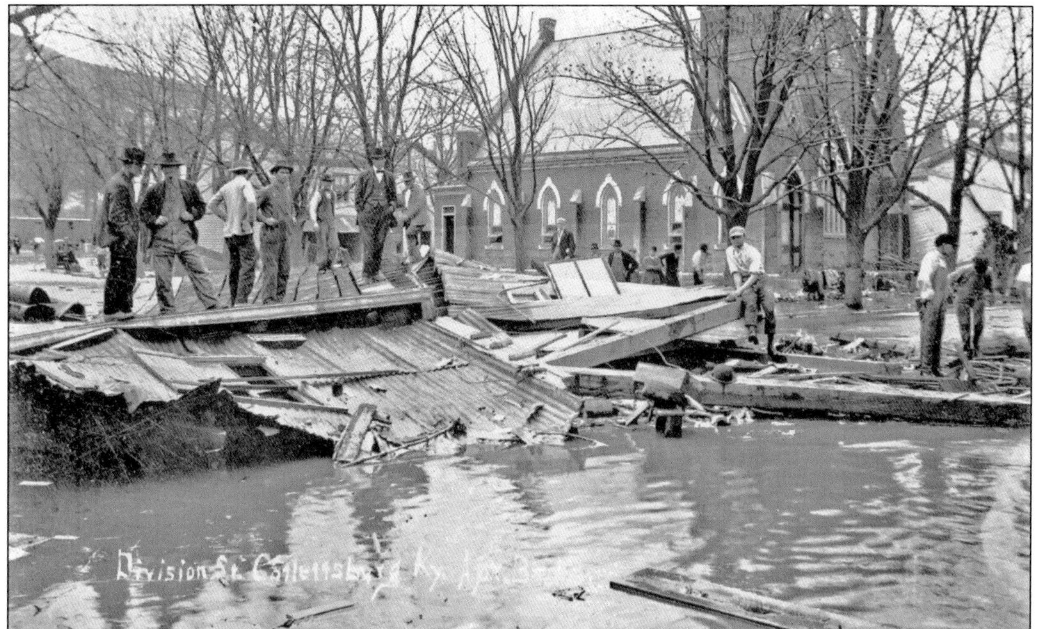

AFTER THE FLOOD. This picture taken along Division Street in Catlettsburg demonstrates the destructiveness of floods. Debris is in the street and along the walkways in the background. Many towns along the Ohio River suffered great loss, similar to the devastation in this photograph from 1913. (Courtesy of the James C. Powers Collection.)

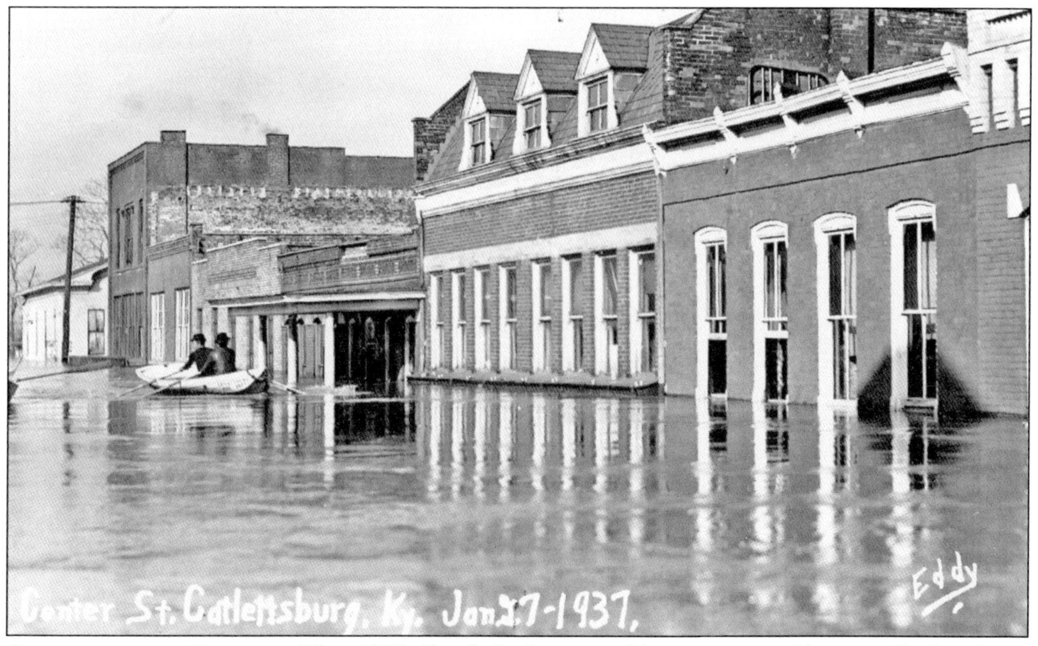

CATLETTSBURG FLOODS. The 1937 flood dealt a terrible economic blow to Catlettsburg. Several historic homes were lost because of this flood. Like Ashland, Ironton, Huntington, and Russell, Catlettsburg built a floodwall to protect the city from the invading Ohio River. Today murals on the flood walls reflect the cities' history in splendid detail. (Courtesy of the James C. Powers Collection.)

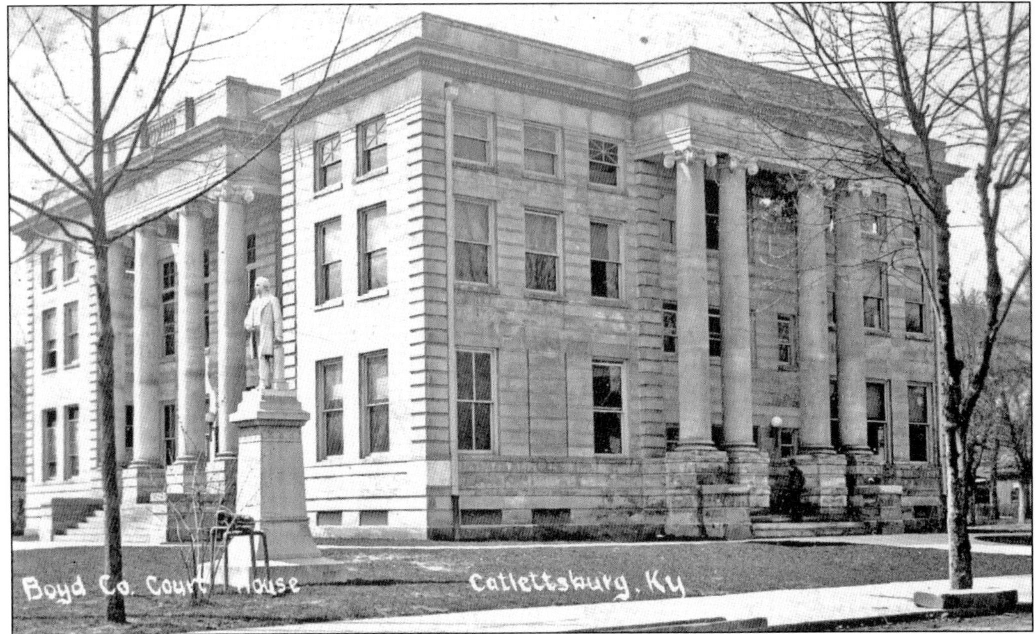

BOYD COUNTY COURTHOUSE. Catlettsburg was incorporated in 1848 and named after local landowner Horatio Catlett. The city was one of the largest timber markets in the world. The Boyd County Courthouse, with its classical Greek columns and statue of John Milton Elliot, is located in the beautiful town. (Courtesy of the James C. Powers Collection.)

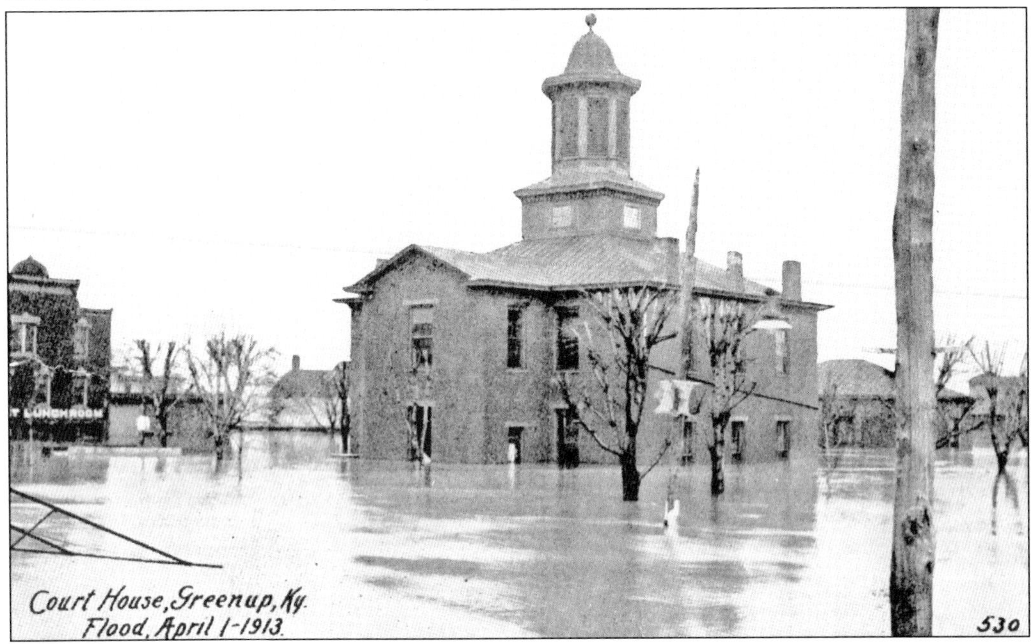

GREENUP UNDER WATER. This photograph from 1913 shows the flood that year running through the old courthouse building downtown. The 1937 flood proved to be too much for the courthouse, and it was replaced not long afterwards with an impressive, permanent structure. The courthouse yards proudly displays historical information regarding some of the county's favorite sons. (Courtesy of the Terry L. Baldridge Collection.)

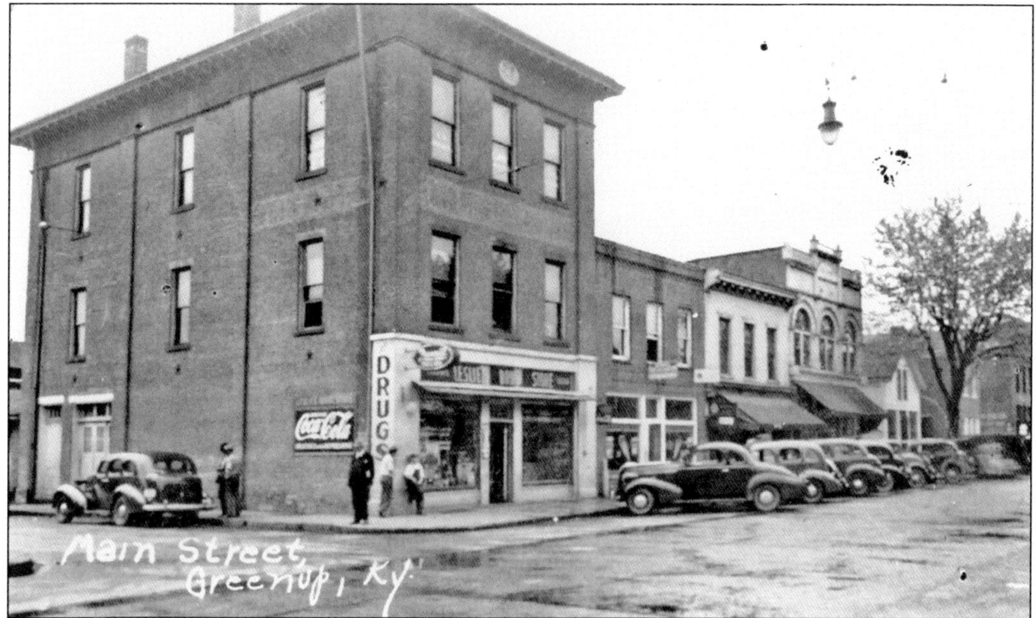

MAIN STREET. The three-story drugstore on southwest corner of Harrison Street and Main Street looks busy in this photograph from 1950. The first four buildings stand today and face the newer courthouse building in downtown Greenup. These streets are packed with eager visitors during the Greenup Old Fashion Days celebration every October. (Courtesy of the Terry L. Baldridge Collection.)

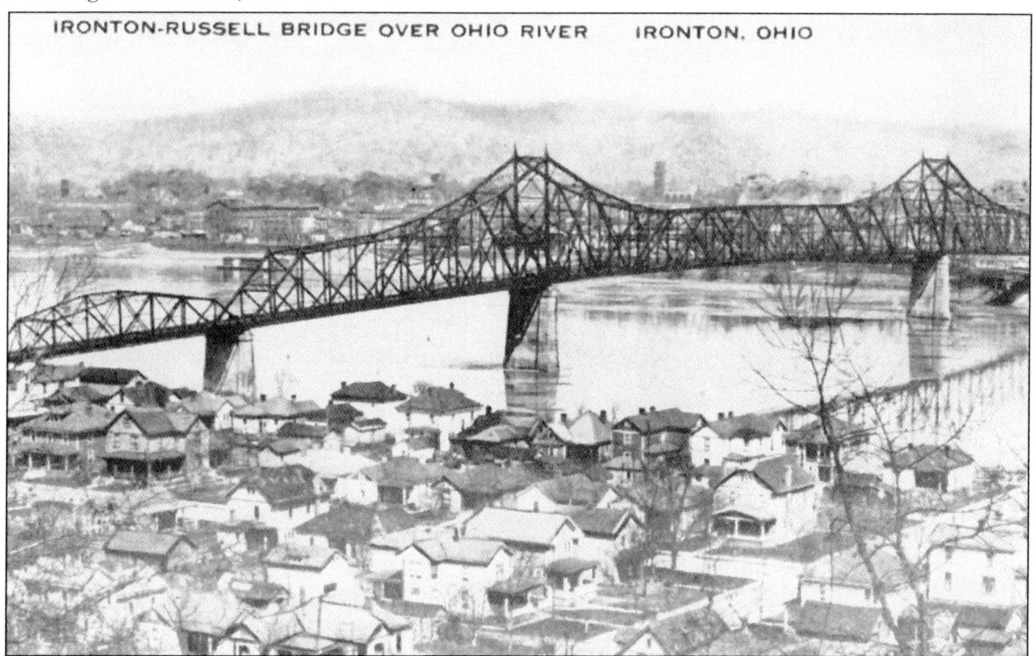

IRONTON-RUSSELL BRIDGE. Built in 1922 by local construction workers, the Ironton-Russell Bridge was the first highway bridge between Cincinnati and Parkersburg. The image shows the bridge from the Russell, Kentucky, side around 1950. The bridge has had a number of face-lifts and updates during its 86-year history. (Courtesy of the James C. Powers Collection.)

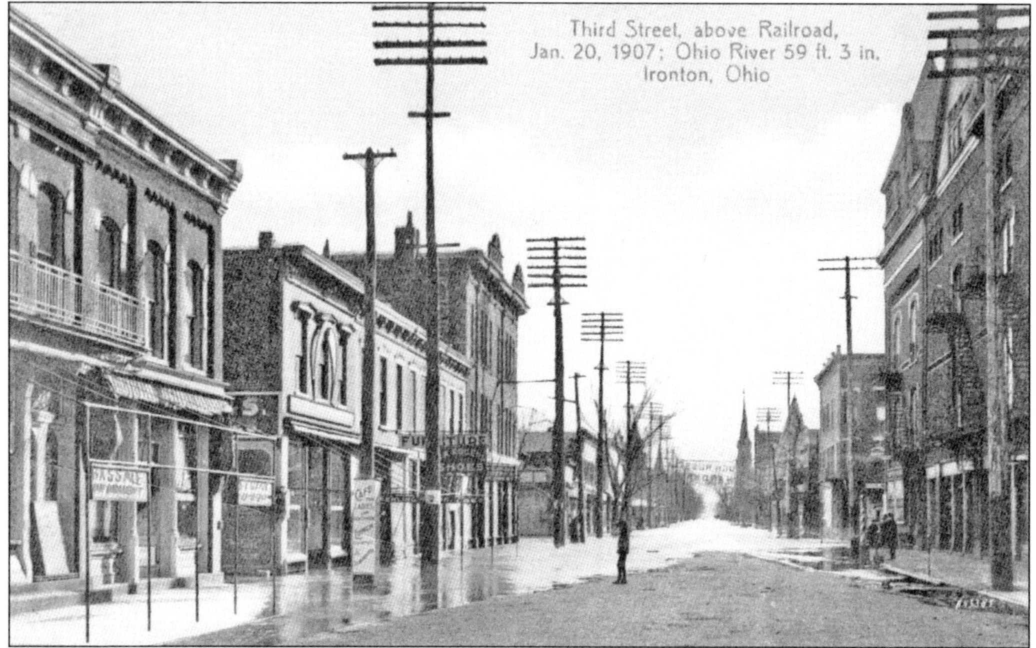

IRONTON FLOODING. Ironton was founded in 1849 by John Campbell and was at one time the largest producer of iron from pig iron in the world. Like Ashland, Ironton is located on the Ohio River in the center of the Hanging Rock region. As shown, the picturesque city was inundated by the river in this 1907 flood. (Courtesy of the James C. Powers Collection.)

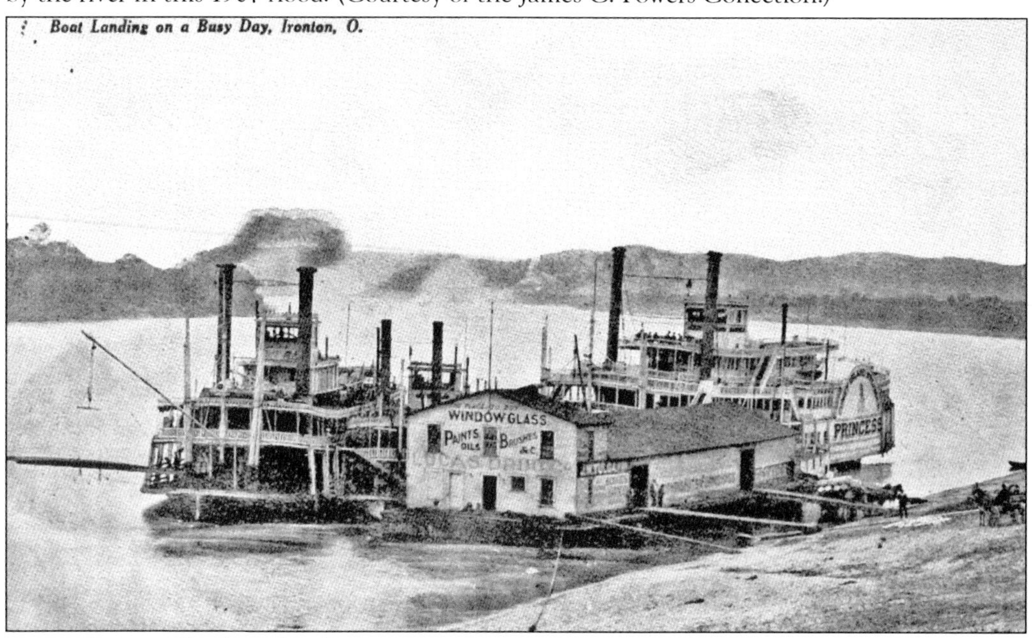

RIVER STORE. The boat landing in Ironton served as a store and a passenger transfer station for many years. In 1919, as the river transport industry was drying up, football became a city sensation. Ironton was home to the famous Ironton Tanks, a professional small-town team that enjoyed almost a decade of winning seasons. The stadium in which they played can be seen today. (Courtesy of the James C. Powers Collection.)

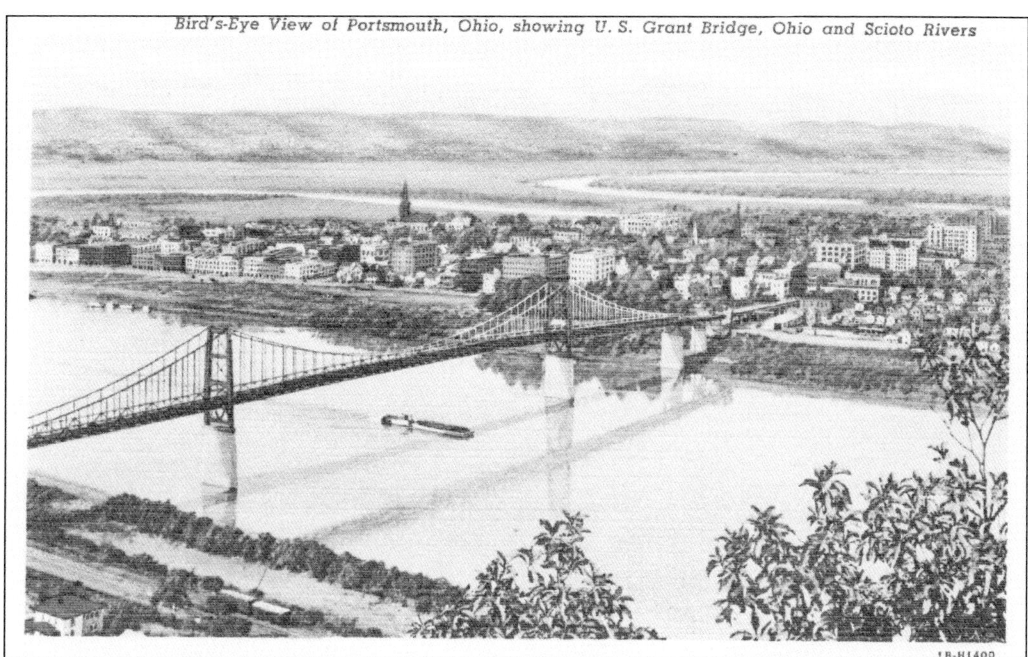

PORTSMOUTH, OHIO. Portsmouth was founded in 1803, but its history began in the 1790s as the village, Alexandria. When the river is at a low state, foundations and artifacts can be seen. Like Ironton, Portsmouth fielded a professional football team throughout the 1920s and early 1930s. The Portsmouth Spartans dominated professional football until they were bought and moved to Detroit. (Courtesy of the James C. Powers Collection.)

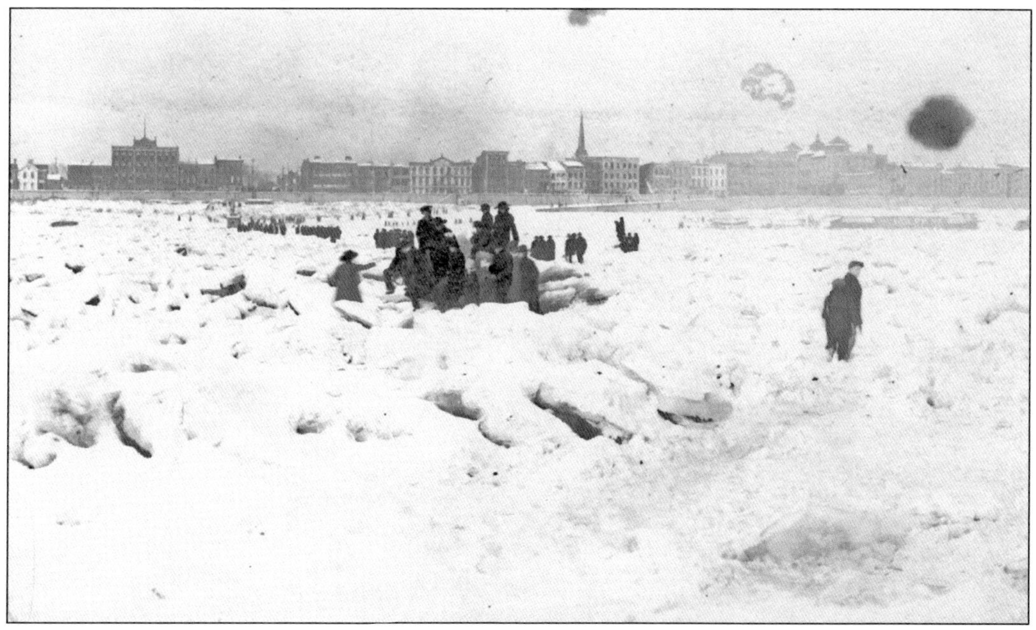

THE FROZEN OHIO RIVER. In the late 1800s and early to mid-1900s, the Ohio River would freeze over with several inches of ice. This photograph looks more like a town in Greenland than Portsmouth, Ohio, around 1910. Many older residents remember walking across the frozen river to deliver livestock. (Courtesy of the James C. Powers Collection.)

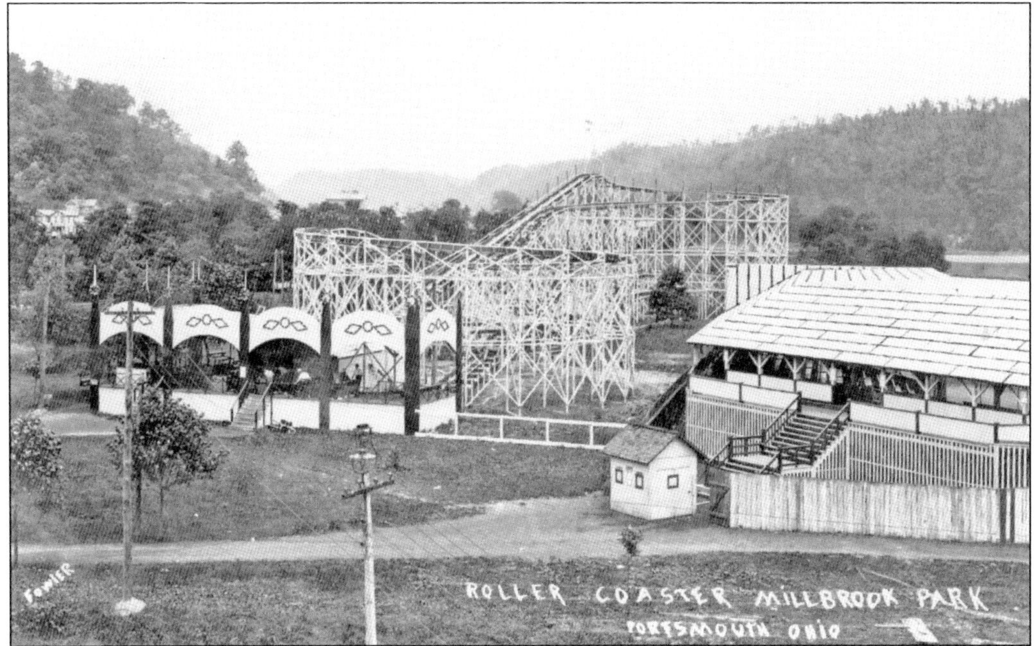

MILLBROOK PARK. Located in New Boston, Ohio, Millbrook Park was the jewel of the three amusement parks in the area. It had one of the largest rollercoasters in the world and was certainly larger than the coasters at Clyffside Park and Camden Park. Millbrook Park discontinued operation after the costly 1913 flood. (Courtesy of the James C. Powers Collection.)

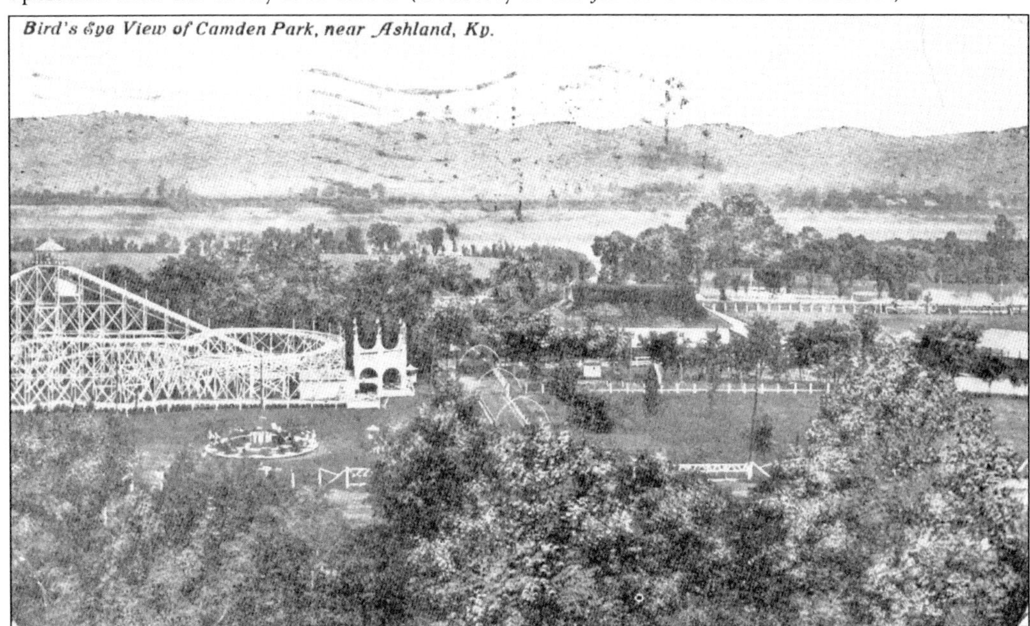

CAMDEN PARK. This park was planned out and constructed by the Camden Interstate Railway as a picnic area in 1903. The streetcar company constructed a large pool, rides, and lights to match Clyffside Park in Ashland. The rollercoaster pictured above was replaced in 1958 by the Big Dipper coaster, which celebrated its 50th annivarsary this year. (Courtesy of the Terry L. Baldridge Collection.)

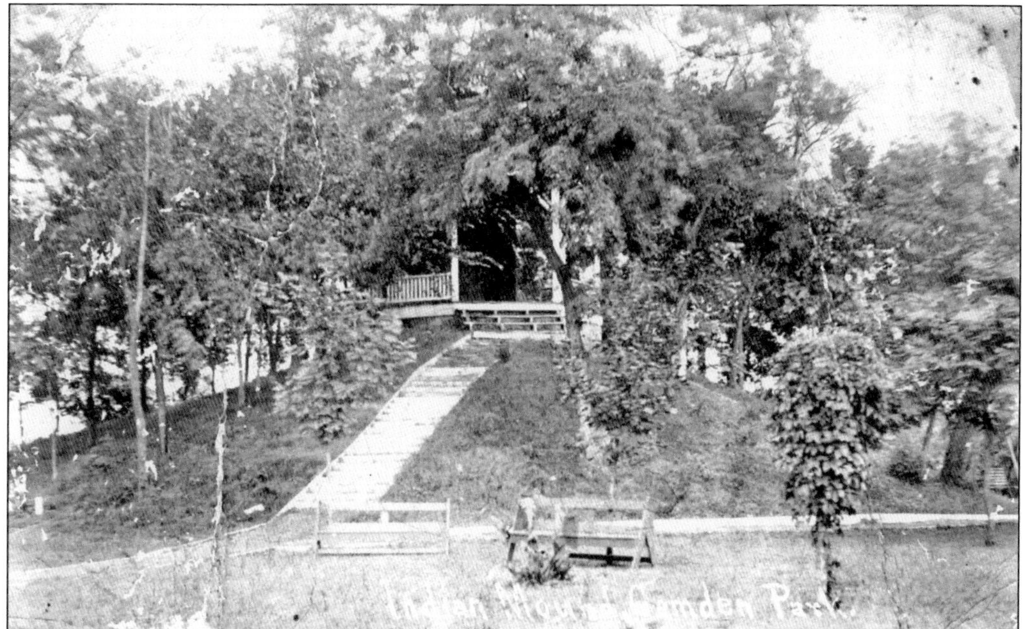

BURIAL MOUND. The Ashland area has many Adena earthworks along the Ohio River. This photograph shows the burial mound located at Camden Park near Huntington, West Virginia. Although the rides and generations coming to this amusement park have changed, the Indian Mound has changed very little from this 1910 image. (Courtesy of the James C. Powers Collection.)

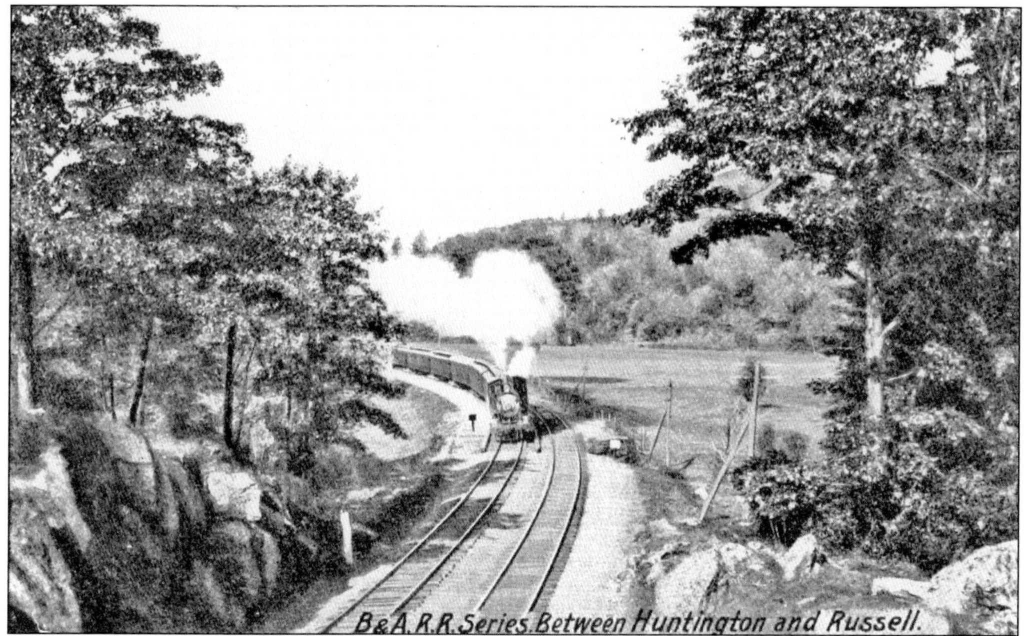

RAILROAD TRAVEL. Rail was the quickest means of travel between Huntington and Ashland. Ashland and the surrounding area have seen almost a dozen railways come and go. Fewer and fewer residents remember what it was like to travel to an area amusement park via the rail lines. (Courtesy of the Terry L. Baldridge Collection.)

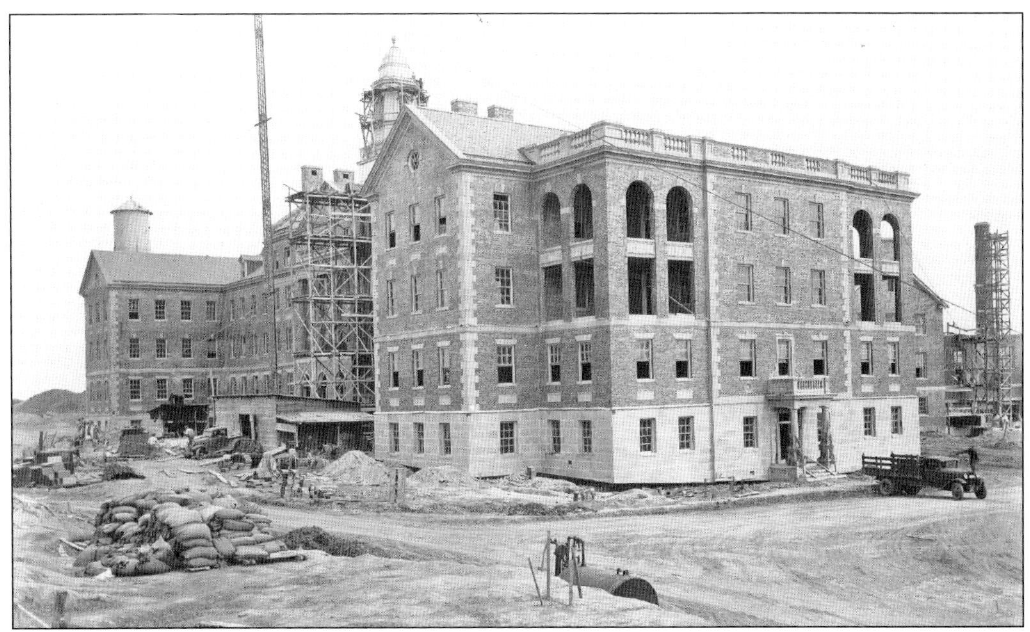

VA MEDICAL CENTER. Pres. Herbert Hoover signed an agreement to purchase over 325 acres of land on which to build the Veterans Administration Hospital. The photograph shows Building One under construction in early 1932. Frank Sears of Charleston, West Virginia, was the first patient to be seen after the hospital opened in October 1932. (Courtesy of the Huntington VA Medical Center Archives and Steve Boyes.)

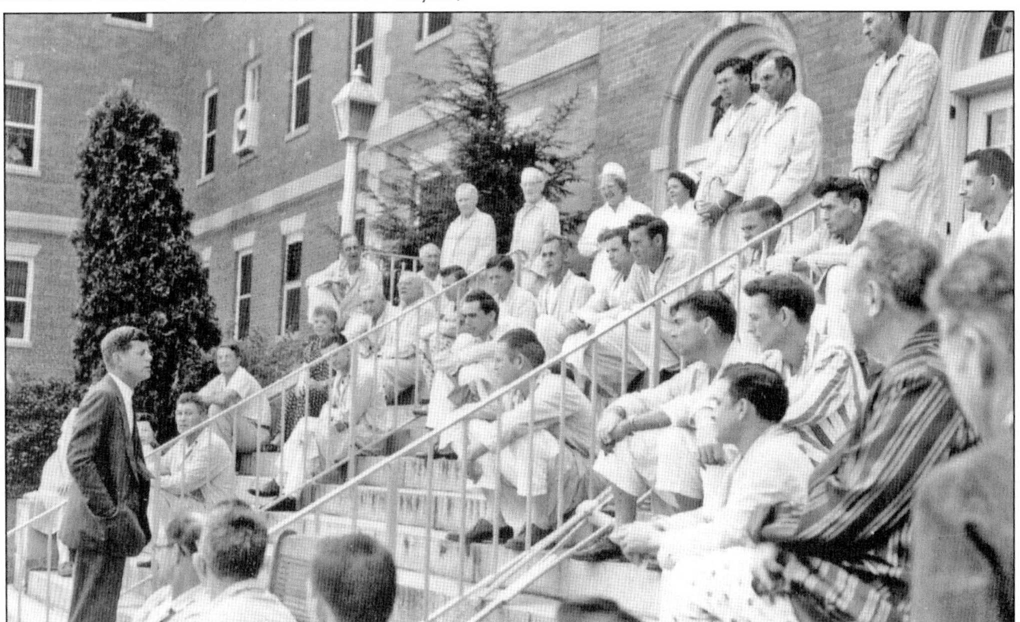

JOHN F. KENNEDY VISITS. Sen. John F. Kennedy visited Huntington, West Virginia, in 1960 as a presidential candidate. The senator took some of his campaign time to discuss issues and concerns with patients at the VA Hospital. Notice that the majority of the men in the photograph are peers of the soon-to-be president. (Courtesy of the Huntington VA Medical Center Archives.)

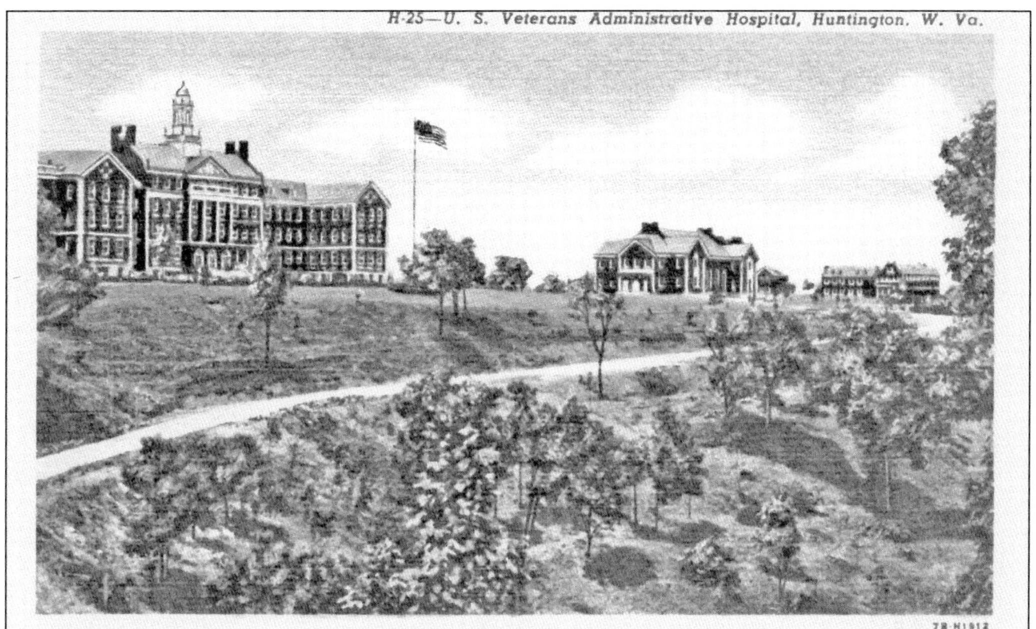

A Tri-State Hospital. The VA Medical Center continues today as the healthcare facility of choice for many veterans in the West Virginia, Kentucky, and Ohio tri-state. The hospital is always looking for ways to improve the quality of life for its veteran patients and their families. (Courtesy of the Terry L. Baldridge Collection.)

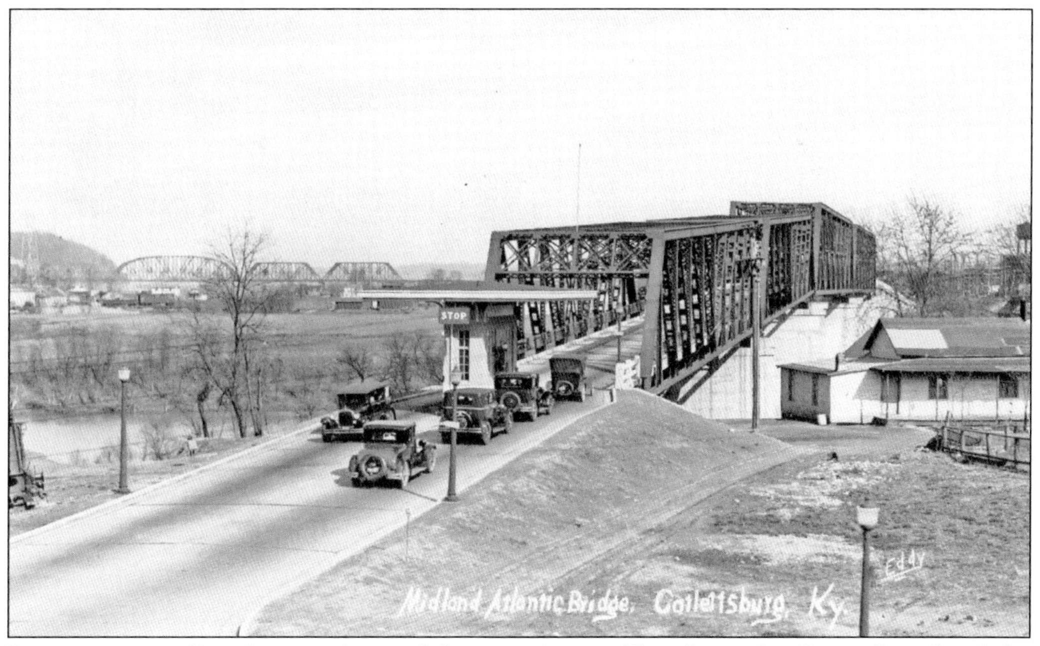

Bridging the Big Sandy. Automobiles stop for a tollbooth on the Kentucky side of the Catlettsburg and Kenova Bridge in the 1930s. The tollbooths are long gone, but people traveling to and from Ashland, Kentucky; Huntington, West Virginia; and Ironton, Ohio, use this bridge, the two central city bridges, and the I-64 bridges. (Courtesy of the James C. Powers Collection.)

Consistent with our mission to preserve history on a local level, this book was printed in South Carolina on American-made paper and manufactured entirely in the United States. Products carrying the accredited Forest Stewardship Council (FSC) label are printed on 100 percent FSC-certified paper.

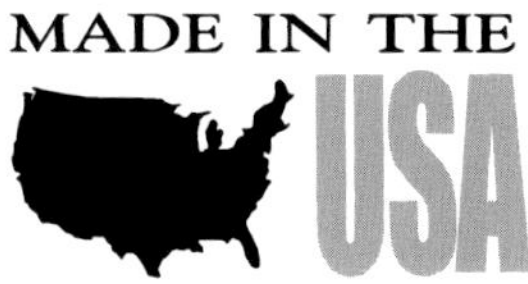